Trees Be Company

An Anthology of Poetry

EDITED BY ANGELA KING & SUSAN CLIFFORD FOR
Common Ground

FOREWORD BY JOHN FOWLES

Published by The Bristol Press

The Bristol Press is an imprint of Bristol Classical Press, 226 North Street, Bedminster, Bristol BS3 1JD.

Published in 1989 by The Bristol Press.

British Library Cataloguing in Publication Data
Trees be company: an anthology of poetry.
  1. Poetry in English. Special subjects. Trees.
Anthologies
I. King, Angela, 1944- II. Clifford, Susan
821'.008'036

ISBN 1-85399-069-8

T

613243

This book has been printed and bound by Short Run Press Ltd., Exeter, Devon, on 100% recycled paper (Five Seasons); the cover is recycled board (Speckletone).

Contents

About this Anthology

Poetry is rich in references to trees and woods and the spirits that we give them. In our own deciduous world, they call the seasons; they live longer and grow bigger than any other creature; they provide feasts for metaphor, symbol and allegory, and they allude to secrets of common culture long trapped in their annual rings.

We feel the time is right to put the cultural arguments about trees and woods alongside the scientific, economic and ecological ones. They need our help.

The intention of this book is to present evidence of our deep cultural need for trees and woods and to inspire people to take care of them.

Trees, and indeed woods, know no distinction between town and country: they are close to everyone. But ironically, concern for loss of rainforest or rising global temperatures (the greenhouse effect) rarely brings us to care more deeply for the trees in our own street, garden or locality. And yet 56% of Britain's trees are affected by acid rain (UN, 1988). Half of the ancient woodlands present in 1945 have been destroyed, replanted with conifers or cleared for cereal production, roads and building development. The October hurricane of 1987 felled 15 million trees. Disease and prejudice take their tithe.

If we are to combat local pollution, make even the slightest impact on global warming, enjoy our surroundings and share them with many other creatures, we need trees: trees here and trees now. If we are to nourish more than our prosaic needs we need their longevity, their beauty, their generosity. We are tied to the global turn of events not simply through the ecosystem, but by a universal and deeper need for trees with roots in many cultures. Trees stand for nature and culture. We shall stand or fall with them.

There are so many poems which demonstrate our imaginative relationship with trees, our selection has been guided by a desire to show that the 20th century is as rich as earlier times and we feel strongly that the contemporary poet's voice should be heard alongside that of the politician and professional environmentalist. We have tried to offer a variety of poets and preoccupations, sometimes sacrificing favourites on the way. Arranging the poems alphabetically by title encourages chance connections. So many poets have found richness in the theme – we had to restrict our selection to poems written in English (with a few exceptions of Welsh, Old English, Irish and Latin). One day perhaps we shall embark on the rest of the world...

We have uncovered poets immersed in nature and also those who would shun such affiliations. We have found mythology and legend, languages of longevity and seasonal revolution, popular politics and the power of places, lost childhood and golden ages gone, prognoses of good or evil, misplaced love, refuge from the world's ills or one's own afflictions, solace and fears, threat and discovery, and – most frequently – a lifting of the soul: all evidence is that if we talk to the trees, they speak back to us.

> One impulse from a vernal wood
> May teach you more of man;
> Of moral evil and of good,
> Than all the sages can.

William Wordsworth

Angela King and Susan Clifford
May 1989

Common Ground
45, Shelton Street
London WC2 9HJ

About Common Ground

Common Ground is working to encourage new ways of looking at the world, to excite people into remembering the richness of the commonplace and the value of the everyday, to savour the symbolisms with which we have endowed nature, to revalue our emotional engagement with places and all that they mean to us and to go on to become actively involved in their care.

We have chosen to focus attention not singularly upon natural history or archaeology or social history or legend or literary traditions but upon their complex combining which is the reality of people's relationship with their places, and which begins in our hearts but gets mediated by our reason.

In attempting to reassert the importance of liberating our subjective response to the world about us we have turned for philosophical help to those who wear their emotions on their sleeve. We work with people from all branches of the arts. Much of what we do attempts to place cultural arguments and evidence beside the scientific, technical and economic rationales which so dominate, and we believe, debilitate our ways of thinking and doing.

Common Ground works through projects:

Trees, Woods and the Green Man is stressing the importance of trees and woods by exploring their aesthetic, spiritual and cultural value as well as their ecological importance. It is doing this through all branches of the arts, exhibitions and publications as well as practical guides to tree care in town and country.

The Parish Maps Project intends to give people more confidence to show what they value in the familiar features of their everyday surroundings. An imaginative map created by local people becomes a starting point for sensitive conservation action. Over 600 community maps are now being made all over Britain, each one reflecting the rich resources and creativity of that particular place. From Australia to North America the idea is being taken up, demonstrating the potential of positive parochialism to be universally relevant.

The New Milestones Project is encouraging a new generation of town, village and countryside sculptures. It hopes to stimulate the creation of small-scale works of the imagination which express our sense of history, our love of place and of the natural world. It is involving local people in commissioning sculptures which will be valued and enduring features in the present and future life of the whole community.

Common Ground is a charity which does not have a membership. Our hope is that using our projects and ideas will help people to become more involved for themselves in their own localities. We are funded by a wide variety of charitable trusts, government agencies, businesses and individuals.

In the hope that you will be inspired to action by this book, Common Ground has also produced a sister volume entitled *In a Nutshell: A manifesto for trees and a guide to growing and protecting them* by Neil Sinden.

Foreword

Snottygogs...this odd dialect word, so uncouth-sounding for something so pretty, somehow lodged in my mind, perhaps for its sheer inappropriateness, from the moment I first heard it. According to Geoffrey Grigson in *The Englishman's Flora* – a poem of a book, though in prose – it comes in this form from Sussex. And what are snottygogs? They are those little carmine-pink berries that festoon the dark green branches of yew, and that attract birds in early winter as ripe cherries do summer children. Yew seeds are poisonous, so are the leaves, but not the coral flesh of the little snottygogs. I have several yews, always busy with tits and goldcrests, in my Dorset garden. One of my favourite trees, its dark 'graveyard' reputation in English folklore (and poetry) is absurd and to my mind convincing proof that the closest mammal to man is not a primate, but the sheep. Only flock-belief, or total swallowing of convention, can explain the profound gloom with which we surround such a charmingly lively and sturdy tree. I suppose it is that since it can, if we are very stupid, harm us, it must be very evil – an infantile logic that informs far too much of our attitude to nature.

According to a recent Greenpeace publication, *Tree Survey of Southern Britain*, yew are doing particularly badly in Dorset; nearly nine out of ten are damaged by various forms of pollution. As soon as I had read the report I rushed out to look at my own. There was a particularly rich crop of snottygogs this last year, and the old trees, such marvellous re-shooters when pruned (one reason I love them), seemed greenly flourishing. As so often these days, the reality of nature outside flagrantly contradicts the doom one reads indoors. Science is crying wolf, it seems, with none yet in sight. Would it were so, but it is not. 1989 began with a formidable warning about our endangered earth from what seemed an unlikely source: *Time* magazine. To what extent we humans are on the brink – a decade, fifty years, a century away – is a matter of dispute; but not that the nemesis is near in any real time scale.

We all know that things are very bad for trees, indeed for all nature, and all over the world; which makes writing of their plight, or making anyone listen to it, near impossible. In *The Dream of the Rood*, one of the earlier poems in this anthology, it is made a glory of the tree that it constituted the Cross and so bore the body of Christ. But it is not Christ who is crucified now; it is the tree itself, and on the bitter gallows of human greed and stupidity. Only suicidal morons, in a world already choking to death, would destroy the best natural air-conditioner creation affords; as well cut our children's throats.

We are all heir to two conflicting souls, or psyches, when it comes to nature: a green one and a black. The first, best symbolized by the tree, still retains, despite the Gadarene influx into our nature-barren cities, at least a memory of what it was to live in balance of a kind with nature, on a green planet. The black soul, which has gained such huge power during these last two centuries, was bred by that disastrously arrogant aspect of Christianity (and other male-dominated religions) which supposed man to be in God's image and duly appointed him, like some hopelessly venal and ultimately crazed gamekeeper, the steward of all creation. Given the proliferating and savagely parasitical species mankind is, that was to place our destiny in the power of the rat, the locust, the plague. The black soul in us both fears and hates nature, and it still drives the majority.

Science, I suspect, helps rather less than we like to suppose or would wish. However well intended, or cogently presented, it tends to anaesthetize. The scientists are the experts, they must know best; I don't. Is not all the power, the knowledge of means, the authority, theirs? I need do nothing, for the very simple reason that I cannot. Science stifles instinctive feeling, and when such feeling concerns nature, it can slip with ominous ease into mere sentimentality. One might dismiss the scientific content of all the poetry here as non-existent; and so conclude that it cannot be serious or worth attention. But such smug dismissal, so typical of our science-tyrannized world, quite simply threatens to end all life on it.

The poems in this anthology remind me very much of the countless fallen leaves that litter the pavements in this time and place where I happen to write: Primrose Hill in London, December. I watch people kick rather crossly through, or fastidiously sidestep, the dead leaves; indeed treat them as most of us treat the detritus of past human feelings, which is what such collections as this represent. Messy and irritating dead leaf, so many blemishes on a supposedly proper modern world. An elderly aunt once told me a long time ago, when I was a little boy in her charge, that dead leaves were human faces. One did not tread carelessly on them, or kick them thoughtlessly aside, as I was wont.

This is how I hope this anthology will be read; whatever the poems' individual value, they are a reminder of what that city-asphyxiated green soul in all of us both was and is. To flick through them without thinking or caring is to kick through human faces, or the minds behind them. Dead leaves, whether literal or on paper, constitute the humus from which all new leaf must grow. In poetry as in life, trees are like humans: they need their pasts to feed their presents.

Destroy either, and you lose all. The black soul will have won, and the last tree died; no leaves to kick through, nor even a small boy left to kick.

John Fowles

Afforestation

It's a population of trees
Colonising the old
Haunts of men; I prefer,
Listening to their talk,
The bare language of grass
To what the woods say,
Standing in black crowds
Under the stars at night
Or in the sun's way.
The grass feeds the sheep;
The sheep give the wool
For warm clothing, but these ——?
I see the cheap times
Against which they grow:
Thin houses for dupes,
Pages of pale trash,
A world that has gone sour
With spruce. Cut them down,
They won't take the weight
Of any of the strong bodies
For which the wind sighs.

R.S. Thomas

Afternoon Tea

Please you, excuse me, good five-o'clock people,
   I've lost my last hatful of words,
And my heart's in the wood up above the church steeple,
   I'd rather have tea with the birds.

Gay Kate's stolen kisses, poor Barnaby's scars,
   John's losses and Mary's gains,
Oh! what do they matter, my dears, to the stars
   Or the glow-worms in the lanes!

I'd rather lie under the tall elm-trees,
  With old rooks talking loud overhead,
To watch a red squirrel run over my knees,
  Very still on my brackeny bed.

And wonder what feathers the wrens will be taking
  For lining their nests next Spring;
Or why the tossed shadow of boughs in a great wind shaking
  Is such a lovely thing.

Charlotte Mew

Alcaic

Out in the deep wood, silence and darkness fall,
down through the wet leaves comes the October mist;
    no sound, but only a blackbird scolding,
        making the mist and the darkness listen.

Peter Levi

The Almond Trees

There's nothing here
this early;
cold sand
cold churning ocean, the Atlantic,
no visible history,

except this stand
of twisted, coppery, sea-almond trees
their shining postures surely
bent as metal, and one

2

foam-haired, salt-grizzled fisherman,
his mongrel growling, whirling on the stick
he pitches him; its spinning rays
'no visible history'
until their lengthened shapes amaze the sun.

By noon,
this further shore of Africa is strewn
with the forked limbs of girls toasting their flesh
in scarves, sunglasses, Pompeian bikinis,

brown daphnes, laurels, they'll all have
like their originals, their sacred grove,
this frieze
of twisted, coppery, sea-almond trees.

The fierce acetylene air
has singed
their writhing trunks with rust, the same
hues as a foundered, peeling barge.
It'll sear a pale skin copper with its flame.

The sand's white-hot ash underheel,
but their aged limbs have got their brazen sheen
from fire. Their bodies fiercely shine!
They're cured,
they endured their furnace.

Aged trees and oiled limbs share a common colour!

Welded in one flame,
huddling naked, stripped of their name,
for Greek or Roman tags, they were lashed
raw by wind, washed
out with salt and fire-dried,
bitterly nourished where their branches died,

their leaves' broad dialect a coarse,
enduring sound
they shared together.

Not as some running hamadryad's cries
rooted, broke slowly into leaf
her nipples peaking to smooth, wooden boles

Their grief
howls seaward through charred, ravaged holes.

One sunburnt body now acknowledges
that past and its own metamorphosis
as, moving from the sun, she kneels to spread
her wrap within the bent arms of this grove
that grieves in silence, like parental love.

Derek Walcott

Alone in the Woods

Alone in the woods I felt
The bitter hostility of the sky and the trees
Nature has taught her creatures to hate
Man that fusses and fumes
Unquiet man
As the sap rises in the trees
As the sap paints the trees a violent green
So rises the wrath of Nature's creatures
At man
So paints the face of Nature a violent green.
Nature is sick at man
Sick at his fuss and fume
Sick at his agonies
Sick at his gaudy mind

That drives his body
Ever more quickly
More and more
In the wrong direction.

Stevie Smith

Amphion

My father left a park to me,
  But it is wild and barren,
A garden too with scarce a tree,
  And waster than a warren:
Yet say the neighbours when they call,
  It is not bad but good land,
And in it is the germ of all
  That grows within the woodland.

O had I lived when song was great
  In days of old Amphion,
And ta'en my fiddle to the gate,
  Nor cared for seed or scion!
And had I lived when song was great,
  And legs of trees were limber,
And ta'en my fiddle to the gate,
  And fiddled in the timber!

'Tis said he had a tuneful tongue,
  Such happy intonation,
Wherever he sat down and sung
  He left a small plantation;
Wherever in a lonely grove
  He set up his forlorn pipes,
The gouty oak began to move,
  And flounder into hornpipes.

The mountain stirred its bushy crown,
  And, as tradition teaches,
Young ashes pirouetted down
  Coquetting with young beeches;
And briony-vine and ivy-wreath
  Ran forward to his rhyming,
And from the valleys underneath
  Came little copses climbing.

The linden broke her ranks and rent
  The woodbine wreaths that bind her,
And down the middle, buzz! she went
  With all her bees behind her;
The poplars, in long order due,
  With cypress promenaded,
The shock-head willows two and two
  By rivers gallopaded.

Came wet-shod alder from the wave,
  Came yews, a dismal coterie;
Each plucked his one foot from the grave,
  Poussetting with a sloe-tree:
Old elms came breaking from the vine,
  The vine streamed out to follow,
And, sweating rosin, plumped the pine
  From many a cloudy hollow.

And wasn't it a sight to see,
  When, ere his song was ended,
Like some great landslip, tree by tree,
  The country-side descended;
And shepherds from the mountain-eaves
  Looked down, half-pleased, half-frightened,
As dashed about the drunken leaves
  The random sunshine lightened!

Oh, nature first was fresh to men,
  And wanton without measure;

6

So youthful and so flexile then,
  You moved her at your pleasure.
Twang out, my fiddle! shake the twigs!
  And make her dance attendance;
Blow, flute, and stir the stiff-set sprigs,
  And scirrhous roots and tendons.

'Tis vain! in such a brassy age
  I could not move a thistle;
The very sparrows in the hedge
  Scarce answer to my whistle;
Or at the most, when three-parts-sick
  With strumming and with scraping,
A jackass heehaws from the rick,
  The passive oxen gaping.

But what is that I hear? a sound
  Like sleepy counsel pleading;
O Lord ! – 'tis in my neighbour's ground,
  The modern Muses reading.
They read Botanic Treatises,
  And Works on Gardening through there,
And Methods of transplanting trees
  To look as if they grew there.

The withered Misses! how they prose
  O'er books of travelled seamen,
And show you slips of all that grows
  From England to Van Diemen.
They read in arbours clipt and cut,
  And alleys, faded places,
By squares of tropic summer shut
  And warmed in crystal cases.

But these, though fed with careful dirt,
  Are neither green nor sappy;
Half-conscious of the garden-squirt,
  The spindlings look unhappy.

Better to me the meanest weed
  That blows upon its mountain,
The vilest herb that runs to seed
  Beside its native fountain.

And I must work through months of toil,
  And years of cultivation,
Upon my proper patch of soil
  To grow my own plantation.
I'll take the showers as they fall,
  I will not vex my bosom:
Enough if at the end of all
  A little garden blossom.

Alfred, Lord Tennyson

Apple Poem

Take the apple from the bowl or bough
Or kitchen table where in gloom it glows
And you will sense, mysteriously, how
Its fragrant and substantial presence throws
A shadow shape of this one's red and green.
Whatever it may be – Rose of Bern,
Spice Pippin, Golden Russet, Hawthorn Dean –
Across the mind and then you may discern
Through every sense the quintessential fruit,
Perfected properties all apples own,
In this platonic shadow; absolute
This pleasing thing that you alone have grown.

Beneath the apple's skin, its green or gold,
Yellow, red or streaked with varied tints,
The white flesh tempts, sharp or sweet, quite cold.
Its blood is colourless; scent teases, hints

8

At othernesses that you can't define;
The taste of innocence, so slow to fade,
Persists like memory. This fruit is wine
And bread; is eucharistic. It has played
Its role in epics, fairy-tales, among
Most races of the earth; made prophecies
Of marriages and kept the Norse Gods young;
Shone like moons on Hesperidian trees.

And here, domestic, familiar as a pet,
Plump as your granny's cheek, prepared to be
Translated into jam or jelly, yet
It still retains a curious mystery.
Forget the holy leaves, the pagan lore,
And that you munch on legends when you eat,
But see, as you crunch closer to the core,
Those little pips, diminutive and neat
Containers aping tiny beetles or
Microscopic purses, little beads,
Each holding in its patient dark a store
Of apples, flowering orchards, countless seeds.

Vernon Scannell

'Autumn again, you wouldn't know in the city'

...Autumn again, you wouldn't know in the city
Gotta come out in a car see the birds
       flock by the yellow bush –
In Autumn, in autumn, this part of the planet's
       famous for red leaves –
Difficult for Man on earth to 'scape the snares of delusion –
    All wrong, the thought process screamed at
                from Infancy,
The Self built with myriad thoughts
       from football to I Am That I Am,

Difficult to stop breathing factory smoke,
Difficult to step out of clothes,
             hard to forget the green parka –
Trees scream & drop
             bright Leaves,
Yea Trees scream & drop bright leaves,
Difficult to get out of bed in the morning
                  in the slums –
Even sex happiness a long drawn-out scheme
                  To keep the mind moving –

Big gray truck rolling down highway
             to unload wares –
Bony white branches of birch relieved of their burden
– overpass, overpass, overpass
          crossing the road, more traffic
             between the cities,
                  More sex carried near and far –
             Blinking tail lights
          To the Veterans hospital where we can all collapse,
Forget Pleasure and Ambition,
          be tranquil and let leaves
          blush, turned on
by the lightningbolt doctrine that rings
                              telephones
          interrupting my pleasurable humiliating dream
             in the locker room
                        last nite? –
Weeping Willow, what's your catastrophe?
          Red Red oak, oh, what's your worry? ...

Allen Ginsberg
                  from Autumn Gold: New England Fall

A Barbican Ash

City pigeons on the air
planing like surfers swirl in their
calm descent, skid on one wing
about a tree where no sapling
was yesterday. Their country cousins,
counties away, now circle in
search of a nest not to be found
between the holed sky and the holed ground.
Like a flag at its masthead frayed
with shot, in this I read
of a tree winched from a wood
to be set in a concrete glade.
Workmen today come packing
its roots with a chemical Spring.

Men are more mobile than trees:
but have, when transplanted to cities,
no mineral extract of manure,
hormone or vitamin to ensure
that their roots survive, carve through the stone
roots, cable roots, strangling my own.

Jon Stallworthy

Bare Almond-Trees

Wet almond-trees, in the rain,
Like iron sticking grimly out of earth;
Black almond trunks, in the rain,
Like iron implements twisted, hideous, out of the earth,
Out of the deep, soft fledge of Sicilian winter-green,
Earth-grass uneatable,
Almond trunks curving blackly, iron-dark, climbing the slopes.

11

Almond-tree, beneath the terrace rail,
Black, rusted, iron trunk,
You have welded your thin stems finer,
Like steel, like sensitive steel in the air,
Grey, lavender, sensitive steel, curving thinly and brittly
    up in a parabola.

What are you doing in the December rain?
Have you a strange electric sensitiveness in your steel tips?
Do you feel the air for electric influences
Like some strange magnetic apparatus?
Do you take in messages, in some strange code,
From heaven's wolfish, wandering electricity, that prowls
    so constantly round Etna?
Do you take the whisper of sulphur from the air?
Do you hear the chemical accents of the sun?
Do you telephone the roar of the waters over the earth?
And from all this, do you make calculations?

Sicily, December's Sicily in a mass of rain
With iron branching blackly, rusted like old, twisted
    implements
And brandishing and stooping over earth's wintry fledge,
    climbing the slopes
Of uneatable soft green!

                                         Taormina.

                                    D.H. Lawrence

The Battle of the Trees

The tops of the beech tree
  Have sprouted of late,
Are changed and renewed
  From their withered state.

When the beech prospers,
  Though spells and litanies
The oak tops entangle,
  There is hope for trees.

I have plundered the fern,
  Through all secrets I spy,
Old Math ap Mathonwy
  Knew no more than I.

With nine sorts of faculty
  God had gifted me:
I am fruits of fruits gathered
  From nine sorts of tree –

Plum, quince, whortle, mulberry,
  Raspberry, pear,
Black cherry and white
  With the sorb in me share.

From my seat at Fefynedd,
  A city that is strong,
I watched the trees and green things
  Hastening along.

Retreating from happiness
  They would fain be set
In forms of the chief letters
  Of the alphabet.

Wayfarers wondered,
  Warriors were dismayed
At renewal of conflicts
  Such as Gwydion made,

At a battle raging
  Under each tongue root
Of a hundred-headed thing,
  A monstrous brute,

A toad with a hundred claws
　Armed at his thighs;
And in his head-recesses
　Raging likewise.

The alders in the front line
　Began the affray.
Willow and rowan-tree
　Were tardy in array.

The holly, dark green,
　Made a resolute stand;
He is armed with many spear points
　Wounding the hand.

With foot-beat of the swift oak
　Heaven and earth rung;
'Stout Guardian of the Door,'
　His name in every tongue.

Great was the gorse in battle,
　And the ivy at his prime;
The hazel was arbiter
　At this charmed time.

Uncouth and savage was the fir,
　Cruel the ash-tree –
Turns not aside a foot-breadth,
　Straight at the heart runs he.

The birch, though very noble,
　Armed himself but late:
A sign not of cowardice
　But of high estate.

The heath gave consolation
　To the toil-spent folk,
The long-enduring poplars
　In battle much broke.

Some of them were cast away
  On the field of fight
Because of holes torn in them
  By the enemy's might.

Very wrathful was the vine
  Whose henchmen are the elms;
I exalt him mightily
  To rulers of realms.

Strong chieftains were the blackthorn
  With his ill fruit,
The unbeloved whitethorn
  Who wears the same suit,

The swift-pursuing reed,
  The broom with his brood,
And the furze but ill-behaved
  Until he is subdued.

The dower-scattering yew
  Stood glum at the fight's fringe,
With the elder slow to burn
  Amid fires that singe,

And the blessed wild apple
  Laughing in pride
From the *Gorchan* of Maelderw
  By the rock side.

In shelter linger
  Privet and woodbine,
Inexperienced in warfare,
  And the courtly pine.

But I, although slighted
 Because I was not big,
Fought, trees, in your array
 On the field of Goddeu Brig.

Robert Graves

'Bear me, Pomona! to thy citron groves'

...Bear me, Pomona! to thy citron groves;
To where the lemon and the piercing lime,
With the deep orange glowing through the green,
Their lighter glories blend. Lay me reclined
Beneath the spreading tamarind, that shakes,
Fanned by the breeze, its fever-cooling fruit.
Deep in the night the massy locust sheds
Quench my hot limbs; or lead me through the maze,
Embowering endless, of the Indian fig;
Or, thrown at gayer ease on some fair brow,
Let me behold, by breezy murmurs cooled,
Broad o'er my head the verdant cedar wave,
And high palmettos lift their graceful shade.
Oh, stretched amid these orchards of the sun,
Give me to drain the cocoa's milky bowl,
And from the palm to draw its freshening wine!
More bounteous far than all the frantic juice
Which Bacchus pours. Nor, on its slender twigs
Low-bending, be the full pomegranate scorned;
Nor, creeping through the woods, the gelid race
Of berries. Oft in humble station dwells
Unboastful worth, above fastidious pomp.

16

Witness, thou best Anana, thou the pride
Of vegetable life, beyond whate'er
The poet's imaged in the golden age:
Quick let me strip thee of thy tufty coat,
Spread thy ambrosial stores, and feast with Jove!...

James Thomson
from The Seasons: Summer

Beech

They will not go. These leaves insist on staying.
Coinage like theirs looked frail six weeks ago.
What hintings at, excitement of delaying,
Almost as if some richer fruits could grow

If leaves hung on against each swipe of storm,
If branches bent but still did not give way.
Today is brushed with sun. The leaves are warm.
I picked one from the pavement and it lay

With borrowed shining on my Winter hand.
Persistence of this nature sends the pulse
Beating more rapidly. When will it end,

That pride of leaves? When will the branches be
Utterly bare, and seem like something else,
Now half-forgotten, no part of a tree?

Elizabeth Jennings

Beech Tree

I planted in February
A bronze-leafed beech,
In the chill brown soil
I spread out its silken fibres.

Protected it from the goats
With wire netting
And fixed it firm against
The worrying wind.

Now it is safe, I said,
April must stir
My precious baby
To greenful loveliness.

It is August now, I have hoped
But I hope no more –
My beech tree will never hide sparrows
From hungry hawks.

Patrick Kavanagh

Binsey Poplars
felled 1879

My aspens dear, whose airy cages quelled,
Quelled or quenched in leaves the leaping sun,
All felled, felled, are all felled;
    Of a fresh and following folded rank
        Not spared, not one
        That dandled a sandalled
    Shadow that swam or sank

18

On meadow and river and wind-wandering weed-
    winding bank.

O if we but knew what we do
        When we delve or hew –
    Hack and rack the growing green!
        Since country is so tender
        To touch, her being so slender,
        That, like this sleek and seeing ball
        But a prick will make no eye at all,
        Where we, even where we mean

        To mend her we end her,
        When we hew or delve:
After-comers cannot guess the beauty been.
    Ten or twelve, only ten or twelve
        Strokes of havoc unselve
            The sweet especial scene,
        Rural scene, a rural scene,
        Sweet especial rural scene.

Gerard Manley Hopkins

Birches

When I see birches bend to left and right
Across the lines of straighter darker trees,
I like to think some boy's been swinging them.
But swinging doesn't bend them down to stay
As ice-storms do. Often you must have seen them
Loaded with ice a sunny winter morning
After a rain. They click upon themselves
As the breeze rises, and turn many-colored
As the stir cracks and crazes their enamel.
Soon the sun's warmth makes them shed crystal shells
Shattering and avalanching on the snow-crust –

Such heaps of broken glass to sweep away
You'd think the inner dome of heaven had fallen.
They are dragged to the withered bracken by the load,
And they seem not to break; though once they are bowed
So low for long, they never right themselves:
You may see their trunks arching in the woods
Years afterwards, trailing their leaves on the ground
Like girls on hands and knees that throw their hair
Before them over their heads to dry in the sun.
But I was going to say when Truth broke in
With all her matter-of-fact about the ice-storm
I should prefer to have some boy bend them
As he went out and in to fetch the cows –
Some boy too far from town to learn baseball,
Whose only play was what he found himself,
Summer or winter, and could play alone.
One by one he subdued his father's trees
By riding them down over and over again
Until he took the stiffness out of them,
And not one but hung limp, not one was left
For him to conquer. He learned all there was
To learn about not launching out too soon
And so not carrying the tree away
Clear to the ground. He always kept his poise
To the top branches, climbing carefully
With the same pains you use to fill a cup
Up to the brim, and even above the brim.
Then he flung outward, feet first, with a swish,
Kicking his way down through the air to the ground.
So was I once myself a swinger of birches.
And so I dream of going back to be.
It's when I'm weary of considerations,
And life is too much like a pathless wood
Where your face burns and tickles with the cobwebs
Broken across it, and one eye is weeping
From a twig's having lashed across it open.
I'd like to get away from earth a while
And then come back to it and begin over.

May no fate willfully misunderstand me
And half grant what I wish and snatch me away
Not to return. Earth's the right place for love:
I don't know where it's likely to go better.
I'd like to go by climbing a birch tree,
And climb black branches up a snow-white trunk
Toward heaven, till the tree could bear no more,
But dipped its top and set me down again.
That would be good both going and coming back.
One could do worse than be a swinger of birches.

Robert Frost

Blunden's Beech

I named it Blunden's Beech; and no one knew
That this – of local beeches – was the best.
Remembering lines by Clare, I'd sometimes rest
Contentful on the cushioned moss that grew
Between its roots. Finches, a flitting crew,
Chirped their concerns. Wiltshire, from east to west
Contained my tree. And Edmund never guessed
How he was there with me till dusk and dew.

Thus, fancy-free from ownership and claim,
The mind can make its legends live and sing
And grow to be the genius of some place.
And thus, where sylvan shadows held a name,
The thought of Poetry will dwell, and bring
To summer's idyll an unheeded grace.

Siegfried Sassoon

Bog oak

A carter's trophy
split for rafters,
a cobwebbed, black,
long-seasoned rib

under the first thatch.
I might tarry
with the moustached
dead, the creel-fillers,

or eavesdrop on
their hopeless wisdom
as a blow-down of smoke
struggles over the half-door

and mizzling rain
blurs the far end
of the cart track.
The softening ruts

lead back to no
'oak groves', no
cutters of mistletoe
in the green clearings.

Perhaps I just make out
Edmund Spenser,
dreaming sunlight,
encroached upon by

geniuses who creep
'out of every corner
of the woodes and glennes'
towards watercress and carrion.

Seamus Heaney

22

'The bushy leafy oak tree'

The bushy leafy oak tree
is highest in the wood,
the forking shoots of hazel
hide sweet hazel-nuts.

The alder is my darling,
all thornless in the gap,
some milk of human kindness
coursing in its sap.

The blackthorn is a jaggy creel
stippled with dark sloes;
green watercress in thatch on wells
where the drinking blackbird goes.

Sweetest of the leafy stalks,
the vetches strew the pathway;
the oyster-grass is my delight,
and the wild strawberry.

Low-set clumps of apple trees
drum down fruit when shaken;
scarlet berries clot like blood
on mountain rowan.

Briars curl in sideways,
arch a stickle back,
draw blood and curl up innocent
to sneak the next attack.

The yew tree in each churchyard
wraps night in its dark hood.
Ivy is a shadowy
genius of the wood.

Holly rears its windbreak,
a door in winter's face;
life-blood on a spear-shaft
darkens the grain of ash.

Birch tree, smooth and blessed,
delicious to the breeze,
high twigs plait and crown it
the queen of trees.

The aspen pales
and whispers, hesitates:
a thousand frightened scuts
race in its leaves.
But what disturbs me most
in the leafy wood
is the to and fro and to and fro
of an oak rod.

trans. *Seamus Heaney*
from Sweeney Astray

Cardiff Elms

Until this summer
through the open roof of the car
their lace was light as rain
against the burning sun.
On a rose-coloured road
they laid their inks,
knew exactly, in the seed,
where in the sky they would reach
precise parameters.

Traffic-jammed under a square
of perfect blue I thirst
for their lake's fingering
shadow, trunk by trunk arching
a cloister between the parks
and pillars of a civic architecture,
older and taller than all of it.

Heat is a salt encrustation.
Walls square up to the sky
without the company of leaves
or the town life of birds.
At the roadside this enormous
firewood, elmwood, the start
of some terrible undoing.

Gillian Clarke

The Cedar

Look from the high window with the eye of wonder
When the sun soars over and the moon dips under.

Look when the sun is coming and the moon is going
On the aspiring creature, on the cedar growing.

Plant or world? are those lights and shadows
Branches, or great air-suspended meadows?

Boles and branches, haunted by the flitting linnet,
Or great hillsides rolling up to cliffs of granite?

Those doomed shapes, thick-clustered on the ledges,
Upright fruit, or dwellings thatched with sedges?

Fair through the eye of innocence returning,
This is a country hanging in the morning;

Scented alps, where nothing but the daylight changes,
Climbing to black walls of mountain ranges;

And under the black walls, under the sky-banners,
The dwellings of the blessed in the green savannahs.

Ruth Pitter

Ceremonies for Candlemasse Eve

Down with the Rosemary and Bayes,
    Down with the Mistleto;
In stead of Holly, now up-raise
    The greener Box (for show.)

The Holly hitherto did sway;
    Let Box now domineere;
Untill the dancing Easter-day,
    Or Easters Eve appeare.

Then youthfull Box which now hath grace,
    Your houses to renew;
Grown old, surrender must his place,
    Unto the crisped Yew.

When Yew is out, then Birch comes in,
    And many Flowers beside;
Both of a fresh, and fragrant kinne
    To honour Whitsontide.

Green Rushes then, and sweetest Bents,
    With cooler Oken boughs;
Come in for comely ornaments,
    To re-adorn the house.
Thus times do shift; each thing his turne do's hold;
New things succeed, as former things grow old.

                               Robert Herrick

The Chalk Pit

'Is this the road that climbs above and bends
Round what was once a chalk pit: now it is
By accident an amphitheatre.
Some ash trees standing ankle-deep in brier
And bramble act the parts, and neither speak
Nor stir.' 'But see: they have fallen, every one,
And brier and bramble have grown over them.'
'That is the place. As usual no one is here.
Hardly can I imagine the drop of the axe,
And the smack that is like an echo, sounding here.'
'I do not understand.' 'Why, what I mean is
That I have seen the place two or three times
At most, and that its emptiness and silence
And stillness haunt me, as if just before
It was not empty, silent, still, but full
Of life of some kind, perhaps tragical.
Has anything unusual happened here?'

'Not that I know of. It is called the Dell.
They have not dug chalk here for a century.
That was the ash trees' age. But I will ask.'
'No. Do not. I prefer to make a tale,
Or better leave it like the end of a play,
Actors and audience and lights all gone;
For so it looks now. In my memory

Again and again I see it, strangely dark,
And vacant of a life but just withdrawn.
We have not seen the woodman with the axe.
Some ghost has left it now as we two came.'

'And yet you doubted if this were the road?'
'Well, sometimes I have thought of it and failed
To place it. No. And I am not quite sure,
Even now, this is it. For another place,
Real or painted, may have combined with it.
Or I myself a long way back in time...'
'Why, as to that, I used to meet a man –
I had forgotten, – searching for birds' nests
Along the road and in the chalk pit too.
The wren's hole was an eye that looked at him
For recognition. Every nest he knew.
He got a stiff neck, by looking this side or that,
Spring after spring, he told me, with his laugh, –
A sort of laugh. He was a visitor,
A man of forty, – smoked and strolled about.
At orts and crosses Pleasure and Pain had played
On his brown features; – I think both had lost; –
Mild and yet wild too. You may know the kind.
And once or twice a woman shared his walks,
A girl of twenty with a brown boy's face,
And hair brown as a thrush or as a nut,
Thick eyebrows, glinting eyes –' 'You have said enough.
A pair, – free thought, free love, – I know the breed:
I shall not mix my fancies up with them.'

'You please yourself. I should prefer the truth
Or nothing. Here, in fact, is nothing at all
Except a silent place that once rang loud,
And trees and us – imperfect friends, we men
And trees since time began; and nevertheless
Between us still we breed a mystery.'

Edward Thomas

The Cherry Tree

In her gnarled sleep it
begins
      though she seems
as unmoving as the statue
of a running man: her
branches caught in a
writhing, her trunk
leaning as if in mid-fall.
When the wind moves
against her grave body
only the youngest twigs
scutter amongst themselves.

But there's something going on
in those twisted brown limbs,
it starts as a need
and it takes over, a need
to push
      push outward
from the center, to
bring what is not
from what is, pushing
till at the tips of the push
something comes about
              and then
pulling it from outside
until yes she has them started
tiny bumps
appear at the ends of twigs.

Then at once they're all here,
she wears them like a coat
a coat of babies,
I almost think that she
preens herself, jubilant at
the thick dazzle of bloom,

that the caught writhing has become
a sinuous wriggle of joy
beneath her fleece.
But she is working still
to feed her children,
there's a lot more yet,
bringing up all she can
a lot of goodness from roots

while the petals drop.
The fleece is gone
as suddenly as it came
and hundreds of babies are left
almost too small to be seen
but they fatten, fatten, get pink
and shine among her leaves.

Now she can repose a bit
they are so fat.
                    She cares less
birds get them, men
pick them, human children wear them
in pairs over their ears
she loses them all.
That's why she made them,
to lose them into the world, she
returns to herself,
she rests, she doesn't care.

She leans into the wind
her trunk shines black
with rain, she sleeps
as black and hard as lava.
She knows nothing about babies.

Thom Gunn

The Cherry Trees

The cherry trees bend over and are shedding
On the old road where all that passed are dead,
Their petals, strewing the grass as for a wedding
This early May morn when there is none to wed.

Edward Thomas

The Christmas Tree

Put out the lights now!
Look at the Tree, the rough tree dazzled
In oriole plumes of flame,
Tinselled with twinkling frost fire, tasselled
With stars and moons – the same
That yesterday hid in the spinney and had no fame
Till we put out the lights now.

Hard are the nights now:
The fields at moonrise turn to agate.
Shadows are cold as jet;
In dyke and furrow, in copse and faggot
The frost's tooth is set;
And stars are the sparks whirled out by the north wind's fret
On the flinty nights now.

So feast your eyes now
On mimic star and moon-cold bauble:
Worlds may wither unseen,
But the Christmas Tree is a tree of fable,
A phoenix in evergreen,
And the world cannot change or chill what its mysteries
    mean
To your hearts and eyes now.

The vision dies now
Candle by candle: the tree that embraced it
Returns to its own kind,
To be earthed again and weather as best it
May the frost and the wind.
Children, it too had its hour – you will not mind
If it lives or dies now.

C. Day Lewis

The Combe

The Combe was ever dark, ancient and dark.
Its mouth is stopped with bramble, thorn, and briar;
And no one scrambles over the sliding chalk
By beech and yew and perishing juniper
Down the half precipices of its sides, with roots
And rabbit holes for steps. The sun of Winter,
And moon of Summer, and all the singing birds
Except the missel-thrush that loves juniper,
Are quite shut out. But far more ancient and dark
The Combe looks since they killed the badger there,
Dug him out and gave him to the hounds,
That most ancient Briton of English beasts.

Edward Thomas

'Come, farmers, then, and learn the form of tendance'

...Come, farmers, then, and learn the form of tendance
Each kind of tree requires; domesticate
The wild by culture. Do not let your land

Lie idle. O what joy to plant with vines
All Ismarus and clothe the great Taburnus
With olives!...
                    ...The moral is
That every tree needs labour, all must be
Forced into furrows, tamed at any cost.
But olives favour truncheons, vines come best
From layers, myrtles best from solid stems,
From suckers hardy hazels, and from seed
The mighty ash, the shady tree whose leaves
Hercules plucked to crown him, and the acorns
Of the Chaonian Father. Likewise spring
From seed the lofty palm tree and the fir
Destined to see the hazards of the deep.
Grafting it is that makes the rugged arbute
Bear walnuts, barren planes rear healthy apples
And chestnuts foster beeches; thanks to this
The manna-ash can blanch with pear-blossom
And pigs munch acorns at the elm tree foot.
        The arts of budding and of grafting differ.
In the former, where the buds push out of the bark
And burst their delicate sheaths, just in the knot,
A narrow slit is made. In this an eye
From an alien tree is set and taught to merge
Into the sappy rind.
In the latter, knotless trunks are trimmed, and there
Wedges are driven deep into the wood,
Then fertile slips inserted. Presently
Up shoots a lofty tree with flourishing boughs,
Marvelling at its unfamiliar leaves
And fruits unlike its own...

Virgil
from The Georgics Book II

The Crab Tree

Here is the crab tree,
Firm and erect,
In spite of the thin soil,
In spite of neglect.
The twisted root grapples
For sap with the rock,
And draws the hard juice
To the succulent top:
Here are wild apples,
Here's a tart crop!

No outlandish grafting
That ever grew soft
In a sweet air of Persia,
Or safe Roman croft;
Unsheltered by steading,
Rock-rooted and grown,
A great tree of Erin,
It stands up alone,
A forest tree spreading
Where forests are gone.

Of all who pass by it
How few in it see
A westering remnant
Of days when Lough Neagh
Flowed up the long dingles
Its blossom had lit,
Old days of glory
Time cannot repeat;
And therefore it mingles
The bitter and sweet.

It takes from the West Wind
The thrust of the main;
It makes from the tension

Of sky and of plain,
Of what clay enacted,
Of living alarm,
A vitalised symbol
Of earth and of storm,
Of Chaos contracted
To intricate form.

Unbreakable wrestler!
What sapling or herb
Has core of such sweetness
And fruit so acerb?
So grim a transmitter
Of life through mishap,
That one wonders whether
If that in the sap,
Is sweet or is bitter
Which makes it stand up.

Oliver St. John Gogarty

Cypress & Cedar

A smell comes off my pencil as I write
in the margins of a sacred Sanskrit text.
By just sufficient candlelight I skim
these scriptures sceptically from hymn to hymn.
The bits I read aloud to you I've Xed
for the little clues they offer to life's light.

I sit in mine, and you sit in your chair.
A sweetness hangs round yours; a foul smell mine.
Though the house still has no windows and no door
and the tin roof's roughly propped with 4 x 4s
that any gale could jolt, our chairs are fine
and both scents battle for the same night air.

Near Chiefland just off US 129,
from the clapboard abbattoir about a mile,
the local sawyer Bob displays his wares:
porch swings, picnic tables, lounging chairs,
rough sawn and nailed together 'cracker' style.
The hand I shake leaves powerful smells on mine.

Beside two piles of shavings, white and red,
one fragrant as a perfume, and one rank
and malodorous from its swampland ooze,
Bob displayed that week's work's chairs for me to choose.
I chose one that was sweet, and one that stank,
and thought about the sweet wood for a bed.

To quote the carpenter he 'stinks o' shite'
and his wife won't sleep with him on cypress days,
but after a day of cedar, so he said,
she comes back eagerly into his bed,
and, as long as he works cedar, there she stays.
Sometimes he scorns the red wood and works white!

Today I've laboured with my hands for hours
sawing fenceposts up for winter; one tough knot
jolted the chainsaw at my face and sprayed
a beetroot cedar dust off the bucked blade,
along with damp earth with its smell of rot,
hurtling beetles, termites in shocked showers.

To get one gatepost free I had to tug
for half an hour, but dragged up from its hole
it smelled, down even to the last four feet
rammed in the ground, still beautifully sweet
as if the grave had given life parole
and left the sour earth perfumed where I'd dug.

Bob gave me a cedar buckle for my belt,
and after the whole day cutting, stacking wood,
damp denim, genitals, 'genuine hide leather'

all these fragrances were bound together
by cedar, and together they smelled good.
It was wonderful the way my trousers smelled.

I can't help but suppose flesh-famished Phèdre
would have swept this prissy, epicene,
big-game hunting stepson Hippolyte,
led by his nose to cedar, off his feet,
and left no play at all for poor Racine,
if she'd soaped her breasts with *Bois de Cèdre*.

If in doubt ask Bob the sawyer's wife!
Pet lovers who can't stand the stink of cat
buy sacks of litter that's been 'cedarized'
and from ancient times the odour's been much prized.
Though not a Pharaoh I too favour that
for freighting my rank remains out of this life.

Why not two cedar chairs? Why go and buy
a reeking cypress chair as a reminder,
as if one's needed, of primeval ooze,
like swamps near Suwannee backroads, or bayous,
stagnation Mother Nature left behind her
hauling Mankind up from mononuclei?

Cypress still has roots in that old stew
paddling its origins in protozoa,
the stew where consciousness that writes and reads
grew its first squat tail from slimy seeds.
I'd've used it for the Ark if I'd been Noah,
though cedar, I know you'll say, would also do.

This place not in the *Blue Guide* or in *Fodor*
between the Suwannee River and the Styx
named by some homesick English classicist
who loved such puns, loathed swamps, and, lonely, pissed
his livelihood away with redneck hicks
and never once enjoyed the cedar's odour,

or put its smoke to snake-deterrent use
prescribed by Virgil in his *Georgics* III
with *chelydrus* here in the US south
construed as the diamondback or cottonmouth
which freed him, some said, from his misery.
Others said liquor, and others still a noose.

And, evenings, he, who'd been an avid reader
of the *Odyssey* and the *Iliad* in Greek,
became an even avider verandah drinker
believing sourmash made a Stoic thinker
though stuck with no paddle up Phlegethon's creek,
and had no wife with clothes chest of sweet cedar.

But you bought one at Bob's place and you keep
your cotton frocks in it, your underwear,
and such a fragrance comes from your doffed bras
as come from uncorked phials in hot bazaars,
and when you take your clothes off and lie bare
your body breathes out cedar while you sleep.

That lonely English exile named the river,
though it could have been someone like me, for whom,
though most evenings on the porch I read and write,
there's often such uneasiness in night
it creates despair in me, or drinker's gloom
that could send later twinges through the liver.

Tonight so far's been peaceful with no lightning.
The pecan trees and hophornbeams are still.
The storm's held off, the candleflame's quite straight,
the fire and wick united in one fate.
Though this quietness that can, one moment, fill
the heart with peace, can, the next, be frightening –

A hog gets gelded with a gruesome squeal
that skids across the quietness of night
to where we're sitting on our dodgy porch.

I reach for Seth Tooke's shotgun and the torch
then realize its 'farmwork' so alright
but my flesh also flinches from the steel.

Peace like a lily pad on swamps of pain –
floating's its only way of being linked.
This consciousness of ours that reads and writes
drifts on a darkness deeper than the night's.
Above that blackness, buoyed on the extinct,
peace, pure-white, floats flowering in the brain,

and fades, as finally the nenuphar
we found on a pewter swamp where two roads ended
was also bound to fade. The head and heart
are neither of them too much good apart
and peace comes in the moments that they're blended
as cypress and cedar at this moment are.

My love, as prone as I am to despair,
I think the world of night's best born in pairs,
one half we'll call the female, one the male,
though neither essence need, in love, prevail.
We sit here in distinctly scented chairs
you, love, in the cedar, me the cypress chair.

Though tomorrow night I might well sit in yours
and you in mine, the blended scent's the same
since I pushed my chair close to your chair
and we read by the one calm candle that we share
in this wilderness that might take years to tame,
this house still with no windows and no doors.

Let the candle cliché come out of the chill –
'the flickering candle on a vast dark plain'
of one lone voice against the state machine,
or Mimi's on cold stairs aren't what I mean
but moments like this now when heart and brain
seem one sole flame that's bright and straight and still.

If it's in Levy County that I die
(though fearing I'd feel homesick as I died
I'd sooner croak in Yorkshire if I could)
I'll have my coffin made of cedar wood
to balance the smell like cypress from inside
and hope the smoke of both blends in the sky,

as both scents from our porch chairs do tonight.
'Tvashti', says this Indian Rig Veda,
'hewed the world out of one tree,' but doesn't tell,
since for durability both do as well,
if the world he made was cypress wood; or cedar
the smell coming off my pencil as I write.

Tony Harrison

Dead Wood

Worn down to stumps, shredded by the wind,
Crushed underfoot in brittle slaty husks,
The forest turned from wood to stone to dust.

The rind of bark peeled off in slivers, shed
Dry spores, mineral resins, scales of scrim,
Scattering huge-leaved branches under the sun.

These giants shrank to pygmies in the glare.
Basilisks flashed their petrifying eyes.
The whole plateau rattled with bones of trees.

Now oil-men bring the few gnarled timbers back
As souvenirs. A lopped stone branch lies there
To hold up books, or prop open a door.

Anthony Thwaite

Delight of Being Alone

I know no greater delight than the sheer delight of being alone
It makes me realise the delicious pleasure of the moon
that she has in travelling by herself: throughout time,
or the splendid growing of an ash-tree
alone, on a hill-side in the north, humming in the wind.

D.H. Lawrence

Dieback

Eyes register their natural frontiers
Over invisible marathons, snakes, grasses,
Retreating to familiarity,
Imagination, mind, my feet and shoes.
This is oceanic country and I want a horse
And to be lonely, lawless and nomadic.
Beneath the Australasian blue
On the Tablelands, the dry pasturage
Rises and falls on continental cadences.
A lifetime dreaming of summers in Scotland
Brings me a big bag of blue childhood
But this is more of sky, an up-above
Illusory with yonder's blue beyond blue.
More birds enter my vocabulary
But I have no names by which to call them:
Eyes chronicle these things, all new to me,
Wordless in an optic archive.
I've seen the land and heard its native tongue,
But I'm its stranger, a pig-ignorant
Pedestrian, watching what he steps on.
Though I've been bumped into by a mad bat
With faulty radar, and bitten by a stoat
In Scotland, nature here is angrier

Than sanity can bear to contemplate.
I could do with grey-green gum-tree shade
And the perfumery of eucalypts,
But this is a landscape of dieback, trees
Whipped by bacterial artistry and flayed
Into nude postures, bark and leafage gone,
A famished gathering of naked Ys.
I can see five animals, including man
In a fast Japanese vehicle, spurting dust
With speed's up-tempo confidence.
Good State, what's stripped your forests bare,
What pastoral crime's been done to you
In this modernity, by carelessness
Or by sap-sipping, hungry beetles?
I haven't got the right, but I care.
Night falls here without sorrow. Truly, it falls
With howling innocence, cold and starry.
Under a slice of moon, the bald forests cry
Standing in their own coffins.

Douglas Dunn

Domus Caedet Arborem

Ever since the great planes were murdered at the end of the gardens
The city, to me, at night has the look of a Spirit brooding crime;
As if the dark houses watching the trees from dark windows
      Were simply biding their time.

Charlotte Mew

Elder

Feigns dead in winter, none lives better.
Chewed by cattle springs up stronger; an odd
Personal smell and unlovable skin;
Straight shoots like organ pipes in cigarette paper.
No nurseryman would sell you an
Elder – 'not bush, not tree, not bad, not good'.
Judas was surely a fragile man
To hang himself from this – 'God's stinking trees'.

In summer it juggles flower-plates in air,
Creamy as cumulus, and berries, each a weasel's eye
Of light. Pretends it's unburnable
(Who burns it sees the Devil), cringes, hides a soul
Of cream plates, purple fruits in a rattle
Of bones. A good example.

P.J. Kavanagh

The Elm

This is the place where Dorothea smiled.
I did not know the reason, nor did she.
But there she stood, and turned, and smiled at me:
A sudden glory had bewitched the child.
The corn at harvest, and a single tree.
This is the place where Dorothea smiled.

Hilaire Belloc

The Elm Beetle

So long I sat and conned
That naked bole
With the strange hieroglyphics scored
That those small priests,
The beetle-grubs, had bored,
Telling of gods and kings and beasts
And the long journey of the soul
Through magic-opened gates
To where the throned Osiris waits,
That when at last I woke
I stepped from an Egyptian tomb
To see the wood's sun-spotted gloom,
And rising cottage smoke
That leaned upon the wind and broke,
Roller-striped fields, and smooth cow-shadowed pond.

Andrew Young

The Elm Decline

The crags crash to the tarn; slow-
motion corrosion of scree.
From scooped corries,
bare as slag,
black sykes ooze
through quarries of broken boulders.
The sump of the tarn
slumps into its mosses – bog
asphodel, sundew, sedges –
a perpetual
sour October
yellowing the moor.

44

　　　　　　　Seven
thousand years ago
trees grew
high as this tarn. The pikes
were stacks and skerries
spiking the green,
the tidal surge
of oak, birch, elm,
ebbing to ochre
and the wrackwood of backend.

　　　　　　　　　Then

round the year Three
Thousand B.C.,
the proportion of elm pollen
preserved in peat
declined from twenty
per cent to four.

　　　　　　Stone axes,
chipped clean from the crag-face,
ripped the hide off the fells.
Spade and plough
scriated the bared flesh,
skewered down to the bone.
The rake flaked into fragments
and kettlehole tarns
were shovelled chock-full
of a rubble of rotting rocks.

　　　　　　　Today
electric landslips
crack the rock;
drills tunnel it;
valleys go under the tap.
Dynamited runnels
channel a poisoned rain,

and the fractured ledges
are scoured and emery'd
by wind-to-wind rubbings
of nuclear dust.

       Soon
the pikes, the old
bottlestops of lava,
will stand scraped bare,
nothing but air round stone
and stone in air,
ground-down stumps
of a skeleton jaw –

       Until
under the scree,
under the riddled rake,
beside the outflow of the reedless lake,
no human eye remains to see
a land-scape man
helped nature make.

Norman Nicholson

The Elms

Air darkens, air cools
And the first rain is heard in the great elms
A drop for each leaf, before it reaches the ground
I am still alive.

John Fuller

The Elm's Home

I

A dark sky blowing over
our backyard maples,
the air already cool,
Brockport begins its autumn.
My mower's drone and power
drift past the first leaves fallen
curled into red and yellow fists.
In a corner of lawn against
an old wire fence against the older woods,
a grove of mushrooms the kids
already hacked umbrellaless with golfclubs
rots into a mush of lumped columns,
pleats and fans.

These are the suburbs
where I loved that tree, our one elm.
Now, an inch under the loam,
its stump is a candle
of slow decay, lighting, above it,
thousands of perfect pearls
tiered like ant-eggs,
and these, by nature, growing so low
my mower's blades will never touch them.

II

My precious secrets come
to this, then? Yes.
Stay away from them,
you careless bastards.

But listen: sometimes,
at night, kneeling

within a dream within
the elm's oval shadow,

I can look down
into my leg-bones,
into my own marrow
clustered with eggs,

small and perfect pearl
mushrooms
living for all my life.
I can look up

into the elm and hear each leaf
whisper in my own breath, *welcome
home, this is your home,
welcome home.*

III

Sun, shine through me,
  for I have lost my body,
    my old elm gone home
  to its earthy city, O
sun, shine through me.

IV

Downward leader flash track
driving: 1,000 miles per second;
inconceivable return track:
87,000 miles per second.

But if we could stop it with our eyes:
its central core, hotter and brighter
than the surface of the sun,
only half-inch to an inch diameter;

its corona envelope, or glow discharge,
ten to twenty feet. Lightning:
our eyeballs' branched after-image. Lightning:
smell of ozone in the air,

pure stroke and electric numen.

V

Last night, heat
lightning branching
the blue-black sky,
alone on our back lawn,
when I closed my eyes for the right time,
when I knelt within the nimbus
where the elm I loved
lived for a hundred years,

when I touched the loam fill over the elm's stump,
its clusters of tiny noctilucent mushrooms,
I saw through them
into the ground, into the elm's dead
luminous roots, the branches of heaven
under the earth, this island home,
my lightning lord,
my home.

William Heyen

Elms under Cloud

Elms, old men with thinned-out hair,
And mouths down-turned, express
The oldness of the English scene:

And up the hill a pale road reaches
To a huge paleness browned with scattered,
Irritated cloud.

The spirit takes the chalky road, and says,
When will the clouds, like curves of love
Above the scene, again be smoothly rolled?

Geoffrey Grigson

Ending up in Kent

I'm leaning out the cottage window, latch
unfastened, trying to see for miles, further.
Postcard-picture me in a country of thatch,
twisted lanes, daub and wattle. I entertain
with coal-fires and gas cylinders.
For all through the year it rains, I freeze.
The neighboring oasts are like spindles,
fat with the wound-up thread of absent summer.
I walk detergent streams, in search of trees.

Someone's put me in a story-book, but kills
every tree before my entrance.
I follow an ordnance map and find
frightening rows of straight and vacant pines.
The earth as barren as the rugs
people in my nearby town put down. Medicine
sting of pine. Listen there, hear nothing. No bird sings
I'm told that insects are the only living things
in that Forestry Commission flat. And slugs.

Gala-day on the Tonbridge-Hastings line
and my landlord's chopping down his chestnut trees.
Two train stops and you're at a famous Waters place
where they renovate shops into postcard prints.

Inside are offices, outside a show of wealth. In me,
when I walk that scenic, cobbled walk, a tall tree
grows crooked, like a money-graph
zigzagging into civic failure. In warm weather
they sell sulphur from the Wells for your pleasure.
Good Health! November and the Guy will burn.
What leaves are left on what trees are left will turn.

Eva Salzman

An English Wood

This valley wood is pledged
To the set shape of things,
And reasonably hedged:
Here are no harpies fledged,
No rocs may clap their wings,
Nor gryphons wave their stings.
Here, poised in quietude,
Calm elementals brood
On the set shape of things:
They fend away alarms
From this green wood.
Here nothing is that harms –
No bulls with lungs of brass,
No toothed or spiny grass,
No tree whose clutching arms
Drink blood when travellers pass,
No mount of glass;
No bardic tongues unfold
Satires or charms.
Only, the lawns are soft,
The tree-stems, grave and old;
Slow branches sway aloft,
The evening air comes cold,

51

The sunset scatters gold.
Small grasses toss and bend,
Small pathways idly tend
Towards no fearful end.

Robert Graves

'Enter these enchanted woods'

I

Enter these enchanted woods,
    You who dare.
Nothing harms beneath the leaves
More than waves a swimmer cleaves.
Toss your heart up with the lark,
Foot at peace with mouse and worm,
    Fair you fare.
Only at a dread of dark
Quaver, and they quit their form:
Thousand eyeballs under hoods
    Have you by the hair.
Enter these enchanted woods,
    You who dare.

II

Here the snake across your path
Stretches in his golden bath:
Mossy-footed squirrels leap
Soft as winnowing plumes of Sleep:
Yaffles on a chuckle skim
Low to laugh from branches dim:
Up the pine, where sits the star,
Rattles deep the moth-winged jar.

Each has business of his own;
But should you distrust a tone,
    Then beware.
Shudder all the haunted roods,
All the eyeballs under hoods
    Shroud you in their glare.
Enter these enchanted woods,
    You who dare.

George Meredith
from The Woods of Westermain

The Fallen Elm

Old elm that murmured in our chimney top
The sweetest anthem autumn ever made
And into mellow whispering calms would drop
When showers fell on thy many coloured shade
And when dark tempests mimic thunder made –
While darkness came as it would strangle light
With the black tempest of a winter night
That rocked thee like a cradle in thy root –
How did I love to hear the winds upbraid
Thy strength without – while all within was mute.
It seasoned comfort to our hearts' desire,
We felt that kind protection like a friend
And edged our chairs up closer to the fire,
Enjoying comfort that was never penned.
Old favourite tree, thou'st seen time's changes lower,
Though change till now did never injure thee;
For time beheld thee as her sacred dower
And nature claimed thee her domestic tree.
Storms came and shook thee many a weary hour,
Yet stedfast to thy home thy roots have been;
Summers of thirst parched round thy homely bower
Till earth grew iron – still thy leaves were green.

The children sought thee in thy summer shade
And made their playhouse rings of stick and stone;
The mavis sang and felt himself alone
While in thy leaves his early nest was made,
And I did feel his happiness mine own,
Nought heeding that our friendship was betrayed,
Friend not inanimate – though stocks and stones
There are, and many formed of flesh and bones.
Thou owned a language by which hearts are stirred
Deeper than by a feeling clothed in word,
And speakest now what's known of every tongue,
Language of pity and the force of wrong.
What cant assumes, what hypocrites will dare,
Speaks home to truth and shows it what they are.
I see a picture which thy fate displays
And learn a lesson from thy destiny;
Self-interest saw thee stand in freedom's ways –
So thy old shadow must a tyrant be.
Thou'st heard the knave, abusing those in power,
Bawl freedom loud and then oppress the free;
Thou'st sheltered hypocrites in many a shower,
That when in power would never shelter thee.
Thou'st heard the knave supply his canting powers
With wrong's illusions when he wanted friends;
That bawled for shelter when he lived in showers
And when clouds vanished made thy shade amends –
With axe at root he felled thee to the ground
And barked of freedom – O I hate the sound
Time hears its visions speak, – and age sublime
Hath made thee a disciple unto time.
– It grows the cant term of enslaving tools
To wrong another by the name of right;
Thus came enclosure – ruin was its guide,
But freedom's cottage soon was thrust aside
And workhouse prisons raised upon the site.
Een nature's dwellings far away from men,
The common heath, became the spoiler's prey;
The rabbit had not where to make his den

And labour's only cow was drove away.
No matter – wrong was right and right was wrong,
And freedom's bawl was sanction to the song.
– Such was thy ruin, music-making elm;
The right of freedom was to injure thine:
As thou wert served, so would they overwhelm
In freedom's name the little that is mine.
And there are knaves that brawl for better laws
And cant of tyranny in stronger power
Who glut their vile unsatiated maws
And freedom's birthright from the weak devour.

John Clare

Felling a Tree

The surge of spirit that goes with using an axe,
The first heat – and calming down till the stiff back's
Unease passed, and the hot moisture came on body.
There under banks of Dane and Roman with the golden
Imperial coloured flower, whose name is lost to me –
Hewing the trunk desperately with upward strokes;
Seeing the chips fly – (it was at shoulder height, the trunk)
The green go, and the white appear –
Who should have been making music, but this had to be done
To earn a cottage shelter, and milk, and a little bread:
To right a body, beautiful as water and honour could make one –
And like the soldier lithe of body in the foremost rank
I stood there, muscle stiff, free of arm, working out fear.
Glad it was the ash tree's hardness not of the oaks', of the iron
     oak.
Sweat dripped from me – but there was no stay and the echoing
     bank
Sent back sharp sounds of hacking and of true straight woodcraft.
Some Roman from the pinewood caught memory and laughed.

Hit, crack and false aim, echoed from the amphitheatre
Of what was Rome before Romulus drew shoulder of Remus
Nearer his own – or Fabius won his salvation of victories.
In resting I thought of the hidden farm and Rome's hidden mild
    yoke
Still on the Gloucester heart strong after love's fill of centuries,
For all the happy, or the quiet, Severn or Leadon streams.
Pondered on music's deep truth, poetry's form or metre,
Rested – and took a thought and stuck onward again,
Who had frozen by Chaulnes out of all caring of pain –
Learnt Roman fortitude at Laventie or Ypres,
Saw bright edge bury dull in the beautiful wood,
Touched splinters so wonderful – half through and soon to come
    down
From that ledge of rock under harebell, the yellow flower – the
    pinewood's crown.
Four inches more – and I should hear the crash and great thunder
Of an ash Crickley had loved for a century, and kept her own.
Thoughts of soldier and musician gathered to me
The desire of conquest ran in my blood, went through me –
There was a battle in my spirit and my blood shared it,
Maisemore – and Gloucester – bred me, and Cotswold reared it,
This great tree standing nobly in the July's day full light
Nearly to fall – my courage broke – and gathered – my breath
    feared it,
My heart – and again I struck, again the splinters and steel glinters
Dazzled my eyes – and the pain and the desperation and near
    victory
Carried me onwards – there were exultations and mockings sunward
Sheer courage, as of boat sailings in equinoctial unsafe squalls,
Stiffened my virtue, and the thing was done. No. Dropped my
    body,
The axe dropped – for a minute, taking breath, and gathering
    the greedy
Courage – looking for rest to the farm and grey loose-piled walls,
Rising like Troilus to the first word of 'Ready',
The last desperate onslaught – took the two inches of too steady
Trunk – on the rock edge it lurched, threatening my labouring life

(Nearly on me). Like Trafalgar's own sails imperiously moving to
    defeat
Across the wide sky unexpected glided and the high bank's pines
    and fell straight
Lower and lower till the crashing of the fellow trees made strife.
The thud of earth, and the full tree lying low in state,
With all its glory of life and sap quick in the veins...
Such beauty, for the farm fires and heat against chilly rains,
Golden glows in the kitchen from what a century made great...

The axe fell from my hand, and I was proud of my hand,
Crickley forgave, for her nobleness, the common fate of trees
As noble or more noble, the oak, the elm that is treacherous,
But dear for her cherishing to this beloved and this rocky land.
Over above all the world there, in a tired glory swerved there,
To a fall, the tree that for long had watched Wales glow strong,
Seen Severn, and farm, and Brecon, Black Mountains times
    without reckon.
And tomorrow would be fuel for the bright kitchen – for brown
    tea, against cold night.

Ivor Gurney

Fence Posts

It might be that horses would be useful
On a snowy morning to take the trail
Down the ridge to visit Steve or Mike and
Faster than going around the gravelled road by car.

So the thought came to fence a part of the forest,
Thin trees and clear the brush,
Ron splits cedar rails and fenceposts
On Black Sands Placer road where he gets
These great old butt logs from the Camptonville sawmill

Why they can't use them I don't know –
They aren't all pecky.
He delivers, too, in a bread van
His grandfather drove in Seattle.

Sapwood posts are a little bit cheaper than heartwood.
I could have bought all heartwood from the start
But then I thought how it doesn't work
To always make a point of getting the best which is why
I sometimes pick out the worse and damaged looking fruit
And vegetables at the market because I know
I actually will enjoy them in any case but
Some people might take them as second choice
And feel sour about it all evening.

With sapwood fenceposts
You ought to soak to make sure they won't rot
In a fifty-five gallon drum with penta 10 to 1
Which is ten gallons of oil and a gallon of
Termite and fungus poison.
I use old crankcase oil to dilute
And that's a good thing to do with it but,
There's not really enough old crank to go around.
The posts should be two feet in the ground.

So, soaking six posts a week at a time
The soaked pile getting bigger week by week,
But the oil only comes up one and a half feet.
I could add kerosene in
At seventy cents a gallon
Which is what it costs when you buy it by the drum
And that's $3.50 to raise the soaking level up
Plus a half a can of penta more, six dollars,
For a hundred and twenty fence posts
On which I saved thirty dollars by getting the sapwood,
But still you have to count your time,

A well-done fence is beautiful.
And horses, too.
Penny wise pound foolish either way.

Fifty Faggots

There they stand, on their ends, the fifty faggots
That once were underwood of hazel and ash
In Jenny Pinks's Copse. Now, by the hedge
Close packed, they make a thicket fancy alone
Can creep through with the mouse and wren. Next Spring
A blackbird or a robin will nest there,
Accustomed to them, thinking they will remain
Whatever is for ever to a bird:
This Spring it is too late; the swift has come.
'Twas a hot day for carrying them up:
Better they will never warm me, though they must
Light several Winters' fires. Before they are done
The war will have ended, many other things
Have ended, maybe, that I can no more
Foresee or more control than robin and wren.

Edward Thomas

'For over-al, wher that I myn eyen caste'

For over-al, wher that I myn eyen caste,
Were trees clad with leves that ay shal laste,
Eche in his kinde, of colour fresh and grene
As emeraude, that joye was to sene.

The bilder ook, and eek the hardy asshe;
The piler elm, the cofre unto careyne:
The boxtree piper; holm to whippes lasshe;
The sayling firr; the cipres, deth to pleyne;
The sheter ew, the asp for shaftes pleyne;
The olyve of pees, and eek the drunken vyne,
The victor palm, the laurer to devyne...

Geoffrey Chaucer
from The Parlement of Foules

'Give me a land of boughs in leaf'

Give me a land of boughs in leaf,
   A land of trees that stand;
Where trees are fallen, there is grief;
   I love no leafless land...

A.E. Housman

Glyn Cynon Wood

Aberdare, Llanwynno through,
all Merthyr to Llanfabon;
there was never a more disastrous thing
than the cutting of Glyn Cynon.

They cut down many a parlour pure
where youth and manhood meet;
in those days of the regular star
Glyn Cynon's woods were sweet.

If a man in sudden plight
took to flight from foe,
for guest-house to the nightingale
in Cynon Vale he'd go.

Many a birch-tree green of cloak
(I'd like to choke the Saxon!)
is now a flaming heap of fire
where iron-workers blacken.

For cutting the branch and bearing away
the wild birds' habitation
may misfortune quickly reach
Rowenna's treacherous children!

Rather should the English be
strung up beneath the seas,
keeping painful house in hell
than felling Cynon's trees.

Upon my oath, I've heard it said
that a herd of the red deer
for Mawddwy's deep dark woods has left,
bereft of its warmth here.

No more the badger's earth we'll sack
nor start a buck from the glade;
no more deer-stalking in my day,
now they've cut Glyn Cynon's shade.

If ever a stag got into a wood
with huntsmen a stride behind,
never again will he turn in his run
with Cynon Wood in mind.

If the flour-white girl once came
to walk along the brook,

Glyn Cynon's wood was always there
as a fair trysting nook.

If as in times gone by men plan
to span the mountain river;
though wood be found for house and church
Glyn Cynon's no provider.

I'd like to call on them a quest
of every honest bird,
where the owl, worthiest in the wood,
as hangman would be heard.

If there's a question who rehearsed
in verse this cruel tale,
it's one who many a tryst has kept
in the depth of Cynon Vale.

Anon

Green Man

Fleet in the forest,
leafshaken, wild in the wood,
flowers tousled in his hair,
garlanded with laurel and with ivy,
the Green Grotesque swoops out of stone and timber.
Locked in a church boss
his eyes start with alarm
at his enclosure. Brown priests agreed
to give his effigy a place.
That would bring the gaffers in,
the maids with May bandeaus,
the mothers full of fears and needing cures.

They could turn an eye
towards the old religion
while they received the new.
Christ nailed to a tree would keep their reverence
front facing; they could fringe
the alter of the new covenant with evergreen
with rosemary to sprig the nosegays left
under the wood-man's stare.
Needs are many and the winter cold,
best to placate all gods.
The Mediterreanean Lord of Life
could promise them a warmer afterlife,
the Forest Sprite green leaves,
a yellow corn and a berried harvest.

Heather Harrison

Green Man in the Garden

Green man in the garden
   Staring from the tree,
Why do you look so long and hard
   Through the pane at me?

Your eyes are dark as holly,
   Of sycamore your horns,
Your bones are made of elder-branch,
   Your teeth are made of thorns.

Your hat is made of ivy-leaf,
   Of bark your dancing shoes,
And evergreen and green and green
   Your jacket and shirt and trews.

Leave your house and leave your land
  And throw away the key,
And never look behind, he creaked,
  And come and live with me.

I bolted up the window,
  I bolted up the door,
I drew the blind that I should find
  The green man never more.

But when I softly turned the stair
  As I went up to bed,
I saw the green man standing there.
  Sleep well, my friend, he said.

Charles Causley

'The groves are down'

The groves are down
                cut down
Groves of Ahab, of Cybele
Pine trees, knobbed twigs
      thick cone and seed
      Cybele's tree this, sacred in groves
Pine of Seami, cedar of Haida
Cut down by the prophets of Israel
      the fairies of Athens
      the thugs of Rome
                both ancient and modern;
Cut down to make room for the suburbs
Bulldozed by Luther and Weyerhaeuser
Crosscut and chainsaw
      squareheads and finns
      high-lead and cat-skidding
Trees down
Creeks choked, trout killed, roads.

Sawmill temples of Jehovah.
Squat black burners 100 feet high
Sending the smoke of our burnt
Live sap and leaf
To his eager nose.

Gary Snyder
from Logging

'The holly and the ivy'

The holly and the ivy,
When they are both full grown,
Of all the trees that are in the wood,
The holly bears the crown:

> *The rising of the sun*
> *And the running of the deer,*
> *The playing of the merry organ,*
> *Sweet singing in the choir.*

The holly bears a blossom,
As white as the lily flower,
And Mary bore sweet Jesus Christ,
To be our sweet Saviour:

The holly bears a berry,
As red as any blood,
And Mary bore sweet Jesus Christ
To do poor sinners good:

The holly bears a prickle,
As sharp as any thorn,
And Mary bore sweet Jesus Christ
On Christmas day in the morn:

The holly bears a bark,
As bitter as any gall,
And Mary bore sweet Jesus Christ
For to redeem us all:

The holly and the ivy,
When they are both full grown,
Of all the trees that are in the wood,
The holly bears the crown:

Anon

Home-Thoughts, from Abroad

I
Oh, to be in England
Now that April's there,
And whoever wakes in England
Sees, some morning, unaware,
That the lowest boughs and the brushwood sheaf
Round the elm-tree bole are in tiny leaf,
While the chaffinch sings on the orchard bough
In England – now!

II
And after April, when May follows,
And the whitethroat builds, and all the swallows!
Hark, where my blossomed pear-tree in the hedge
Leans to the field and scatters on the clover
Bossoms and dewdrops – at the bent spray's edge –
That's the wise thrush; he sings each song twice over,
Lest you should think he never could recapture
The first fine careless rapture!

And though the fields look rough with hoary dew
All will be gay when noontide wakes anew
The buttercups, the little children's dower
– Far brighter than this gaudy melon-flower!

Robert Browning

'How long does it take to make the woods?'

How long does it take to make the woods?
As long as it takes to make the world.
The woods is present as the world is, the presence
of all its past, and of all its time to come.
It is always finished, it is always being made, the act
of its making forever greater than the act of its destruction.
It is a part of eternity, for its end and beginning
belong to the end and beginning of all things,
the beginning lost in the end, the end in the beginning.

What is the way to the woods, how do you go there?
By climbing up through the six days' field,
kept in all the body's years, the body's
sorrow, weariness, and joy. By passing through
the narrow gate on the far side of that field
where the pasture grass of the body's life gives way
to the high, original standing of the trees.
By coming into the shadow, the shadow
of the grace of the strait way's ending,
the shadow of the mercy of light.

Why must the gate be narrow?
Because you cannot pass beyond it burdened.
To come into the woods you must leave behind
the six days' world, all of it, all of its plans and hopes.

You must come without weapon or tool, alone,
expecting nothing, remembering nothing,
into the ease of sight, the brotherhood of eye and leaf.

Wendell Berry
from Sabbaths

'Hwaet! A dream came to me at deep midnight'

Hwaet!
A dream came to me
        at deep midnight
when humankind
        kept their beds
– the dream of dreams!
        I shall declare it.

It seemed I saw the Tree itself
borne on the air, light wound about it,
– a beam of brightest wood, a beacon clad
in overlapping gold, glancing gems
fair at its foot, and five stones
set in a crux flashed from the crosstree...

...Yet lying there a long while
I beheld, sorrowing, the Healer's Tree
till it seemed that I heard how it broke silence,
best of wood, and began to speak:

'Over that long remove my mind ranges
back to the holt where I was hewn down;
from my own stem I was struck away,
        dragged off by strong enemies,
wrought into a roadside scaffold,
        They made me a hoist for wrongdoers.

The soldiers on their shoulders bore me,
      until on a hill-top they set me up;
many enemies made me fast there.
      Then I saw, marching toward me,
mankind's brave King;
      He came to climb upon me.

I dared not break or bend aside
against God's will, though the ground itself
shook at my feet. Fast I stood,
who falling could have felled them all.

Almighty God ungirded Him,
      eager to mount the gallows,
unafraid in the sight of many:
      He would set free mankind.
I shook when His arms embraced me
      but I durst not bow to ground,
stoop to Earth's surface.
      Stand fast I must.

I was reared up, a rood.
      I raised the great King,
liege lord of the heavens,
      dared not lean from the true.
They drove me through with dark nails:
      on me are the deep wounds manifest,
wide-mouthed hate-dents.
      I durst not harm any of them.
How they mocked at us both!
      I was all moist with blood
sprung from the Man's side
      after He sent forth His soul.

Wry wierds a-many I underwent
up on that hill-top; saw the Lord of Hosts
stretched out stark. Darkness shrouded
the King's corse. Clouds wrapped

its clear shining. A shade went out
wan under cloud-pall. All creation wept,
keened the King's death. Christ was on the Cross...

Anon
from the Dream of the Rood

In a Wood

Pale beech and pine so blue,
    Set in one clay,
Bough to bough cannot you
    Live out your day?
When the rains skim and skip,
Why mar sweet comradeship,
Blighting with poison-drip
    Neighbourly spray?

Heart-halt and spirit-lame,
    City-opprest,
Unto this wood I came
    As to a nest;
Dreaming that sylvan peace
Offered the harrowed ease –
Nature a soft release
    From men's unrest.

But, having entered in,
    Great growths and small
Show them to men akin –
    Combatants all!
Sycamore shoulders oak,
Bines the slim sapling yoke,
Ivy-spun halters choke
    Elms stout and tall.

Touches from ash, O wych,
　　Sting you like scorn!
You, too, brave hollies, twitch
　　Sidelong from thorn.
Even the rank poplars bear
Lothly a rival's air,
Cankering in black despair
　　If overborne.

Thomas Hardy

'In midwinter a wood was'

In midwinter a wood was
where the sand-coloured deer ran
through quietness.
It was a marvellous thing
to see those deer running.

Softer than ashes
snow lay all winter where they ran,
and in the wood a holly tree was.
God, it was a marvellous thing
to see the deer running.

Between lime trunks grey or green
branch-headed stags went by
silently trotting.
A holly tree dark and crimson
sprouted at the wood's centre, thick and high
without a whisper, no other berry so fine.

Outside the wood was black midwinter,
over the downs that reared so solemn
wind rushed in gales, and strong here

wrapped around wood and holly fire
(where deer among the close limes ran)
with a storming circle of its thunder.
Under the trees it was a marvellous thing
to see the deer running.

Peter Levi

'In somer, when the shawes be sheyne'

In somer, when the shawes be sheyne
    And leves be large and long,
Hit is full mery in feyre foreste
    To here the foulys song;

To se the dere draw to the dale
    And leve the hilles hee,
And shadow hem in the leves grene
    Vnder the grene-wode tre...

Anon
from The Ballad of Robyn Hode
and the Munke

In the Woods

Always at this time there is the bankrupt plant:
autumn afflicts the failed machinery of ferns with rust.
The foliage is full of broken windows.
The birch trees shed their aluminium crust,

and the cedar drops its complicated cogs.
The roof of things has fallen in –
these paprika patches on the factory floor
are corrugated remnants of protective tin.

Oddments blacken strangely on a nearby fence:
rags, an old glove in a liquorice droop,
washleathers warp with dull black holly claws.
It is a sad, abandoned, oddly human group.

The glove is singular. You cannot try it on.
It is too small. Besides, it has no fingers.
It is more like something surgical –
the unpleasant shape of stumpy enigmas.

Below, a nylon sock curls up like a dead animal.
Through a hole in the toe, a glint of teeth.
Over there, the remains of a fire –
pigeon feathers in a narrow ashy wreath.

And everywhere egg-shells, egg-shells,
so light they stir with the gentlest breath –
a breakfast of papery skulls. The Omelette Man
has eaten here and manufactured death.

Craig Raine

In Westerham Woods

Two lovers here once carved their name,
A heart between them like a flame;
Now these two lovers' names depart
From either side a broken heart.

Andrew Young

73

'I saw in Louisiana a live-oak growing'

I saw in Louisiana a live-oak growing,
All alone stood it and the moss hung down from the
      branches,
Without any companion it grew there uttering joyous leaves
      of dark green,
And its look, rude, unbending, lusty, made me think of
      myself,
But I wonder'd how it could utter joyous leaves standing
      alone there without its friend near, for I knew I could not,
And I broke off a twig with a certain number of leaves upon
      it, and twined around it a little moss,
And brought it away, and I have placed it in sight in my
      room,
It is not needed to remind me as of my own dear friends,
(For I believe lately I think of little else than of them,)
Yet it remains to me a curious token, it makes me think of
      manly love;
For all that, and though the live-oak glistens there in
      Louisiana solitary in a wide flat space,
Uttering joyous leaves all its life without a friend a lover
      near,
I know very well I could not.

Walt Whitman

'I see the oak's bride in the oak's grasp'

I see the oak's bride in the oak's grasp.

Nuptials among prehistoric insects
The tremulous convulsion
The inching hydra strength
Among frilled lizards

74

Dropping twigs, and acorns, and leaves.
The oak is in bliss
Its roots
Lift arms that are a supplication
Crippled with stigmata
Like the sea-carved cliffs earth lifts
Loaded with dumb, uttering effigies
The oak seems to die and to be dead
In its love-act.

As I lie under it

In a brown leaf nostalgia

An acorn stupor.

Ted Hughes
from Gaudete

'I think that I shall never see'

I think that I shall never see
A poem as lovely as a tree,
Poems are made by fools like me
But only God can make a tree.

Alfred (Joyce) Kilmer

'It is not growing like a tree'

It is not growing like a tree
In bulk, doth make Man better be;
Or standing long an oak, three hundred year,

To fall a log at last, dry, bald, and sere:
    A lily of a day
    Is fairer far in May,
    Although it fall and die that night;
    It was the plant and flower of Light.
In small proportions we just beauties see;
And in short measures life may perfect be.

Ben Jonson

'The land of Y Llain was on the high marsh'

...The land of Y Llain was on the high marsh
on the border between Caron-is-Clawdd and Padarn Odwyn
slanting from Cae Top down to Y Waun,
and beyond Cae Top was a glade of dark trees –
pines and tall larches – to break the cold wind,
the wind from the north.
And there were the small four-sided fields
like checkerboard, or a patchwork quilt,
and around each of the fields, a hedge.

    My father planted the hedges farthest from the house, –
the hedges of Cae Top and Cae Brwyn, –
myself a youngster at his heels
putting the plants in his hand:
three hawthorns and a beech-tree,
three hawthorns and a beech-tree in turn;
his feet measuring the distance between them along the top of the
    ditch,
squeezing them solidly into the loose earth-and-chalk.
Then the patterned wiring outside them –
the square posts of peeled oak-wood
sunk deep in the living earth –
and I getting to turn the wiring-engine on the post

while he did the stapling,
the hammer ringing in my ears with the pounding.
And I daring on the sly
to send a telegram back over the taut wires
to the other children at the far end of the ditch,
the note of music raising its pitch
with each turn I gave the old wiring-engine's handle.
      My grandfather, said my father, had planted the Middle Field
   – Cae Cwteri, Cae Polion, Cae Troi –
but generations we knew nothing at all about,
except for the mark of their handiwork on Cae Lloi and Cae Moch
had planted the tall strong stout-trunked trees round the house,
and set sweet-plums here and there in the hedges.
      And there we children would be
safe in a fold in the ditch under the hedges,
the dried leaves a coverlet to keep us warm
(like the babes in the story hidden with leaves by the birds).
The breeze that trickled through the trunks of the hedges
was not enough to ruffle the wren's and the robin's feathers:
but above the hedges and the trees, above the house,
aloft in the firmament, the wind was
tumbling the clouds, tickling them till their white laughter
was unruly hysteria like children on a kitchen floor,
till the excess of play turns suddenly strange
and the laughter's whiteness scowls, and darkens,
and the tears burst forth, and the clouds escape
in a race from the wind, from the tickling and the tumbling,
escaping headlong from the wind's provocation –
the pursuing wind outside me,
and I fast in the fold in the ditch beneath the leaves
listening to its sound, outside,
with nothing at all occuring within what I am
because of the care and craft of generations of my fathers
planting their hedges prudently to shelter me in my day, –
nothing – despite my wishing and wishing...

                              J. Kitchener Davies
               from The Sound of the Wind that is Blowing

The Leaf

'How beautifully it falls,' you said,
As a leaf turned and twirled
On invisible wind upheld,
How airily to ground
Prolongs its flight.

You for a leaf-fall forgot
Old age, loneliness,
Body's weary frame,
Crippled hands, failing sense,
Unkind world and its pain.

What did that small leaf sign
To you, troth its gold
Plight 'twixt you and what unseen
Messenger to the heart
From a fair, simple land?

Kathleen Raine

'Living a good way up a mountain'

...Living a good way up a mountain
Above the natural line of trees,
We nurture saplings, ache for torn
Or wounded cedar, oak or thorn
And mourn fatalities.

Trees are annual calendars
And their expressive flags have taught us
To greet the spring. They're twiggy babels
For many birds; pencils and tables
To please our daughters' daughters.

The lifetime that they take to grow
Is rarely ours. We feel a bond
Like that with age: memorabilia
To be respected, grave, familiar,
A little feared or fond.

We note the fruiting of the rowan,
If it's the year for bullace or
For sloe, or how much higher stand
The valiant Blackheath walnut and
The Oxford sycamore.

But most regret in this last winter
The passing of an ancient ash
Which air, that changed location at
Unlikely speed, disturbed and flat-
tened with an unheard crash.

But now, although it leans upon
One hinge of bark, new leafage shoots
From stumps the guilty wind has healed.
It dipped its elbows in the field
And there established roots.

If only our unrooted lives
When felled could simply change direction
And all our tall assumptions both
Be trimmed and find amazing growth,
A perfect resurrection!

The tree has found a way of walking
Not as our childhood stories told us
Through sudden supernatural strength
But through first tumbling its full length
Then growing from its shoulders...

John Fuller
from The Grey and the Green

London Trees

Out of the roads of London springs the forest,
Over and underworld, the veritable Eden
Here we have planted for our solitude,
Those planes, where thoughts unblamed among the leaves
    may run.

Sensing us, the trees tremble in their sleep,
The living leaves recoil before our fires.
Baring to us war-charred and broken branches,
And seeing theirs, we for our own destruction weep.

And women, sore at heart, trying to pray
Unravel the young buds with anxious fingers
Searching for God, who has gone far away,
Yet still at evening in the green world lingers.

Obedient still to Him, the toiling trees
Lift up their fountains, where still waters rise
Upwards into life, filled from the surrounding skies
To quench the sorrows thirsting in the world's eyes.

Kathleen Raine

The Long-Tailed Tits

I stopped to hear it clear,
The sound of water tinkling near,
Although I knew no dowser could
Turn hazel-fork in that beech-wood.

Then on the high tree-tops
With rising runs and jerks and stops
Like water stones break into bits
Flowed the cascade of long-tailed tits.

Andrew Young

'Loveliest of trees, the cherry now'

Loveliest of trees, the cherry now
Is hung with bloom along the bough,
And stands about the woodland ride
Wearing white for Eastertide.

Now, of my threescore years and ten,
Twenty will not come again,
And take from seventy springs a score,
It only leaves me fifty more.

And since to look at things in bloom
Fifty springs are little room,
About the woodlands I will go
To see the cherry hung with snow.

A.E. Housman
from A Shropshire Lad

The Magic Apple Tree

Sealed in rainlight one
November sleepwalking afternoon streets
I remembered Samuel Palmer's garden
Waterhouse in Shoreham, and at once
I knew: that the chill of wet

brown streets was no more literal
than the yellow he laid there against
his unnatural blue   because
together they worked upon me like
an icon   infantine

he called his vision / so it was
with the early makers of icons, who
worked humbly, choosing wood without resin.
They stilled their spirits before using the gold
and while the brightness held under the *kvass*
their colours too induced
the peculiar joy of abandoning restlessness

and now in streets where only white
mac or car metal catches the failing
light, if we sing of
the red and the blue and the texture of goat hair,
there is no deceit in our prophecy:
for even now our brackish waters can
be sweetened by a strange tree.

                    Elaine Feinstein

Maple and Starlings

Over my head, a maple fills with starlings
against the evening sky.
I won't move, I won't speak.
The maple will hold them as long as it does.

In a few seconds, the maple rising above me blossomed
with starlings. Darker than evening, darker than leaves,
they flew from nowhere to here for the first time.
I knew maple and starlings for the first time.

This evening, the maple above me turned to starlings.
A few moments, and everything was over, nothing
changed. The starlings flew from nowhere they remember.
The maple stands for nothing in the evening air.

How long had it been evening?
As long as starlings' shadows
were blowing through the maples.
As long as leaves were flying.

Over my head, a maple fills with evening,
releases flows of starlings,
or receives them,
wherever they came from, wherever they're going.

The maple growing into the evening above me fills
with starlings. For a few seconds, it's been as though
I've not been here to say *maple*, and *starlings*.
For a few seconds, the evening has darkened with starlings.

Someone has been dreaming: maple, starlings,
an evening second by second being its own darkness.
A maple rising in the dark air: Starlings
from nowhere to nowhere. A maple. Starlings.

William Heyen

Maple and Sumach

Maple and sumach down this autumn ride –
Look, in what scarlet character they speak!
For this their russet and rejoicing week
Trees spend a year of sunsets on their pride.
You leaves drenched with the lifeblood of the year –
What flamingo dawns have wavered from the east,

What eves have crimsoned to their toppling crest
To give the fame and transience that you wear!
Leaf-low he shall lie soon: but no such blaze
Briefly can cheer man's ashen, harsh decline;
His fall is short of pride, he bleeds within
And paler creeps to the dead end of his days.
O light's abandon and the fire-crest sky
Speak in me now for all who are to die!

C. Day Lewis

The May-Tree

As if when a man was striding on an errand
of adult importance requiring a brief-case
a scruffy child should slip her hand in his
and he be obliged to accept her and protect her,
like this, today, the may came in my mind:
the responsibility.
                         Though she's no child –
I've looked at her for eighteen years from the window
and she was already old when we came to this house.
Her hair straggles and one shoulder's
a little higher than the other,
result of the careless way she's been flail-cut,
She's fruitful – so-so. Fieldfares take their toll.
But she's had to be tough: she isn't beautiful.

She grows against the wire of the farmer's field,
a tree, definitely, having a naked
visible trunk unlike the opulent
Palmeresque bushes behind her in the pasture.
Now they, when they're in bloom, are radiant
they can cause temporary transmutations
even in computer-friendly minds.

But she even I, her nearest sister, hadn't much
thought about till one day when two men came by
and stopped the tractor with the flail, got down
and shook her about and looked her over,
Was it worthwhile to keep an aging haw?
and I found myself running and trying not to scream
trying to discover I who was always craven
authority to hold their wanton hands.

Who smiled reassurance. Just trimming.
They knew at once what was the matter,
had seen women taken in this way before.
Their smiles had more than a sprinkling of scorn.

You don't bring may blossom into the house!
Everyone's mother taught them that.
Don't be afraid, Mother, don't be afraid
if I bring it indoors inside my head
loving and learning the tree that is over-against me:
I'm so afraid they will cut the may-tree down.

We can't carry the world, heroic, cracking:
Atlas was a man's misguided myth.
But let's carry a clod each
link arms and lift up a spring language
bud and break out and bring in better times.

Kim Taplin

The Memorial Trees

Here in the public garden deep with shade
        The branches cluster, filtering the sun,
And as they sway, the gaining patterns fade
        Across the paths and steps, and from the gun

Set into concrete, pointing up, dull green,
　　Where olive trees enclose it row on row.
Enlaced above the barrel like a screen
　　Their leaves are grey and silver as they blow

As if intended to conceal its aim;
　　But tags of metal gleam from every tree
Where bark encroaches on a soldier's name
　　Dulled by the bitter moisture from the sea;

It wanders in the leaves and makes them stir.
　　Dry leaves, and ancient on the victim's head
But hung with fruit, a pulse of what they were;
　　Now they are turned to trees, the living dead,

Yielders before the wind, graspers for life,
　　For ever rooted where they understood
The angel shrieking with the grafting knife
　　When the bombardment splintered in the wood.

Then saplings, and the shovelfuls of earth
　　And grieving fingers spreading tender roots
Again at others' hands. But this was birth,
　　To plant their dying with life's attributes,

The anguish of the living here revealed;
　　When every autumn of the monument
With each rich pressing of the fruit must yield
　　A trickle bright as pain for nourishment.

Michael Vince

Never Tell

The saplings of the green-tipped birch
Draw my foot from bondage:
Let no boy know your secret!

Oak saplings in the grove
Draw my foot from its chain:
Tell no secret to a maid!

Anon

The New Tree

Planted a tree the afternoon before
what has become the first evening of autumn
(eucalyptus-spring in Australia),
wind dropped and clouds moved on, mid-August storms
seemingly gone. And now the moon, almost
at full, a thin-worn disk of beaten tawny
metal foil, or crumpled papery fallen
eucalyptus leaf, hovers above the hawthorn
and the bramble hedges, unkempt corner
of my northern garden, as I cross the lawn
to touch the newly planted tree, its short
rose-madder stems and glaucous foliage, once more,
and wonder if its roots can feel the draw
of the antipodes, the pull from that far shore;
confirm again that everything's in order,
and wish it well until tomorrow's dawn.

Ruth Fainlight

'No weekends for the gods now. Wars'

...No weekends for the gods now. Wars
flicker, earth licks its open sores,
fresh breakage, fresh promotions, chance
assassinations, no advance.

Only man thinning out his kind
sounds through the Sabbath noon, the blind
swipe of the pruner and his knife
busy about the tree of life...

Robert Lowell
from Waking Early Sunday Morning

No-man's Wood

Shall I have jealous thoughts to nurse,
When I behold a rich man's house?
Not though his windows, thick as stars,
    Number the days in every year;
I, with one window for each month,
    Am rich in four or five to spare.

But when I count his shrubberies,
His fountains there, and clumps of trees,
Over the palings of his park
    I leap with my primeval blood;
Down wild ravines to Ocean's rocks,
    Clean through the heart of No-man's Wood.

W.H. Davies

'Nor less attractive is the woodland scene'

Nor less attractive is the woodland scene,
Diversified with trees of ev'ry growth,
Alike, yet various. Here the gray smooth trunks
Of ash, or lime, or beech, distinctly shine,
Within the twilight of their distant shades;

There, lost behind a rising ground, the wood
Seems sunk and shorten'd to its topmost boughs.
No tree in all the grove but has its charms,
Though each its hue peculiar; paler some,
And of a wannish gray; the willow such
And poplar, that with silver lines his leaf,
And ash far-stretching his umbrageous arm;
Of deeper green the elm; and deeper still,
Lord of the woods, the long-surviving oak.
Some glossy-leav'd, and shining in the sun,
The maple, and the beech of oily nuts
Prolific, and the lime at dewy eve
Diffusing odours: not unnoted pass
The sycamore, capricious in attire,
Now green, now tawny, and, ere autumn yet
Have chang'd the woods, in scarlet honours bright.
O'er these, but far beyond (a spacious map
Of hill and valley interpos'd between),
The Ouse, dividing the well-water'd land,
Now glitters in the sun, and now retires,
As bashful, yet impatient to be seen.

William Cowper
from The Task

Not After Plutarch

'Comfort me with apples'

parallel lives of one mind in two climes
this is my present reality –
beginning with rivers running reflective water
with wind nearest comparison of spirit
and apple orchards of forgotten tribes

fruit trees grown gaunt and tall
the apples small tough-skinned as berries
rough but tendersweet to teeth
used to crack hazel nuts or the long-sheathed filbert

this from the equator is the far isle
of the blest the happiest immortal hyperboreans
now I am sure this haunting of apple-eating
and gathering long painted ladders baskets
and measures heaped up grass lumpy
with tumbled harvest is the childhood be-
ginning of the discovery of Avalon
where the sun sets and all those western clouds
and shadowy hills are stained with human dreams

forget the fright of Eden deep is the Vale
of Avalon with sleep and mellow apple fruitage

Mary Casey

'Now I am here, what thou wilt do with me'

...Now I am here, what thou wilt do with me
　　None of my books will show:
I reade, and sigh, and wish I were a tree;
　　For sure then I should grow
To fruit or shade: at least some bird would trust
Her household to me, and I should be just...

George Herbert
from The Temple (Affliction I)

'Now, my co-mates and brothers in exile'

Duke Senior: Now, my co-mates and brothers in exile,
Hath not old customs made this life more sweet
Than that of painted pomp? Are not these woods
More free from peril than the envious court!
Here feel we not the penalty of Adam,
The seasons' difference; as the icy fang
And churlish chiding of the winter's wind,
Which when it bites and blows upon my body,
Even till I shrink with cold, I smile and say
'This is no flattery; these are counsellors
That feelingly persuade me what I am'.
Sweet are the uses of adversity;
Which, like the toad, ugly and venomous,
Wears yet a precious jewel in his head;
And this our life, exempt from public haunt,
Finds tongues in trees, books in the running brooks,
Sermons in stones, and good in everything.
I would not change it.

William Shakespeare
from As You Like It

'O Rosalind! these trees shall be my books'

Orlando: O Rosalind! these trees shall be my books,
And in their barks my thoughts I'll character,
That every eye which in this forest looks
Shall see thy virtue witness'd everywhere.
Run, run, Orlando; carve on every tree,
The fair, the chaste, and unexpressive she.

William Shakespeare
from As You Like It

Oak

Slow in growth, late in putting out leaves,
And the full leaves dark, austere,
Neither the flower nor the fruit sweet
Save to the harsh jay's tongue, squirrel's and boar's,
Oak has an earthward urge, each bough dithers,
Now rising, now jerked aside, twisted back,
Only the bulk of the lower trunk keeps
A straight course, only the massed foliage together
Rounds a shape out of knots and zigzags.

But when other trees, even the late-leaved ash,
Slow-growing walnut, wide-branching beech and linden
Sway in a summer wind, poplar and willow bend,
Oak alone looks compact, in a stillness hides
Black stumps of limbs that blight or blast bared;
And for death reserves its more durable substance.
On wide floorboards four centuries old,
Sloping, yet scarcely worn, I can walk
And in words not oaken, those of my time, diminished,
Mark them that never were a monument
But plain utility, and mark the diminution,
Loss of that patient tree, loss of the skills
That matched the patience, shaping hard wood
To outlast the worker and outlast the user;
How by oak beams, worm-eaten,
This cottage stands, when brick and plaster have crumbled,
In casements of oak the leaded panes rest
Where new frames, new doors, mere deal, again and again have
rotted.

Michael Hamburger

Oak Duir

June 10 – July 7

I put my head in the bag of leaves
and breathed green. Coarse sourjuiced crushed
smell of wet summers, that sharp male taste;
foliate-faced I sucked green with each breath,
spaced out on oak. The fine drenching rain
felt seasidey. We walked the gleaming lane
that ribbons from hill to hill, slowly, dodging
odd Sunday cars, to our knees in tangled stalks,
flowering grasses, red cloverheads weighed down
with so much wet, the ditches murmuring.

Wine from oakleaves is tawny, tastes dark
and woody, midsummer evening fires, the sweet
smoke of peat. It is strong, climbs down deep
and blazes. It comes from the young growth;
the tender pink-flushed clusters of new leaf
offer themselves at a touch, break free
in showers of droplets, stalked green and sapped
like frankincense. You pour boiling water
on the stripped leaves: they smell of fresh tea.
The brew is bitter and brown; it could cure leather.

I sipped at last year's wine; thought, from now on
the nights draw in. The season's prime lay
stewed in a bin, filling our house with summer.
(I'm autumnal, best in receding light
in the dark half of the year.) Next day
I strained the stuff, added yeast and sweetness,
set the warm juice to work. Those clear green leaves
are bloodless now, bleached out: I have
their essence bottled up, breathed in, elixir of all
oaks in me, as the sun inches south.

Hilary Llewellyn-Williams
from Tree Calendar

93

'The oak inns creak in their joints as light declines'

The oak inns creak in their joints as light declines
from the ale-coloured skies of Warwickshire.
Autumn has blown the froth from the foaming orchards,
so white-haired regulars draw chairs nearer the grate
to spit on logs that crackle into leaves of fire.
But they grow deafer, not sure if what they hear
is the drone of the abbeys from matins to compline,
or the hornet's nest of a chain saw working late
on the knoll up there back of the Norman chapel.
Evening loosens the moth, the owl shifts its weight,
a fish-mouthed moon swims up from wavering elms,
but four old men are out on the garden benches,
talking of the bows they have drawn, their strings of wenches,
their coined eyes shrewdly glittering like the Thames'
estuaries. I heard their old talk carried
through cables laid across the Atlantic bed,
their gossip rustles like an apple orchard's
in my own head, and I can drop their names
like familiars – those bastard grandsires
whose maker granted them a primal pardon –
because the worm that cores the rotting apple
of the world and the hornet's chain saw cannot touch the words
of Shallow or Silence in their fading garden.

Derek Walcott

The Old Elm Tree by the River

Shrugging in the flight of its leaves,
it is dying. Death is slowly
standing up in its trunk and branches
like a camouflaged hunter. In the night
I am wakened by one of its branches
crashing down, heavy as a wall, and then

94

lie sleepless, the world changed.
That is a life I know the country by.
Mine is a life I know the country by.
Willing to live and die, we stand here,
timely and at home, neighborly as two men.
Our place is changing in us as we stand,
and we hold up the weight that will bring us down.
In us the land enacts its history.
When we stood it was beneath us, and was
the strength by which we held to it
and stood, the daylight over it
a mighty blessing we cannot bear for long.

Wendell Berry

The Old Oak Tree

I sit beneath your leaves, old oak,
 You mighty one of all the trees;
Within whose hollow trunk a man
 Could stable his big horse with ease.

I see your knuckles hard and strong,
 But have no fear they'll come to blows;
Your life is long, and mine is short,
 But which has known the greater woes?

Thou hast not seen starved women here,
 Or man gone mad because ill-fed –
Who stares at stones in city streets,
 Mistaking them for hunks of bread.

Thou hast not felt the shivering backs
 Of homeless children lying down
And sleeping in the cold, night air –
 Like doors and walls, in London town.

Knowing thou hast not known such shame,
    And only storms have come thy way,
Methinks I could in comfort spend
    My summer with thee, day by day.

To lie by day in thy green shade,
    And in thy hollow rest at night;
And through the open doorway see
    The stars turn over leaves of light.

W.H. Davies

'Old Yew, which graspest at the stones'

Old Yew, which graspest at the stones
    That name the under-lying dead,
    Thy fibres net the dreamless head,
Thy roots are wrapt about the bones.

The seasons bring the flower again,
    And bring the firstling to the flock;
    And in the dusk of thee, the clock
Beats out the little lives of men.

O not for thee the glow, the bloom,
    Who changest not in any gale,
    Nor branding summer suns avail
To touch thy thousand years of gloom:

And gazing on thee, sullen tree,
    Sick for thy stubborn hardihood,
    I seem to fail from out my blood
And grow incorporate into thee.

Alfred, Lord Tennyson

On a Tree Fallen Across the Road
(To Hear Us Talk)

The tree the tempest with a crash of wood
Throws down in front of us is not to bar
Our passage to our journey's end for good,
But just to ask us who we think we are

Insisting always on our own way so.
She likes to halt us in our runner tracks,
And make us get down in a foot of snow
Debating what to do without an axe.

And yet she knows obstruction is in vain:
We will not be put off the final goal
We have it hidden in us to attain,
Not though we have to seize earth by the pole

And, tired of aimless circling in one place,
Steer straight off after something into space.

Robert Frost

Pine

Growing up under the weight of wardrobes,
we have awarded ourselves pine. The old veneers
have been stripped away. A Swedish wife welcomes u:
with her frank stare and enlightened ideas.

White wood, bright wood, your blonde shavings
fall away like the curls of a pampered child.
My fingers drift across the grainy fingerprints,
the dusty contours, the tumuli and cliffs.

97

Only these knots hold me, like some feud
from the past – the bad migraines
mother used to get, or a ridge of low pressure
swishing its cloudbursts on the childhood fête.

But we will chamfer all that. When you called
this morning I was clearing our old dresser
of its tea-rings and nicks, the yellow sawdust
heaping up like salt-sift in a glass.

It's a walk through sand-dunes down to the sea,
the space where honesty might begin,
if we knew how, no corners to hide in,
the coming clean of our loyalties, and lies.

Blake Morrison

Pine-Trees and the Sky: Evening

I'd watched the sorrow of the evening sky,
And smelt the sea, and earth, and the warm clover,
And heard the waves, and the seagull's mocking cry.

And in them all was only the old cry,
That song they always sing – 'The best is over!
You may remember now, and think, and sigh,
O silly lover!'
And I was tired and sick that all was over,
And because I,
For all my thinking, never could recover
One moment of the good hours that were over.
And I was sorry and sick, and wished to die.

Then from the sad west turning wearily,
I saw the pines against the white north sky,
Very beautiful, and still, and bending over

Their sharp black heads against a quiet sky.
And there was peace in them; and I
Was happy, and forgot to play the lover,
And laughed, and did no longer wish to die;
Being glad of you, O pine-trees and the sky!

Rupert Brooke
Lulworth, 8th July 1907

The Plantation

Any point in that wood
Was a centre, birch trunks
Ghosting your bearings,
Improvising charmed rings

Wherever you stopped.
Though you walked a straight line
It might be a circle you travelled
With toadstools and stumps

Always repeating themselves.
Or did you re-pass them?
Here were bleyberries quilting the floor,
The black char of a fire

And having found them once
You were sure to find them again.
Someone had always been there
Though always you were alone.

Lovers, birdwatchers,
Campers, gipsies and tramps
Left some trace of their trades
Or their excrement.

Hedging the road so
It invited all comers
To the hush and the mush
Of its whispering treadmill,

Its limits defined,
So they thought, from outside.
They must have been thankful
For the hum of the traffic

If they ventured in
Past the picnickers' belt
Or began to recall
Tales of fog on the mountains.

You had to come back
To learn how to lose yourself,
To be pilot and stray – witch,
Hansel and Gretel in one.

Seamus Heaney

Planting Trees

In the mating of trees,
the pollen grain entering invisible
the domed room of the winds, survives
the ghost of the old forest
that stood here when we came. The ground
invites it, and it will not be gone.
I become the familiar of that ghost
and its ally, carrying in a bucket
twenty trees smaller than weeds,
and I plant them along the way
of the departure of the ancient host.
I return to the ground its original music.
It will rise out of the horizon

100

of the grass, and over the heads
of the weeds, and it will rise over
the horizon of men's heads. As I age
in the world it will rise and spread,
and be for this place horizon
and orison, the voice of its winds.
I have made myself a dream to dream
of its rising, that has gentled my nights.
Let me desire and wish well the life
these trees may live when I
no longer rise in the mornings
to be pleased by the green of them
shining, and their shadows on the ground,
and the sound of the wind in them.

Wendell Berry

A Poison Tree

I was angry with my friend:
I told my wrath, my wrath did end.
I was angry with my foe:
I told it not, my wrath did grow.

And I water'd it in fears,
Night and morning with my tears;
And I sunned it with smiles,
And with soft deceitful wiles.

And it grew both day and night,
Till it bore an apple bright;
And my foe beheld it shine,
And he knew that it was mine,

And into my garden stole
When the night had veil'd the pole:
In the morning glad I see
My foe outstretch'd beneath the tree.

William Blake

The Poplar Field

The poplars are fell'd; farewell to the shade
And the whispering sound of the cool colonnade;
The winds play no longer and sing in the leaves,
Nor Ouse on his bosom their image receives.

Twelve years have elapsed since I first took a view
Of my favourite field and the bank where they grew:
And now in the grass behold they are laid,
And the tree is my seat that once lent me a shade.

The blackbird has fled to another retreat,
Where the hazards afford him a screen from the heat;
And the scene where his melody charm'd me before
Resounds with his sweet-flowing ditty no more.

My fugitive years are all hasting away,
And I must ere long lie as lowly as they,
With a turf on my breast and a stone at my head,
Ere another such grove shall arise in its stead.

'Tis a sight to engage me, if anything can,
To muse on the perishing pleasures of man;
Though his life be a dream, his enjoyments, I see,
Have a being less durable even than he.

William Cowper

Poplars

I walked under the tall poplars that my father planted
On a day in April when I was a boy
Running beside the heap of saplings
From which he picked the straightest spears of sky.

The sun was shining that day
As he shone for the Tuatha De Danann
And no one was old or sad
For life was just beginning

Patrick Kavanagh

Ronsard's Lament for the Cutting of the Forest of Gastine

Old forest, tall household of the birds, no more
Will nimble deer browse as they did before
Deep in your peaceful shade, and your green mane
No more will gentle summer's sun and rain.
No more will the amorous shepherd come to sit
Against a tree, his sheepdog at his feet,
To play upon his four-holed flute in praise
Of pretty Janet and her pleasing ways.
All will be mute, Echo be still for good.
There will be a field where your great trees stood,
Their airy shadows shifting in the light. Now
You will feel the coulter and the plow.
Your deep silence gone, breathless with fear,
Satyr and Pan will not again come here.
Farewell, old hall of the wind's high harmony,
Where I first made my lyre's tongues agree;

Where Calliope, so beautiful and good,
Gave me the love of her great sisterhood,
As if she cast a hundred roses over me;
Where Euterpe at her own breast nourished me.
Farewell, old trees, farewell, high sacred heads,
Once honored with rites and flowers, holy deeds,
Disdained by travellers now, your death their plight
Who burn in the summer sky's naked light –
Who, knowing no more your fresh green shade,
Curse your destroyers, wishing them destroyed.
Farewell, old oaks, once honoured by our creed
As fellow citizens, Dodonean seed,
Jupiter's trees, that first gave food to men,
Ungrateful men, who did not understand
Beneficence – a people utterly gross
To massacre these fathers who nourished us.
The man who trusts this world will not be free
Of grief. How true, O gods, is that philosophy
Which says that all things in the end will perish,
That by the deaths of forms new forms will flourish.
In time, a peak in Tempe's Vale will stand,
And Mount Athos will be a bottomland;
Neptune's fields, in time, will stand in grain.
All forms will pass, matter alone remain.

Wendell Berry

'Shut, too, in a tower of words, I mark'

...Shut, too, in a tower of words, I mark
On the horizon walking like the trees
The wordy shapes of women, and the rows
Of the star-gestured children in the park.
Some let me make you of the vowelled beeches,

Some of the oaken voices, from the roots
Of many a thorny shire tell you notes,
Some let me make you of the water's speeches...

Dylan Thomas
from Especially when the October Wind

The Silver Tree

In a hot steamed up room five girls are spinning
a tree made of silver paper, growing
from a trunk so clumsy only a child
could be taken in by it. Its girth outstrips
the attenuated branches that tumble
from its crown and drop down to the floor where
they coil and lengthen, lovelier than hair,
a genuine silver tree they seem to spin
out of themselves. Their fingers diminish,
twine with foil, are sucked out of their sleeves.
It is the triumph of Aluminium.

And just as they become the tree, the tree
becomes them. They thrive on ambiguity.
As the tree grows they grow, although
infinitely more slowly, and enter into
the frieze where mothers and smart daughters dance
in a cold pastoral. Ice is eating them.

It is desire for perpetuity,
the film rerunning as they petrify
and the forest throws its lank arms about them.
They hang like fruit, sucked out, perfect, until
imaginary gods pass by and cut them down.

George Szirtes

A Single Tree

You ask for more rungs in the ladder I
Built against the solitary tree:
Your legs still short, your brother up already.
So in wind I fix it, and I find
As I lean smoking, back against the tree,
Seagulls driving plovers from their ground,

A picture of two figures, both still young,
Who come across this ladder sagging, rotten,
Leant against a hedge-tree long forgotten,
And wonder at the nearness of each rung;
Watched by their father, trying not to long
To join them or wish again this day
Of wind and gulls and peewits fighting, crying,
Nostalgic falseness in the air, sighing sighing,
Though that was in his mind. So, today,
He takes two cold boys home and gives them food,
Glad he shared with them a single tree
Before they walked without him to the wood.

P.J. Kavanagh

'The solemn work of building up the pyre'

...The solemn work of building up the pyre
Was done in splendour and they laid a fire
That reached to heaven in a cone of green.
The arms were twenty fathoms broad – I mean
The boughs and branches heaped upon the ground –
And straw in piles had first been loaded round.
   But how they made the funeral fires flame,
Or what the trees by number or by name
– Oak, fir-tree, birch, aspen and poplar too,
Ilex and alder, willow, elm and yew,

Box, chestnut, plane, ash, laurel, thorn and lime,
Beech, hazel, whipple-tree – I lack the time
To tell you, or who felled them, nor can tell
How their poor gods ran up and down the dell
All disinherited of habitation,
Robbed of their quiet and in desolation,
The nymph and dryad of the forest lawn,
The hamadryad and the subtle faun,
These I pass over, birds and beasts as well
That fled in terror when the forest fell,
Nor shall I say how in the sudden light
Of the unwonted sun the dell took fright,
Nor how the fire first was couched in straw,
Then in dry sticks thrice severed with a saw,
Then in green wood with spice among the stems
And then in cloth-of-gold with precious gems
And many a flower-garland in the stir
Of breathing incense and the scent of myrrh;
Nor how Arcita lay among it all,
Nor of the wealth and splendour of his pall
Nor yet how Emily thrust in the fire
As custom was and lit the funeral pyre...

Geoffrey Chaucer
from The Knight's Tale

Some Trees

These are amazing: each
Joining a neighbor, as though speech
Were a still performance.
Arranging by chance

To meet as far this morning
From the world as agreeing
With it, you and I
Are suddenly what the trees try

To tell us we are:
That their merely being there
Means something; that soon
We may touch, love, explain.

And glad not to have invented
Such comeliness, we are surrounded:
A silence already filled with noises,
A canvas on which emerges

A chorus of smiles, a winter morning.
Placed in a puzzling light, and moving,
Our days put on such reticence
These accents seem their own defense.

John Ashbery

Song of the Open Road

I think that I shall never see
A billboard lovely as a tree.
Indeed, unless the billboards fall
I'll never see a tree at all.

Ogden Nash

Song of the Stand-pipe

Look the trees are dying in the drought
beech and birch keel over
shallow roots clutch at crumbling earth
copper and silver become uncurrent

beaten too soon into autumn
yet the leaden plane
sheds again
its patched hide
with seventeenth century resilience
whatever civil war
the elements embark on
sun against rain
it stands
making its rough balls to propagate
citizen not recorded in the wild state
hybrid
tough cockney
that will uproot the paving stones
if we should ever
decamp
and lace its branches beautifully
over the crumpled streets.
When elm and oak
are bugged and broken
like love it will be here
nave and aisles
when the next first men
come wondering back
into the tumbled city
to begin again.

Maureen Duffy

South Wind

Where have you been, South Wind, this May-day
    morning, –
With larks aloft, or skimming with the swallow,
Or with blackbirds in a green, sun-glinted thicket?

Oh, I heard you like a tyrant in the valley;
Your ruffian haste shook the young, blossoming orchards;
You clapped rude hands, hallooing round the chimney,
And white your pennons streamed along the river.

You have robbed the bee, South Wind, in your adventure,
Blustering with gentle flowers; but I forgave you
When you stole to me shyly with scent of hawthorn.

Siegfried Sassoon

Stovewood

two thousand years of fog and sucking minerals
     from the soil,
Russian river ox-team & small black train
     haul to mill;
fresh-sawed rough cut by wagon
     and built into a barn;
tear it down and split it up
     and stick it in a stove.

Gary Snyder

'Survivor sole, and hardly such, of all'

Survivor sole, and hardly such, of all
That once liv'd here thy brethren, at my birth
(Since which I number three-score winters past)
A shatter'd veteran, hollow-trunk'd perhaps
As now, and with excoriate forks deform,
Relics of ages! Could a mind, imbued
With truth from heav'n, created thing adore,

I might with rev'rence kneel and worship thee.

It seems idolatry with some excuse
When our forefather Druids in their oaks
Imagin'd sanctity. The conscience yet
Unpurified by an authentic act
Of amnesty, the meed of blood divine,
Lov'd not the light, but gloomy into gloom
Of thickest shades, like Adam after taste
Of fruit proscrib'd, as to a refuge, fled.

Thou wast a bauble once; a cup and ball,
Which babes might play with; and the thievish jay
Seeking her food, with ease might have purloin'd
The auburn nut that held thee, swallowing down
Thy yet close-folded latitude of boughs
And all thine embryo vastness, at a gulp.
But Fate thy growth decreed: autumnal rains
Beneath thy parent tree mellow'd the soil
Design'd thy cradle, and a skipping deer,
With pointed hoof dibbling the glebe, prepar'd
The soft receptacle in which secure
Thy rudiments should sleep the winter through.

So Fancy dreams – Disprove it, if ye can,
Ye reas'ners broad awake, whose busy search
Of argument, employ'd too oft amiss,
Sifts half the pleasures of short life away.

Thou fell'st mature, and in the loamy clod
Swelling, with vegetative force instinct
Didst burst thine egg, as theirs the fabled Twins,
Now stars; two lobes, protruding, pair'd exact:
A leaf succeeded, and another leaf,
And all the elements thy puny growth
Fost'ring propitious, thou becam'st a twig.

Who liv'd when thou wast such? Oh couldst thou speak,
As in Dodona once thy kindred trees
Oracular, I would not curious ask
The future, best unknown, but at thy mouth
Inquisitive, the less ambiguous past.

By thee I might correct, erroneous oft,

The clock of history, facts and events
Timing more punctual, unrecorded facts
Recov'ring, and misstated setting right –
Desp'rate attempt, till trees shall speak again!
    Time made thee what thou wast – King of the woods;
And time hath made thee what thou art – a cave
For owls to roost in. Once thy spreading boughs
O'erhung the champain; and the numerous flock
That graz'd it stood beneath that ample cope
Uncrowded yet safe-shelter'd from the storm.
No flock frequents thee now. Thou hast outliv'd
Thy popularity and art become
(Unless verse rescue thee awhile) a thing
Forgotten, as the foliage of thy youth.
    While thus through all the stages thou hast push'd
Of treeship, first a seedling hid in grass,
Then twig, then sapling, and, as century roll'd
Slow after century, a giant bulk
Of girth enormous, with moss-cushioned root
Upheav'd above the soil, and sides imboss'd
With prominent wens globose, till at the last
The rottenness, which Time is charg'd t' inflict
On other mighty ones, found also thee –
What exhibitions various hath the world
Witness'd of mutability in all
That we account most durable below!
Change is the diet, on which all subsist
Created changeable, and change at last
Destroys them. – Skies uncertain now the heat
Transmitting cloudless, and the solar beam
Now quenching in a boundless sea of clouds, –
Calm and alternate storm, moisture and drought,
Invigorate by turns the springs of life
In all that live, plant, animal, and man,
And in conclusion mar them. Nature's threads,
Fine passing thought, ev'n in her coarsest works,
Delight in agitation, yet sustain
The force that agitates, not unimpaired,

But, worn by frequent impulse, to the cause
Of their best tone their dissolution owe.
        Thought cannot spend itself, comparing still
The great and little of thy lot, thy growth
From almost nullity into a state
Of matchless grandeur, and declension thence
Slow into such magnificent decay.
Time was, when, settling on thy leaf, a fly
Could shake thee to the root – and time has been
When tempests could not. At thy firmest age
Thou hadst within thy bole solid contents
That might have ribb'd the sides or plank'd the deck
Of some flagg'd admiral; and tortuous arms,
The ship-wright's darling treasure, didst present
To the four-quarter'd winds, robust and bold,
Warp'd into tough knee-timber, many a load.
But the axe spar'd thee; in those thriftier days
Oaks fell not, hewn by thousands, to supply
The bottomless demands of contest wag'd
For senatorial honours. Thus to Time
The task was left to whittle thee away
With his sly scythe, whose ever-nibbling edge
Noiseless, an atom and an atom more
Disjoining from the rest, has, unobserv'd,
Achiev'd a labour, which had, far and wide,
(By man perform'd) made all the forest ring...

William Cowper
from Yardley Oak

The Tables Turned

Up! up! my friend, and clear your looks,
Why all this toil and trouble?
Up! up! my friend, and quit your books,
Or surely you'll grow double.

The sun above the mountain's head,
A freshening lustre mellow,
Through all the long green fields has spread,
His first sweet evening yellow.

Books! 'tis a dull and endless strife,
Come, hear the woodland linnet,
How sweet his music; on my life
There's more of wisdom in it.

And hark! how blithe the throstle sings!
And he is no mean preacher;
Come forth into the light of things
Let Nature be your teacher.

She has a world of ready wealth,
Our minds and hearts to bless –
Spontaneous wisdom breathed by health,
Truth breathed by chearfulness.

One impulse from a vernal wood
May teach you more of man;
Of moral evil and of good,
Than all the sages can.

Sweet is the lore which nature brings;
Our meddling intellect
Misshapes the beauteous forms of things; –
– We murder to dissect.

Enough of science and of art;
Close up these barren leaves;
Come forth, and bring with you a heart
That watches and receives.

William Wordsworth

The Tall Fruit-Trees

I'll lop them, it will be easier so to tend them;
> *Then we may clean them, and gather the fruit with ease;*
> *No one can do with these great old orchard trees,*
Dirty, shady, unwieldy – don't try to defend them.

O promise to do them one or two at a time then –
> That will make you twenty years in going the rounds:
Then the tall tops for me will be out of bounds,
> Surely I shall no longer be able to climb then.

But while I am able O let me ascend the plum-tree
> And poke my head out at the top, where the lovely view
Has a foreground of scarlet plums with a wash of blue,
> And I am away from earth in the starling's country.

And for a few years yet spend a day in the pear-tree,
> Squirming and stretching, plagued by the wasps and the twigs,
Scratches all over me, bruised in the arms and legs,
> Coming down whacked at last from the great old bare tree –

And yet not wholly bare, for his topmost steeple
> Still flaunts a fair wreath of a dozen, the best of all;
Ha, he beat me at last, for he was so tall –
> He will not give his best work up to greedy people.

And there is the huge gaunt apple-tree, dead man's seedling,
> With five great limbs, spreading twenty feet from the ground;
How he makes us stagger the longest ladder around,
> So heavy – yet four feet short of the ladder we're needing.

Some years he's good for bushels of small red apples
> That keep well enough, and roast well enough by the fire,
But every year he is young and brave with desire,
> Smothered in rosy wreaths that the sunlight dapples.

Dappled with sunlight and bright with the May-time raindrop,
> Mighty from age and youthful with tender bloom,

He heaves up brightness and scent to our highest room,
    Brushes the dormer-window with shining maintop.

We'll take in a bit more ground, and plant it with limber
    Maidens on dwarfing stocks, at twelve feet apart;
But the great old trees are the real loves of my heart,
    Mountains of blossom and fruit on the stalwart timber.

Ruth Pitter

'There grew a goodly tree him faire beside'

There grew a goodly tree him faire beside,
    Loaden with fruit and apples rosie red,
    As they in pure vermilion had beene dide,
    Whereof great vertues ouer all were red:
    For happie life to all, which thereon fed,
    And life eke euerlasting did befall:
    Great God it planted in that blessed sted
    With his almightie hand, and did it call
The tree of life, the crime of our first fathers fall.

In all the world like was not to be found,
    Saue in that soile, where all good things did grow,
    And freely sprong out of the fruitfull ground,
    As incorrupted Nature did them sow,
    Till that dread Dragon all did ouerthrow.
    Another like faire tree eke grew thereby,
    Whereof who so did eat, eftsoones did know
    Both good and ill: O mornefull memory:
That tree through one mans fault hath doen vs all to dy.

Edmund Spenser
from the Book of the Faerie Queene

'There is an old tale goes that Herne the Hunter'

Mrs Page: There is an old tale goes that Herne the Hunter,
Sometime a keeper here in Windsor Forest,
Doth all the winter-time, at still midnight,
Walk round about an oak, with great ragg'd horns;
And there he blasts the tree, and takes the cattle,
And makes milche-kine yield blood, and shakes a chain
In a most hideous and dreadful manner.
You have heard of such a spirit, and well you know
The superstitious idle-headed eld
Receiv'd, and did deliver to our age,
This tale of Herne the Hunter for a truth.
Page: Why yet there want not many that do fear
In deep of night to walk by this Herne's oak.
But what of this?
Mrs Ford: Marry, this is our device –
That Falstaff at that oak shall meet with us,
Disguis'd, like Herne, with huge horns on his head.

William Shakespeare
from The Merry Wives of Windsor

'There is a thorn; it looks so old'

There is a thorn; it looks so old,
In truth you'd find it hard to say,
How it could ever have been young,
It looks so old and grey.
Not higher than a two-years' child,
It stands erect this aged thorn;
No leaves it has, no thorny points;
It is a mass of knotted joints,
A wretched thing forlorn.
It stands erect, and like a stone
With lichens it is overgrown.

Like rock or stone, it is o'ergrown
With lichens to the very top,
And hung with heavy tufts of moss,
A melancholy crop:
Up from the earth these mosses creep,
And this poor thorn they clasp it round
So close, you'd say that they were bent
With plain and manifest intent,
To drag it to the ground;
And all had joined in one endeavour
To bury this poor thorn for ever...

William Wordsworth
from The Thorn

'There was an old lady whose folly'

There was an old lady whose folly,
Induced her to sit in a holly:
Wherefrom by a thorn, her gown being torn,
She quickly become melancholly.

Edward Lear

'There was an old man in a tree'

There was an old man in a tree,
Whose whiskers were lovely to see;
But the birds of the air, pluck'd them perfectly bare,
To make themselves nests in that tree.

Edward Lear

The Thicket

I

My weald of tales, my beech leaves, my bronze.
A world of trees shades the land's shadow.
Under the tribe's winter, roots of iron,

Roots of grain; and at the thicket's heart
A man's tread, a bird-cry, the glitter
Of a pool rippled with a stone blade,

His last gift. My green eye shuts. Slowly
Drops of light in the night sky falter
My gifts for him: The Hunter, the Plough.

II

Through the trees, through the ferns, through the dark:
A blade shrived with the eyes of a beast
And its five wounds. Armour chafes the spell

Of the wood, my runes, my tree-letters
Mumble in stones. Deeper the heart folds
Leaves about the rood's axe-shaft, a grove

Where the scaled Worm, the Ravager, lurks.
Through my paths, through my thorns, through my tale
The earl's bard tracks him and will not err.

III

The duke's forest domain. Here his verge
Of grant harbours in their old fastness
His loyal-made beasts, the boar, the stag,

The archers' spoils; now they divide them
And sojourn here in the branched covert.
Manor and parlance, the haunch is theirs.

Faint carols of the horn – young Roland
Quartered in the blood of Harold – chase
Home to the toils a mort for Rufus.

IV

I heard this ballad in the green wood
Where the king's deer rustle in the brake
And it ransomed my heart merrily.

A man's face peers from the tangled oaks,
Arrows bristle in the poor slain deer,
An antlered head grinning like a man.

The song curls out from the forest edge,
Where rooks drop to the castle tower,
And the wood-doves call, Law, Law, Outlaw.

V

The land till dusk. Limbs of a torn elm
Lapse in thin blue smoke. Your kindled hearth
Fades in the dome of the common-weal:

A man gathering a few dry sticks,
Masters who gather fields together.
From hedgerow and ditch of a new world

The ship of state, keeled with oak, lunges
Into the western beam, where poor Jack
Harrows hell in the Virginia woods.

VI

Eyes of fire peering from the forest –
I heard the hammering of iron
Where the hidden streams are dammed in ponds.

I looked for you, your bundles of sticks,
Hazel, chestnut, hurdles, poles for hops:
Fence-posts and the forbidden hedge-rows.

I walked further up the mill-valley.
Charcoal and white-heat have bleared my hands.
Darker smoke than these comes down the line.

VII

There the lawn slopes out into the grain.
Close to the house, walks of fir and ash
Screen the chaste delights of company.

Art extends the long wooded vista
Where sense and taste dapple in the shade,
As a path winds through the tidy grove

To the home of the god Silvanus.
Here my lord may peruse in autumn
The green margin of Rome's dead pages.

VIII

A life of the woods. The oak and elm
The beech and the fir, fell to my axe,
To be cut to shape in the ship-yard.

So a ship took me and death met me
Where the sound living in the dead wood
Is drowned in the green heart of the waves.

Weaker than the beams I took work from,
Among spars and splinters of the fleet,
My head nods towards a bare foreland.

IX

Dark places of a year uncommon,
Felled trunks bright red with speckles of rot,
Shapes of leaves moving over the heath.

I stumbled here. Failure, self-grandeur
Harvest the swollen grain. My ruin
Of the farm swarms with ivy, owl-hoots.

Here I hang. The shrill tongues of rick-fires
Light home my fellow good Captain Swing,
Scrawl our names on a roll of thunder.

X

Dull weight of the bird with bright feathers.
The dark wood casts its net over us.
My lord's men and the dead moon are out.

A fox hounded into the green web.
Horsemen are out, swathes of trees are down,
Field-men caught by vermin in a snare

Where the hares caper under the law.
All the wild ones running in the wood
Dance to my tune, at my belt, tonight.

XI

Mourning and mourning for the lost woods
My lord's debts have felled, the dear thicket
Where small creatures lived, lost to the plough,

The land I looked for was innocence.
Solitary in the fields I watched
A world furious and imperfect

Drawing clear from the melancholy
Of a shrouded elm in a thorn hedge –
A beauty I could not understand.

XII

Ghosts of the world-wood: the trees are felled,
Stumps; puny saplings which replace them
Will outgrow me and then outlive me.

Feeble traceries of twigs, the past
Thrusts from the black mould of the present.
There is a deep thicket to move through,

Tangles, smarts, and patches of soft grass,
Disease and drought, till the trees are felled
And bare ground grows a little clearer.

Michael Vince

'This night I walk through a forest in my head'

This night I walk through a forest in my head;
    In each tree's heart a lute, waiting the skill
    Of hand to chisel it, is musical,
    Already with a song stirring the glade;

All the hard wood cries to the stars that float
    Among the leaves, bird-sweet and shrill,
    Though no wires stretch nor delicate fingers mete
    Out their divisions, nor lute-master's skill.

And so, bewildered like one newly dead
    Who finds the myrtle-groves of Hades strange
    Country to him, I go among the trees

Seeking your image flickering through the shade,
    A madman's fire, and thus deluded range
    Cold hollows of my skull and echoing silences.

John Heath-Stubbs

'Thrise happie hee, who by some shadie Grove'

Thrise happie hee, who by some shadie Grove
Farre from the clamorous World doth live his owne,
Though solitarie, yet who is not alone,
But doth converse with that *Eternall Love*.
O how more sweet is Birds harmonious Mone,
Or the soft Sobbings of the widow'd Dove?
Than those smoothe Whisp'rings neare a Princes Throne,
Which Good make doubtfull, doe the Evill approve.
O how more sweet is *Zephyres* wholesome Breath,
And Sighs perfum'd, which doe the Flowres unfold,
Than that Applause vaine *Honour* doth bequeath?
How sweete are Streames to Poyson drunke in Gold?
    The World is full of Horrours, Falshoods, Slights,
    Woods silent Shades have only trûe Delights.

William Drummond

Throwing a Tree

New Forest

The two executioners stalk along over the knolls,
Bearing two axes with heavy heads shining and wide,
And a long limp two-handled saw toothed for cutting great boles,
And so they approach the proud tree that bears the death-mark on
     its side.

Jackets doffed they swing axes and chop away just above ground,
And the chips fly about and lie white on the moss and fallen
     leaves;
Till a broad deep gash in the bark is hewn all the way round,
And one of them tries to hook upward a rope, which at last he
     achieves.

The saw then begins, till the top of the tall giant shivers:
The shivers are seen to grow greater each cut than before:
They edge out the saw, tug the rope; but the tree only quivers,
And kneeling and sawing again, they step back and try pulling once
     more.

Then, lastly, the living mast sways, further sways: with a shout
Job and Ike rush aside. Reached the end of its long staying
     powers
The tree crashes downward: it shakes all its neighbours
     throughout,
And two hundred years' steady growth has been ended in less than
     two hours.

Thomas Hardy

Timber

In the avenues of yesterday
A tree might have a thing to say.
    Horsemen then heard
    From the branches a word
That sent them serious on their way.

A tree, – a beam, a box, a crutch,
Costing so little or so much;
      Wainscot or stair,
      Barge, baby's chair,
A pier, a flute, a mill, a hutch.

That tree uprooted lying there
Will make such things with knack and care,
      Unless you hear
      From its boughs too clear
The word that has whitened the traveiler's hair.

Edmund Blunden

To a Late Poplar

Not yet half-drest
O tardy bride!
And the priest
And the bridegroom and the guests
Have been waiting a full hour.

The meadow choir
Is playing the wedding march
Two fields away,
And squirrels are already leaping in ecstasy
Among leaf-full branches.

Patrick Kavanagh

To a Tree in London

(*Clement's Inn*)

Here you stay
Night and day,
Never, never going away!

Do you ache
When we take
Holiday for our health's sake?

Wish for feet
When the heat
Scalds you in the brick-built street,

That you might
Climb the height
Where your ancestry saw light,

Find a brook
In some nook
There to purge your swarthy look?

No. You read
Trees to need
Smoke like earth whereon to feed...

Have no sense
That far hence
Air is sweet in a blue immense,

Thus, black, blind,
You have opined
Nothing of your brightest kind;

Never seen
Miles of green,
Smelt the landscape's sweet serene.

Thomas Hardy

To Make a Tree

Take wood, seasoned or green,
    rough-hewn or planed.
Take first one four-square beam
    twice a man's height,
then graft a second, half that,
    on to it
cross-wise and near the top,
    cunningly joined.
Dig socket. Plant upright.
    Hope it will root,
hope sap will rise. If not,
    keep tools at hand
and, when the time is ripe,
    nail up the fruit.

Paul Hyland

Tree

Grotesquely shaped, this stubbed tree craves a madman's
    eye,
its convoluted pipes lie tortured on the air,
twist black, turn back to fanged twigs and attitudes,
its dusty leaves quite stunted, still it will not die.

In rousing spring its frugal green was last to bud,
in autumn will be the first to anticipate the fall.
Now, aimlessly, I give it human attributes:
its mud-coloured bark, sick flesh; sap, a victim's blood.

As, sometimes, a child, contorting his plastic face
to make another laugh, is told to cease his play
lest abstract fate solidifies both lips and eyes,
horrifically, to one perpetual grimace;

so, perhaps, this maimed structure postured once and
       thus –
a buffoon amidst these oaks. Then laughter shook
untimely leaves down till avenging lightning struck,
petrified the attitude, a spectacle for us.

August – other trees conform, are properly dressed;
but this funny one exists for funny children,
easy to climb, easy to insult, or throw stones at,
and only urgent lovers in its shade will rest.

Yet this pauper, this caliban tree, let good men praise,
for it survives, and that's enough; more, on gala nights,
with copper beech and silver birch it too can soar
unanchored, free, in prosperous moonlight and amaze.

Dannie Abse

A Tree

Under unending interrogation by wind
Tortured by huge scaldings of light
Tries to confess all but could not
Bleed a word

Stripped to its root letter, cruciform
Contorted
Tried to tell all

Through crooking of elbows
Twitching of finger-ends.

Finally
Resigned
To be dumb.

Lets what happens to it happen.

Ted Hughes

The Tree

I stood still and was a tree amid the wood,
Knowing the truth of things unseen before;
Of Daphne and the laurel bow
And that god-feasting couple old
That grew elm-oak amid the wold.
'Twas not until the gods had been
Kindly entreated, and been brought within
Unto the hearth of their heart's home
That they might do this wonder thing;
Nathless I have been a tree amid the wood
And many a new thing understood
That was rank folly to my head before.

Ezra Pound

The Tree

This child, shovelling away
what remains of snow –
a batter of ash and crystals –
knows nothing of the pattern
his bent back lifts
above his own reflection:

130

its climbs the street-lamp's stem
and cross-bar, branching
to take in all the lines
from gutter, gable, slates
and chimney-crowns to the high
pillar of a mill chimney
on a colourless damp sky:
there in its topmost air
and eyrie rears that tree
his bending sends up
from a treeless street, its roots
in the eye and in the net the shining
flagstones spread at his feet.

Charles Tomlinson

The Tree

Tree, lend me this root,
That I may sit here at your foot
And watch these hawking flies that wheel
And perch on the air's hand
And red-thighed bees
That fan the dust with their wings' breeze.
Do you not feel me on your heel,
My bone against your bone?
Or are you in such slumber sunk,
Woodpeckers knocking at your trunk
Find you are not at home?
To winds you are not dumb;
Then tell me, if you understand:
When your thick timber has been hewn,
Its boards in floors and fences sewn,
And you no more a tree,
Where will your dryad be?

Andrew Young

Tree Fall

The saw rasps the morning into logs
that chart a tree's slow foundering
sinking to a barky knee, a marooned stump
island in the woven green lawn.
Its head of mermaid hair drops, jerks on a hangman rope
its spread arms own gallows fork the clear sky
where the young executioner swings Tarzan
though the urban jungle, silhouetted
in stark bravado every window fills
to watch, admire up there mid-July
half naked in a sudden sunburst
as the top bows to his overgrown powerdrill
we tame at home to trim the prunus
that burgeons white hopes in the Spring.
Blinded by sun moths stagger drunk with sleep
from their doomed leaf beds. Silent in the ripped air
predator thrush and blackbird let them go.
This was a false acacia, immigrant
a locust tree, John Baptist fed on
with honey for desert breakfast, native
from the New World three hundred years ago.
The tree fellers prise its spread fingers
from their grip on the earth.
I take up a slice of trunk fallen to the ground
its sunshield kept bare of other life
as the ash drips its poison onto the soil
at its feet, an invisible wall
that moats and guards it round.
My slice shows annuities: late spring, drought, flood
mapped in its rings, graphed so fine my naked eye
can't tell them round. Maybe this morning
has shipwrecked two centuries and Mozart
is playing at the inmost ring. From Cologne bridge
you can see beyond mythical Christpoint
back to when we were children of the wood spirits
and knew what we did when we cut down trees.

132

See that ringed jetty? Its timbers plot
where the ships tied up with oil, gods
wine, cooking pots, the centuries before the axe.
I hold an ache, oak corn in my palm.
The earth will make it a chronometer
and I can only guess at the time it will
tick over when the lasersaw brings it down.

Maureen Duffy

The Tree in the Goods Yard

So sigh, that hearkening pasts arouse
In the magic circle of your boughs, –
So timelessly, on sound's deep sea,
Sail your unfurled melody,
            My small dark Tree.

Who set you in this smoky yard
None tells me; it might seem too hard
A fate for a tree whose place should be
With a sounding proud-plumed company
            By a glittering sea.

And yet you live with liking here,
Are well, have some brocade to wear,
And solitary, mysteriously
Revoice light airs as sighs, which free
            Tombed worlds for me.

Edmund Blunden

133

Tree-kill

Chip chop
Chip chop
Down comes a tree

Chip chop
Wallop plop
Help, its fallen on me!

Chip chop
Chip chop
Down comes another

Chip chop
Wheee! bop!
That one fell on mother

Chip chop
Chip chop
Crush on daddys head!

Chip chop
Please stop
Or else we'll *all* be dead!

Spike Milligan

The Tree of Guilt

When first we knew it, gibbet-bare
It scrawled an omen on the air,
But later, in its wealth of leaf,
Looked too lush to hang a thief;

And from its branches muffled doves
Drummed out the purchasable loves
Which far below them were purveyed
On credit through the slinking shade.

And what a cooing trade was done
Around that tree-trunk anyone
Could guess who saw the countless hearts
Carved in its bark transfixed with darts;

So entering this enchanted zone
Anyone would add his own
Cut neatly with a pocket knife,
There for his life and the tree's life.

And having thus signed on the line
Anyone claimed his anodyne
And, drinking it, was lulled asleep
By doves and insects, deep and deep,

Till he finds later, waking cold,
The leaves fallen, himself old,
And his carved heart, though vastly grown,
Not recognizably his own.

The dove's is now the raven's day
And there is interest yet to pay;
And in those branches, gibbet-bare,
Is that a noose that dangles there?

Louis MacNeice

Tree of Heaven

Harvard has famous elms, Boston its maples,
Somerville, weeds.

Nothing thrives on the city's neglect like ailanthus.
It fattens, and breeds.
While oaks, beeches – Massachusetts natives –
Shrink back, poisoned by the Interstate,
Stinking ailanthus feeds
On the pear-drop scent of car body-shops,
The green oil-slick on the pavement:
Immigrant trees.

They are everywhere: at the roots of supermarkets;
They attack
Garbage skips, parking lots, doorways of seedy
Italian restaurants, creeping surreptitiously:
Buckle and crack
The backs of the sidewalks, bursting skywards
To glimpse the blue Boston roofline through the fumes.
On the rank railroad tracks
They stitch up the left behind push-carts and milk-crates,
Undoing the past.

Soon bolted gable-high, they don't age well; their branches snap,
The cheap sticks split.
One strong wind can tear ailanthus' roots right out
And skittle it.
Seeding furtively behind the peeling porches, musty, dark
Back-rooms of funeral homes and junk-shops, sloughing samaras,
They seem the opposite
Of a tree's true, permanent embodiment of place. And yet,
Though they're ephemeral, you can't get rid of them; they are
Wholly appropriate.

Ineradicable Heaven-Tree: feather-leaves fanning
The stifling yard,
Where an old man sits cursing its stragglers that sap
The statue of Mary among his tomatoes,
It wheedles its hard
Suckers through shallow dust; drops hayfever flowers,

136

A litter of rusty keys; and nothing about it
Is lovely, apart
From its name and its green shoots, mending the damage
It springs from, like scars.

Katrina Porteous

Tree Party

Your health, Master Willow. Contrive me a bat
To strike a red ball; apart from that
In the last resort I must hang my harp on you.

Your health, Master Oak. You emblem of strength,
Why must your doings be done at such length?
Beware lest the ironclad ages catch up with you.

Your health, Master Blackthorn. Be live and be quick,
Provide the black priest with a big black stick
That his ignorant flock may go straight for the fear of you.

Your health, Master Palm. If you brew us some toddy
To deliver us out of by means of the body,
We will burn all our bridges and rickshaws in praise of you.

Your health, Master Pine. Though sailing be past
Let you fly your own colours upon your own mast
And rig us a crow's nest to keep a look out from you.

Your health, Master Elm. Of giants arboreal
Poets have found you the most immemorial
And yet the big winds may discover the fault in you.

Your health, Master Hazel. On Hallow-e'en
Your nuts are to gather but not to be seen
Are the twittering ghosts that perforce are alive in you.

Your health, Master Holly. Of all the trees
That decorate parlour walls you please
Yet who would have thought you had so much blood in you?

Your health, Master Apple. Your topmost bough
Entices us to come climbing now
For all that old rumour there might be a snake in you.

Your health, Master Redwood. The record is yours
For the girth that astounds, the sap that endures,
But where are the creatures that once came to nest in you?

Your health, Master Banyan, but do not get drunk
Or you may not distinguish your limbs from your trunk
And the sense of Above and Below will be lost on you.

Your health, Master Bo-Tree. If Buddha should come
Yet again, yet again make your branches keep mum
That his words yet again may drop honey by leave of you.

Your health, Master Yew. My bones are few
And I fully admit my rent is due,
But do not be vexed, I will postdate a cheque for you.

Louis MacNeice

Trees

Trees, our mute companions,
looming through the winter mist
from the side of the road, lit for a moment
in passing by the car's headlamps:
ash and oak, chestnut and yew;
witnesses, huge mild
beings who suffer the consequence
of sharing our planet and cannot move

away from any evil we
subject them to, whose silent
absolution hides the scars of our sins,
who always forgive – yet still assume
the attributes of judges, not victims.

Ruth Fainlight

The Trees

The trees are coming into leaf
Like something almost being said;
The recent buds relax and spread,
Their greenness is a kind of grief.

Is it that they are born again
And we grow old? No, they die too.
Their yearly trick of looking new
Is written down in rings of grain.

Yet still the unresting castles thresh
In fullgrown thickness every May.
Last year is dead, they seem to say,
Begin afresh, afresh, afresh.

Philip Larkin

Trees Be Company

When zummer's burnen het's a-shed
Upon the droopen grasses head,
A-drevèn under sheädy leaves
The workvo'k in their snow-white sleeves,
We then mid yearn to clim' the height,
    Where thorns be white, above the vern;

An' air do turn the zunsheen's might
 To softer light too weak to burn –
  On woodless downs we mid be free,
  But lowland trees be company.

Though downs mid show a wider view
O' green a-reachen into blue
Than roads a-winden in the glen,
An' ringen wi' the sounds o' men;
The thissle's crown o' red an' blue
 In Fall's cwold dew do wither brown,
An' larks come down 'ithin the lew,
  As storms do brew, an' skies do frown –
  An' though the down do let us free,
  The lowland trees be company.

Where birds do zing, below the zun,
In trees above the blue-smok'd tun,
An' sheädes o' stems do overstratch
The mossy path 'ithin the hatch;
If leaves be bright up over head,
 When Maÿ do shed its glitt'ren light;
Or, in the blight o'Fall, do spread
  A yollow bed avore our zight –
  Whatever season it mid be,
  The trees be always company.

When dusky night do nearly hide
The path along the hedge's zide,
An' daylight's hwomely sounds be still
But sounds o'water at the mill;
Then if noo feäce we long'd to greet
 Could come to meet our lwonesome treäce;
Or if noo peäce o' weary veet,
  However fleet, could reach its pleäce –
  However lwonesome we mid be,
  The trees would still be company.

William Barnes

140

Trees in a Town

Why must they fell two chestnuts on the road?
I did not see the lorry and its load
Before a wall had grown where they had stood,
I wish I thought that sphinxlike block was good
Builders have raised, to brood upon the loss
Of those two chestnuts where the two roads cross.
In spite of all the gain some say has been,
How can my eyes accept the altered scene?
How often, checked here on my way to work
By the instant luck of life, I saw themes fork
Into the boughs, where thought could learn as much
As sight will learn, till it is taught by touch.
In March abounding sunlight drenched the tree,
But still those sticky buds would not set free
Their secret fledgling silk of crumpled fronds
Held in the icy trance of winter's bonds.
Summer's wide green brought gloom where eyes could range
Up the dark foliage of attentive change;
But soon that gloom was battered by a squall,
Then the long, yellow leaves were first to fall.

After, in a frost, when all the boughs were bare,
What sudden grace the trees would print on air.
Call either tree a book for men to read
In any season; and then ask what need
A foursquare building had to pull them down.
I can forgive the traffic of this town
Its noise and brutal speed, but only just.
Metal and brick and glass above the dust
Smile on the road and on the lawn between.
What else is there the planners have not seen?
A fig-tree, thick with fruit which never grows
Ripe in our sun. When June is here it throws
Young, yellow fruit to the pavement while, unspent,
The broad leaves thrive and spread a fertile scent,
Warm memory of abundant nature's loins.

The shrivelled figs grow hard as ringing coins,
Seeming to prove the toll-gate has been paid
Out of that garden to the builder's trade.
How patient is the shadow those leaves cast:
They rob the Present who despoil the Past;
In all Utility's cold eye has seen
Beauty's profusion yields to what is mean,
And yet a fallen leaf can still express
Man's exile, his lost innocence, his dress.

Trees in a town, how long will they survive
The merchant's axe for all that looks alive?
How shall miraculous blossom, leaf and seed
Breathe life into the body lulled by speed,
Racing to nothing in an asphalt place?
Something is lost. The trees' obstructive grace
Seems to slick progress wasteful and obscene,
Whose highway must be useful and be clean.

Vernon Watkins

The Trees in Tubs

Little laurel trees, your roots can find
No mountain, yet your leaves extend
Beyond your own world, into mine
Perennial wands, unfolding in my thought
The budding evergreen of time.

Kathleen Raine

A Tree Song

Of all the trees that grow so fair,
    Old England to adorn,
Greater are none beneath the Sun
    Than Oak, and Ash, and Thorn.
Sing Oak, and Ash, and Thorn, good sirs,
    (All of a Midsummer morn!)
Surely we sing no little thing
    In Oak, and Ash, and Thorn!

Oak of Clay lived many a day
    Or ever Æneas began.
Ash of the Loam was a lady at home
    When Brut was an outlaw man.
Thorn of the Down saw New Troy Town
    (From which was London born);
Witness hereby the ancientry
    Of Oak, and Ash, and Thorn!

Yew that is old in churchyard-mould,
    He breedeth a mighty bow.
Alder for shoes do wise men choose,
    And beech for cups also.
But when ye have killed, and your bowl is spilled,
    And your shoes are clean outworn,
Back ye must speed for all that ye need
    To Oak, and Ash, and Thorn!

Ellum she hateth mankind, and waiteth
    Till every gust be laid
To drop a limb on the head of him
    That anyway trusts her shade.
But whether a lad be sober or sad,
    Or mellow with ale from the horn,
He will take no wrong when he lieth along
    'Neath Oak, and Ash, and Thorn!

Oh, do not tell the Priest our plight,
  Or he would call it a sin;
But – we have been out in the woods all night,
  A-conjuring Summer in!
And we bring you news by word of mouth –
  Good news for cattle and corn –
Now is the Sun come up from the South
  With Oak, and Ash, and Thorn!

Sing Oak, and Ash, and Thorn, good sirs
  (All of a Midsummer morn)!
England shall bide till Judgment Tide
  By Oak, and Ash, and Thorn!

Rudyard Kipling

A Tree Telling of Orpheus

White dawn. Stillness.   When the rippling began
    I took it for sea-wind, coming to our valley with rumors
    of salt, of treeless horizons. But the white fog
didn't stir; the leaves of my brothers remained outstretched,
unmoving.
        Yet the rippling drew nearer – and then
my own outermost branches began to tingle, almost as if
fire had been lit below them, too close, and their twig-tips
were drying and curling.
            Yet I was not afraid, only
            deeply alert.

I was the first to see him, for I grew
        out on the pasture slope, beyond the forest.
He was a man, it seemed: the two
moving stems, the short trunk, the two
arm-branches, flexible, each with five leafless
                    twigs at their ends,

and the head that's crowned by brown or gold grass,
bearing a face not like the beaked face of a bird,
       more like a flower's.
              He carried a burden made of
some cut branch bent while it was green,
strands of a vine tight-stretched across it. From this,
when he touched it, and from his voice
which unlike the wind's voice had no need of our
leaves and branches to complete its sound,
                     came the ripple.
But it was now no longer a ripple (he had come near and
stopped in my first shadow) it was a wave that bathed me
      as if rain
         rose from below and around me
      instead of falling.
And what I felt was no longer a dry tingling:
      I seemed to be singing as he sang, I seemed to know
      what the lark knows; all my sap
        was mounting towards the sun that by now
         had risen, the mist was rising, the grass
was drying, yet my roots felt music moisten them
deep under earth.

      He came still closer, leaned on my trunk:
      the bark thrilled like a leaf still-folded.
Music! There was no twig of me not
            trembling with joy and fear.

Then as he sang
it was no longer sounds only that made the music:
he spoke, and as no tree listens I listened, and language
      came into my roots
           out of the earth,
    into my bark
        out of the air,
      into the pores of my greenest shoots
        gently as dew
and there was no word he sang but I knew its meaning.

145

He told of journeys,
              of where sun and moon go while we stand in dark,
        of an earth-journey he dreamed he would take some day
deeper than roots...
He told of the dreams of man, wars, passions, griefs,
                and I, a tree, understood words – ah, it seemed
my thick bark would split like a sapling's that
                                grew too fast in the spring
when a late frost wounds it.

                                Fire he sang,
that trees fear, and I, a tree, rejoiced in its flames.
New buds broke forth from me though it was full summer.
        As though his lyre (now I knew its name)
              were both frost and fire, its chords flamed
up to the crown of me.
                  I was seed again.
                        I was fern in the swamp.
                                  I was coal.

And at the heart of my wood
(so close I was to becoming man or a god)
          there was a kind of silence, a kind of sickness,
              something akin to what men call boredom,
                                          something
(the poem descended a scale, a stream over stones)
          that gives to a candle a coldness
                    in the midst of its burning, he said.

It was then,
          when in the blaze of his power that
                          reached me and changed me
            I thought I should fall my length,
that the singer began
                to leave me.   Slowly
          moved from my noon shadow
                                  to open light,
words leaping and dancing over his shoulders
back to me

> rivery sweep of lyre-tones becoming

slowly again

> ripple.

And I

> in terror

> > but not in doubt of

> > > what I must do

in anguish, in haste,

> > wrenched from the earth root after root,

the soil heaving and cracking, the moss tearing asunder –
and behind me the others: my brothers
forgotten since dawn. In the forest
they too had heard,
and were pulling their roots in pain
out of a thousand years' layers of dead leaves,

> > rolling the rocks away,

> > > > breaking themselves

> > > > > out of

> > > > > their depths.

You would have thought we would lose the sound of the lyre,

> > > of the singing

so dreadful the storm-sounds were, where there was no storm,

> > > no wind but the rush of our

> > > branches moving, our trunks breasting the air.

> > > But the music!

> > > > The music reached us.

Clumsily,

> > stumbling over our own roots,

> > rustling our leaves

> > > > > in answer,

we moved, we followed.

All day we followed, up hill and down.

> > > > We learned to dance,

for he would stop, where the ground was flat,

> > > > and words he said

taught us to leap and to wind in and out

147

around one another   in figures   the lyre's measure designed.
The singer
              laughed till he wept to see us, he was so glad.
                                    At sunset
we came to this place I stand in, this knoll
with its ancient grove that was bare grass then.
              In the last light of that day his song became
farewell.
          He stilled our longing.
          He sang our sun-dried roots back into earth,
watered them: all-night rain of music so quiet
                            we could almost
              not hear it in the
                    moonless dark.
By dawn he was gone.
              We have stood here since,
in our new life.
          We have waited.
                  He does not return.
It is said he made his earth-journey, and lost
what he sought.
          It is said they felled him
and cut up his limbs for firewood.
                  And it is said
his head still sang and was swept out to sea singing.
Perhaps he will not return.
                But what we have lived
comes back to us.
          We see more.
              We feel, as our rings increase,
something that lifts our branches, that stretches our furthest
                                leaf-tips
further.
          The wind, the birds,
                  do not sound poorer but clearer,
recalling our agony, and the way we danced.
The music!

Denise Levertov

148

The Tree-Trunks

How often were these trees
With multipartite vaults and traceries
Pillars of a cathedral
Aisled like Abingdon Church on Thames;
Now rusty gold crowns fall
From heads of old gods and their dames.

Here I am young again,
Young with the youth of Saturn's reign,
So young or old I feel that awe,
Spark in their night of nescience,
Men felt before they raised a saw
Or lying Homer passed his hat for pence.

Andrew Young

Two Japanese Maples

How can the snow,
Come all that way,
Remember to stay
In the twigs of these
Two delicate trees
In tufts just so
And be Japanese
And yet still know
With the dogwood and spruce
To flurry and play
At fast & loose
As the U.S.A.?

William Meredith

149

Under the Oak

You, if you were sensible,
When I tell you the stars flash signals, each one
    dreadful,
You would not turn and answer me
"The night is wonderful."

Even you, if you knew
How this darkness soaks me through and through,
    and infuses
Unholy fear in my essence, you would pause to
    distinguish
What hurts from what amuses.

For I tell you
Beneath this powerful tree, my whole soul's fluid
Oozes away from me as a sacrifice steam
At the knife of a Druid.

Again I tell you, I bleed, I am bound with withies,
My life runs out.
I tell you my blood runs out on the floor of this oak.
Gout upon gout.

Above me springs the blood-born mistletoe
In the shady smoke.
But who are you, twittering to and fro
Beneath the oak?

What thing better are you, what worse?
What have you to do with the mysteries
Of this ancient place, of my ancient curse?
What place have you in my histories?

D.H. Lawrence

Under Trees

Yellow tunnels under the trees, long avenues
Long as the whole of time:
A single aimless man
Carries a black garden broom.
He is too far to hear him
Wading through the leaves, down autumn
Tunnels, under yellow leaves, long avenues.

Geoffrey Grigson

Upper Lambourne

Up the ash-tree climbs the ivy,
　　Up the ivy climbs the sun,
With a twenty-thousand pattering
　　Has a valley breeze begun,
Feathery ash, neglected elder,
　　Shift the shade and make it run–

Shift the shade toward the nettles,
　　And the nettles set it free
To streak the stained Carrara headstone
　　Where, in nineteen-twenty-three,
He who trained a hundred winners
　　Paid the Final Entrance Fee.

Leathery limbs of Upper Lambourne,
　　Leathery skin from sun and wind,
Leathery breeches, spreading stables,
　　Shining saddles left behind –
To the down the string of horses
　　Moving out of sight and mind.

Feathery ash in leathery Lambourne
    Waves above the sarsen stone,
And Edwardian plantations
    So coniferously moan
As to make the swelling downland,
    Far-surrounding, seem their own.

John Betjeman

Urgent

Villages pass under the plough
In England, where there was plague,
And lets time slide over parishes
The way hedges are torn out.
Bulldozers flatten a hill:
Even continents slip.
Everything must elide or kill
As the wild aurochs died;
And our elms. We have
Barely a minute now.

Sheila Wingfield

'The very leaves of the acacia-tree are London'

The very leaves of the acacia-tree are London;
London tap-water fills out the fuschia buds in the back garden,
Blackbirds pull London worms out of the sour soil,
The woodlice, centipedes, eat London, the wasps even.
London air through stomata of myriad leaves
And million lungs of London breathes.

Chlorophyll and haemoglobin do what life can
To purify, to return this great explosion
To sanity of leaf and wing.
Gradual and gentle the growth of London Pride,
And sparrows are free of all the time in the world:
Less than a window-pane between.

Kathleen Raine

Violet and Oak

Down through the trees is my green walk:
It is so narrow there and dark
That all the end, that's seen afar,
Is a dot of daylight, like a star.
When I had walked half-way or more,
I saw a pretty, small, blue flower;
And, looking closer, I espied
A small green stranger at her side.
If that flower's sweetheart lives to die
A natural death, thought I –
What will have happened by then
To a world of ever restless men?
'My little new-born oak,' I said,
'If my soul lives when I am dead,
I'll have an hour or more with you
Five hundred years from now!
When your straight back's so strong that though
Your leaves were lead on every bough,
It would not break – I'll think of you
When, weak and small, your sweetheart was
A little violet in the grass.'

W.H. Davies

153

Virgin in a Tree

How this tart fable instructs
And mocks! Here's the parody of that moral mousetrap
Set in the proverbs stitched on samplers
Approving chased girls who get them to a tree
And put on bark's nun-black

Habit which deflects
All amorous arrows. For to sheathe the virgin shape
In a scabbard of wood baffles pursuers,
Whether goat-thighed or god-haloed. Ever since that first Daphne
Switched her incomparable back

For a bay-tree hide, respect's
Twined to her hard limbs like ivy: the puritan lip
Cries: 'Celebrate Syrinx whose demurs
Won her the frog-colored skin, pale pith and watery
Bed of a reed. Look:

Pine-needle armor protects
Pitys from Pan's assault! And though age drop
Their leafy crown, their fame soars,
Eclipsing Eva, Cleo and Helen of Troy:
For which of those would speak

For a fashion that constricts
White bodies in a wooden girdle, root to top
Unfaced, unformed, the nipple-flowers
Shrouded to suckle darkness? Only they
Who keep cool and holy make

Over and over. And still the heaven
Of final surfeit is just as far
From the door as ever. What happens between us
Happens in darkness, vanishes
Easy and often as each breath.

Sylvia Plath

Walking in Autumn
for Diana Lodge

We have overshot the wood.
The track has led us beyond trees
to the tarmac edge. Too late now
at dusk to return a different way,
hazarding barbed wire or an unknown bull.
We turn back onto the darkening path.
Pale under-leaves of whitebeam, alder
gleam at our feet like stranded fish
or Hansel's stones.
A wren, unseen, churrs alarm:
each tree drains to blackness.
Halfway now, we know
by the leaning crab-apple:
feet crunching into mud
the hard slippery yellow moons.
We hurry without reason
stumbling over roots and stones.
A night creature lurches, cries out,
crashes through brambles.
Skin shrinks inside our clothes;
almost we run
falling through darkness to the wood's end,
the gate into the sloping field.
Home is lights and woodsmoke, voices –
and, our breath caught, not trembling now,
a strange reluctance to enter within doors.

Frances Horovitz

Walnut St., Oak St., Sycamore St., etc.

So this is what happened
to the names of the trees!

155

I heard them fly up,
whistling, out of the woods.
But I did not know
where they had gone.

Wendell Berry

'A waste of time! till Industry approached'

...A waste of time! till Industry approached,
And roused him from his miserable sloth;
His faculties unfolded; pointed out
Where lavish Nature the directing hand
Of Art demanded; showed him how to raise
His feeble force by the mechanic powers,
To dig the mineral from the vaulted earth,
On what to turn the piercing rage of fire,
On what the torrent, and the gathered blast;
Gave the tall ancient forest to his axe;
Taught him to chip the wood, and hew the stone,
Till by degrees the finished fabric rose;
Tore from his limbs the blood-polluted fur,
And wrapt them in the woolly vestment warm,
Or bright in glossy silk, and flowing lawn;
With wholesome viands filled his table, poured
The generous glass around, inspired to wake
The life-refining soul of decent wit;
Nor stopped at barren bare necessity;
But, still advancing bolder, led him on
To pomp, to pleasure, elegance, and grace;
And, breathing high ambition through his soul,
Set science, wisdom, glory in his view,
And bade him be the lord of all below.
        Then gathering men their natural powers combined,
And formed a public; to the general good

Submitting, aiming, and conducting all.
For this the patriot-council met, the full,
The free, and fairly represented whole;
For this they planned the holy guardian laws,
Distinguished orders, animated arts,
And, with joint force Oppression chaining, set
Imperial Justice at the helm, yet still
To them accountable: nor slavish dreamed
That toiling millions must resign their weal
And all the honey of their search to such
As for themselves alone themselves have raised.
      Hence every form of cultivated life
In order set, protected, and inspired
Into perfection wrought. Uniting all,
Society grew numerous, high, polite,
And happy. Nurse of art, the city reared
In beauteous pride her tower-encircled head;
And, stretching street on street, by thousands drew,
From twining woody haunts, or the tough yew
To bows strong-straining, her aspiring sons...

James Thomson
from The Seasons: Autumn

The Way Through the Woods

They shut the road through the woods
Seventy years ago.
Weather and rain have undone it again,
And now you would never know
There was once a road through the woods
Before they planted the trees.
It is underneath the coppice and heath
And the thin anemones.
Only the keeper sees

157

That, where the ring-dove broods,
And the badgers roll at ease,
There was once a road through the woods.

Yet, if you enter the woods
Of a summer evening late,
When the night-air cools on the trout-ringed pools
Where the otter whistles his mate,
(They fear not men in the woods,
Because they see so few.)
You will hear the beat of a horse's feet,
And the swish of a skirt in the dew,
Steadily cantering through
The misty solitudes,
As though they perfectly knew
The old lost road through the woods...
But there is no road through the woods.

Rudyard Kipling

'When first the Eye this Forrest sees'

...When first the Eye this Forrest sees
It seems indeed as *Wood* not *Trees*:
As if their Neighbourhood so old
To one great Trunk them all did mold.
There the huge Bulk takes place, as ment
To thrust up a *Fifth Element*;
And stretches still so closely wedg'd
As if the Night within were hedg'd...

Andrew Marvell
from Upon Appleton House,
to my Lord Fairfax

'When there pressed in from the porch an appalling figure'

...When there pressed in from the porch an appalling figure,
Who in height outstripped all earthly men.
From throat to thigh he was thickset and square;
His loins and limbs were so long and great
That he was half a giant on earth, I believe,
Yet mainly and most of all a man he seemed,
And the handsomest of horsemen, though huge, at that;
For though at back and at breast his body was broad,
His hips and haunches were elegant and small,
And perfectly proportioned were all parts of the man,
    As seen.
    Amazed at the hue of him,
    A foe with furious mien,
    Men gaped, for the giant grim
    Was coloured a gorgeous green.

And garments of green girt the fellow about –
A two-third length tunic, tight at the waist,
A comely cloak on top, accomplished with lining
Of the finest fur to be found, manifest to all,
Marvellous fur-trimmed material, with matching hood
Lying back from his locks and laid on his shoulders;
Fitly held-up hose, in hue the same green,
That was caught at the calf, with clinking spurs beneath
Of bright gold on bases of embroidered silk,
With shields for the shanks and shins when riding.
And verily his vesture was all vivid green,
So were the bars on his belt and the brilliants set
In ravishing array on his rich accoutrements.
It would be tedious to tell a tithe of the trifles
Embossed and embroidered, such as birds and flies,
In green gay and gaudy, with gold in the middle,
About himself and his saddle on silken work.
The breast-hangings of the horse, its haughty crupper,
The enamelled knobs and nails on its bridle,

And the stirrups that he stood on, were all stained with the same;
So were the saddle-bows and splendid tail-straps,
That ever glimmered and glinted with their green stones.
The steed that he spurred on was similar in hue
      To the sight,
   Green and huge of grain,
   Mettlesome in might
   And brusque with bit and rein –
   A steed to serve that knight!

Yes, garbed all in green was the gallant rider.
His hair, like his horse in hue, hung light,
Clustering in curls like a cloak round his shoulders,
And a great bushy beard on his breast flowing down,
With the lovely locks hanging loose from his head,
Was shorn below the shoulder, sheared right round,
So that half his arms were under the encircling hair,
Covered as by a king's cape, that closes at the neck.
The mane of that mighty horse, much like the beard,
Well crisped and combed, was copiously plaited
With twists of twining gold, twinkling in the green,
First a green gossamer, a golden one next.
His flowing tail and forelock followed suit,
And both were bound with bands of bright green,
Ornamented to the end with exquisite stones,
While a thong running thwart threaded on high
Many bright golden bells, burnished and ringing.
Such a horse, such a horseman, in the whole wide world
Was never seen or observed by those assembled before,
      Not one.
   Lightning-like he seemed
   And swift to strike and stun.
   His dreadful blows, men deemed,
   Once dealt, meant death was done.

Yet hauberk and helmet had he none,
Nor plastron nor plate-armour proper to combat,
Nor shield for shoving, nor sharp spear for lunging;
But he held a holly cluster in one hand, holly

That is greenest when groves are gaunt and bare,
And an axe in his other hand, huge and monstrous,
An axe fell and fearsome, fit for a fable;
For fully forty inches frowned the head.
Its handle-base was hued in green, in hammered gold and steel.
The blade was burnished bright, with a broad edge,
Acutely honed for cutting, as keenest razors are.
The grim man gripped it by its great strong handle,
Which was wound with iron all the way to the end,
And graven in green with graceful designs...

Anon
from Sir Gawain and the Green Knight

Wind and Tree

In the way that the most of the wind
Happens where there are trees,

Most of the world is centred
About ourselves.

Often where the wind has gathered
The trees together and together,

One tree will take
Another in her arms and hold.

Their branches that are grinding
Madly together and together,

It is no real fire.
They are breaking each other.

Often I think I should be like
The single tree, going nowhere,

161

Since my own arm could not and would not
Break the other. Yet by my broken bones

I tell new weather.

Paul Muldoon

A Wind Flashes the Grass

Leaves pour blackly across.
We cling to the earth, with glistening eyes, pierced afresh by the
tree's cry.

And the incomprehensible cry
From the boughs, in the wind
Sets us listening for below words,
Meanings that will not part from the rock.

The trees thunder in unison, on a gloomy afternoon
And the ploughman grows anxious, his tractor becomes terrible.
His memory litters downwind
And the shadow of his bones tosses darkly on the air.

The trees suddenly storm to a stop, in a hush
Against the sky, where the field ends.
They crowd there shuddering
And wary, like horses bewildered by lightning.

The stirring of their twigs against the dark, travelling sky
Is the oracle of the earth.

They too are afraid they too are momentary
Streams rivers of shadow

Ted Hughes

Winter

The tree still bends over the lake,
And I try to recall our love,
Our love which had a thousand leaves.

Sheila Wingfield

Winter the Huntsman

Through his iron glades
Rides Winter the Huntsman.
All colour fades
As his horn is heard sighing.

Far through the forest
His wild hooves crash and thunder
Till many a mighty branch
Is torn asunder.

And the red reynard creeps
To his hole near the river,
The copper leaves fall
And the bare trees shiver.

As night creeps from the ground,
Hides each tree from its brother,
And each dying sound
Reveals yet another.

Is it Winter the Huntsman
Who gallops through his iron glades,
Cracking his cruel whip
To the gathering shades?

Osbert Sitwell

163

The Winter Trees

Against the evening sky the trees are black,
Iron themselves against the iron rails;
The hurrying crowds seek cinemas or homes,
A cosy hour where warmth will mock the wind.
They do not look at trees now summer's gone,
For fallen with their leaves are those glad days
Of sand and sea and ships, of swallows, lambs,
Of cricket teams, and walking long in woods.

Standing among the trees, a shadow bends
And picks a cigarette-end from the ground;
It lifts the collar of an overcoat,
And blows upon its hands and stamps its feet –
For this is winter, chastiser of the free,
This is the winter, kind only to the bound.

Clifford Dyment

Winter Trees

The wet dawn inks are doing their blue dissolve.
On their blotter of fog the trees
Seem a botanical drawing –
Memories growing, ring on ring,
A series of weddings.

Knowing neither abortions nor bitchery,
Truer than women,
They seed so effortlessly!
Tasting the winds, that are footless,
Waist-deep in history –

164

Full of wings, otherwordliness.
In this, they are Ledas.
O mother of leaves and sweetness
Who are these pietàs?
The shadows of ringdoves chanting, but easing nothing.

Sylvia Plath

The Wood

A wood.
A man entered;
thought he knew the way
through. The old furies
attended. Did he emerge
in his right mind? The same
man? How many years
passed? Aeons? What is
the right mind? What does
'same' mean? No change of clothes
for the furies? Fast
as they are cut down
the trees grow, new
handles for axes.
There is a rumour from the heart
of the wood: brow
furrowed, mind
smooth, somebody huddles
in wide contemplation – Buddha,
Plato, Blake, Jung –
the name changes, identity
remains, pure being waiting
to be come at. Is it the self
that he mislaid? Is it why

he entered, ignoring
the warning of the labyrinth
without end? How many times
over must he begin again?

                    R.S. Thomas

'The wooden-shouldered tree is wild and high'

The wooden-shouldered tree is wild and high,
it is a plane-tree lighted inwardly,
it imprisons the sun in a cloth of leaf.
That will escape from this world though,
the tree is deliberate, it is life,
it has a musty smell and a shadow.

Bigger breasted than birds, it is breathing,
hangs with a weightless weight on everything,
having considered the sun from time to time
which vanishes in incense and yellow light:
is as silent as fog, the winter gleam
of a small sun and the birds in their flight.

It is courageous and it is alive,
this tree is nine parts of what I believe:
freedom lies in the inward of nature,
and this tree is green fire in a world of trees,
catches blue air, is neither pure nor impure,
but is alive. It is alive and dies.

                    Peter Levi

Wooding

From windows in the Home, old people
stared across the park, watching us
force rhododendron branches back
and trample nettles till the cedar logs

appeared. We must have looked minute:
a father and two sons no more than silhouettes
which stooped, and staggered comically
to where a trailer stood half darkened

by the wall. It took an hour.
And afterwards, to see us fooling
round the green wet-smelling load,
they would have thought us happy.

There we were: me running, my brother
kicking leaves, and each of us decked out
with split sweet chestnut husks
as spiky nipples on our coats.

The whole short afternoon we spoke
of anything except your death,
and then, next day, beyond that
blank enormous wall we buried you,

still destitute of ways to show our grief.

Andrew Motion

The Wood of the Self-Murdered

The trees against the mountain's groin
Pitch wigwams in a zigzag line.
Pelts of pine and spruce and fir
Are tented in the cloudy air;

167

The western light slides down the wide
Slant of the branches of brown hide.

No creature tracks the furry dark,
Not owl nor weasel is awake;
The winds grunts by and rubs its flanks
And hears the groans of rocking trunks,
And the dead drip of the red rain
As the mist blankets down again.

On every twig and branch are risen
Blobs of blood like dark red resin
That drizzle to the ground and stain
Grass and brambleleaf and thorn;
The bark is blistered and the wood
Crusted with scabs and boils of blood.

These are the wooden souls of men
Who broke the life in their own bone;
With rope round neck or knife in throat
They turned their backs upon the light,
And now their fears creak in the breeze,
In blood-red darkness, turned to trees.

Beneath the soil the long shoots bore
To limestone and to iron ore,
Where through the rock that waters ooze
Red as the sap in the live trees,
And becks swill seaward, rich as wine,
The haemorrhage of the split mine.

Empires and towns are buried here
That stabbed themselves or died of fear.
Towers and terraces crack and fall,
And sink into the sandy soil,
And, bleeding like a running sore,
Do penance in the broken ore.

Norman Nicholson

Wood Rides

Who hath not felt the influence that so calms
The weary mind in summers sultry hours
When wandering thickest woods beneath the arms
Of ancient oaks and brushing nameless flowers
That verge the little ride who hath not made
A minutes waste of time and sat him down
Upon a pleasant swell to gaze awhile
On crowding ferns bluebells and hazel leaves
And showers of lady smocks so called by toil
When boys sprote gathering sit on stulps and weave
Garlands while barkmen pill the fallen tree
– Then mid the green variety to start
Who hath (not) met that mood from turmoil free
And felt a placid joy refreshed at heart

John Clare

Woods

I part the out thrusting branches
and come in beneath
the blessed and the blessing trees.
Though I am silent
there is singing around me.
Though I am dark
there is vision around me.
Though I am heavy
there is flight around me.

Wendell Berry

'Ye fallen avenues! once more I mourn'

Ye fallen avenues! once more I mourn
Your fate unmerited, once more rejoice
That yet a remnant of your race survives.
How airy and how light the graceful arch,
Yet awful as the consecrated roof
Re-echoing pious anthems! while beneath
The chequer'd earth seems restless as a flood
Brush'd by the wind. So sportive is the light
Shot through the boughs, it dances as they dance,
Shadow and sunshine intermingling quick,
And darkening and enlightening, as the leaves
Play wanton, every moment, every spot.

William Cowper
from The Task

'You lingering sparse leaves of me on winter-nearing boughs'

You lingering sparse leaves of me on winter-nearing boughs,
And I some well-shorn tree of field or orchard-row;
You tokens diminute and lorn – (not now the flush of May,
    or July clover-bloom – no grain of August now;)
You pallid banner-staves – you pennants valueless – you
    over-stay'd of time,
Yet my soul-dearest leaves confirming all the rest,
The faithfulest – hardiest – last.

Walt Whitman

'Y was a Yew'

Y was a yew,
Which flourished and grew,
By a quiet abode
Near the side of a road.

       y!
Dark little Yew!

Edward Lear

Acknowledgements

It seemed a simple journey – but once we had begun we were overwhelmed with the diversity of routes we could take.

We have to heap thanks upon Susan Forrester and Kim Taplin for sending us along some of the richest paths. Kim has written an inspirational book *Tongues in Trees – trees in the English literary imagination* (Green Books 1989). We are grateful to the Arts Council for the wonderful 20th century Poetry Library now at the South Bank Centre and to the Library of University College London. Michael Bird, Kim Richardson and everyone at Bristol Classical Press deserve our thanks for their helpfulness and cheerful patience and Simon Bishop who designed the cover of this book and *In A Nutshell*. We are grateful to Angela Verren-Taunt for so generously allowing us to use the wonderful Ben Nicholson Tree extensively in our Trees, Woods and the Green Man campaign which has been funded by the London Boroughs Grant Scheme, the Department of the Environment, the Nature Conservancy Council, The Ernest Cook Trust and a London based Trust.

John Fowles' writing with its powerful allusions to nature has been important to us for a long time – we are very grateful for a provocative Foreword.

Our greatest thanks, of course, must go to the poets, from our contemporaries to those whose names we will never know, for giving us such riches. We thank all the poets, publishers and executors who have kindly given permission, and particularly Mavis Pindard at Faber and Faber for friendly, clear and candid help when we first entered the copyright jungle. We have had many warm letters and good wishes: thank you all.

Out of 900 poems with trees at their centre that we found on this first foray we have had to leave out many favourites – but we hope that the breadth and variety of this, our selection, gives pause for thought and lures you to further reading; with this in mind we include formal copyright acknowledgements with full references below. These pages form an extension of the copyright page. We have tried very hard to trace copyright holders – we apologise if there are any omissions or mistakes. We would be grateful if you could write to us so that we can correctly attribute and thank the people concerned.

A – Z List of Poets and their Poems with Sources and Acknowledgements

Anon

'In somer, when the shawes be sheyne' *from* The Ballad of Robyn Hode and the Munke (traditional)
The Oxford Book of Ballads ed. J. Kinsley, Oxford University Press 1969

'Hwaet! A dream came to me at deep midnight' *from* The Dream of the Rood (pre-7th century)
The Earliest English Poems translated & Introduced by Michael Alexander, Penguin Classics 1966, 1977 (© Michael Alexander 1966, 1967; reproduced by permission of Penguin Books Ltd)

'The holly and the ivy' (traditional)
The Oxford Book of Carols by P. Dearmer, R. Vaughan Williams and M. Shaw, O.U.P. 1928

Glyn Cynon Wood (16th century)

Never Tell (13th century)
Oxford Book of Welsh Verse in English O.U.P. 1983

'When there pressed in from the porch an appalling figure' *from Sir Gawain and the Green Knight* translated by Brian Stone, Penguin Classics 1959, 1964, 1974 (© Brian Stone 1959, 1964, 1974; reproduced by permission of Penguin Books Ltd)

Abse, Dannie, 1923-

Tree
White Coat, Purple Coat Hutchinson 1989 and Persea Books U.S. 1989 (© Dannie Abse & Hutchinson 1989)

Ashbery, John, 1927-
Some Trees
The Faber Book of Contemporary American Poetry ed. Helen
Vendler, Faber & Faber 1986 (© John Ashbery 1986)

Barnes, William, 1801-1886
Trees Be Company
William Barnes – The Dorset Poet The Dovecote Press 1984

Belloc, Hilaire, 1870-1953
The Elm
Complete Verse Duckworth 1970 (© H. Belloc 1970 by permission
of Duckworth)

Berry, Wendell, 1934-
Walnut St., Oak St.,Sycamore St., etc.
Ronsard's Lament for the Cutting of the Forest of Gastine
Woods
A Part North Point Press 1980 (© Wendell Berry 1980; reprinted
by permission)

'How long does it take to make the woods'
Sabbaths North Point Press 1987 (© Wendell Berry 1987;
reprinted by permission)

Planting Trees
The Old Elm Tree by the River
Collected Poems 1957-82 North Point Press 1985 (© Wendell
Berry 1985; reprinted by permission)

Betjeman, John, 1906-1984
Upper Lambourne
John Betjeman's Collected Poems John Murray 1980 (© John
Betjeman 1980; reprinted by permission John Murray
(Publishers) Ltd)

Blake, William, 1757-1827
A Poison Tree
Songs of Experience
The Complete Writings of William Blake ed. G. Keynes, O.U.P.
1966

Blunden, Edmund, 1896-1974
>The Tree in the Goods Yard
>*After the Bombing* Macmillan 1949 (© Edmund Blunden 1949)
>
>Timber
>*Selected Poems* Carcanet Press 1982 (© Edmund Blunden 1982)

Brooke, Rupert, 1887-1915
>Pine-Trees and the Sky: Evening
>*The Poetical Works of Rupert Brooke* ed. Geoffrey Keynes, Faber & Faber 1946

Browning, Robert, 1812-1889
>Home-Thoughts, From Abroad
>*Poetical Works 1833-1864* ed. Ian Jack, O.U.P. 1970

Casey, Mary, 1915-1980
>Not After Plutarch
>*Full Circle* The Enitharmon Press 1981 (© Mary Casey 1981 with thanks to Gerard Casey)

Causley, Charles, 1917-
>Green Man in the Garden
>*Collected Poems* Macmillan 1975 (© Charles Causley 1975)

Chaucer, Geoffrey, 1340?-1400
>'The solemn work of building up the pyre' *from*
>The Knight's Tale, *The Canterbury Tales* translated by Nevill Coghill, Penguin Classics 1951, 1958, 1960 (© Nevill Coghill 1951, 1958, 1960; reproduced by permission of Penguin Books Ltd)
>
>'For over-al, wher that I myn eyen caste' *from* The Parlement of Foules
>*Chaucer – Complete Works* ed. Walter Skent, O.U.P. 1976

Clare, John, 1793-1864
>The Fallen Elm
>Wood Rides
>*John Clare The Midsummer Cushion* ed. A. Tibble, Mid Northumberland Arts Group & Carcanet Press 1979

Clarke, Gillian, 1937-
    Cardiff Elms
    Selected Poems Carcanet Press 1985 (© Gillian Clarke 1985;
    thanks to the author & Carcanet Press)

Cowper, William, 1731-1800
    The Poplar Field
    'Survivor sole, and hardly such, of all' *from* Yardley Oak
    'Ye fallen avenues! once more I mourn'
    'Nor less attractive is the woodland scene,'
    from The Task I & II
    Oxford University Press various sources

Davies, W.H., 1870-1940
    No-man's Wood
    Violet and Oak
    The Old Oak Tree
    The Complete Poems of W.H. Davies Jonathan Cape 1963 (© W.H.
    Davies and Jonathan Cape Ltd 1963; with thanks to the executors
    of the W.H. Davies Estate, Jonathan Cape, and Weslyan
    University Press.)

Day Lewis, C., 1904-1972
    The Christmas Tree
    Maple and Sumach
    Poems of C. Day Lewis 1925-72 chosen by Ian Parsons, Jonathan
    Cape 1977 (© C. Day Lewis 1977; with thanks to the executors of
    the Estate of C. Day Lewis and to Jonathan Cape Ltd)

Drummond, William, 1585-1649
    'Thrise happie hee, who by some shadie Grove'

Duffy, Maureen, 1933-
    Tree Fall
    Song of the Stand Pipe
    Collected Poems 1949-84 Hamish Hamilton 1985 (© Maureen
    Duffy 1985)

Dunn, Douglas, 1942-
    Dieback
    Northlight Faber & Faber 1988

(© Douglas Dunn 1988; reprinted by permission of the author and
Faber & Faber Ltd)

Dyment, Clifford, 1914-
The Winter Trees
Collected Poems by Clifford Dyment J.M. Dent 1970 (© Clifford
Dyment 1970)

Fainlight, Ruth, 1931-
The New Tree
Trees
Sibyls and Others Hutchinson 1980 (© Ruth Fainlight 1980)

Feinstein, Elaine, 1930-
The Magic Apple Tree
The Magic Apple Tree Hutchinson 1971 (© Elaine Feinstein 1971;
reprinted by permission Century Hutchinson Ltd)

Frost, Robert, 1874-1963
On a Tree Fallen Across the Road
Birches
The Poetry of Robert Frost ed. Edward Connery Lathem, Jonathan
Cape 1971 (© Robert Frost 1971; with thanks to the Estate of
Robert Frost, to the editor and to Jonathan Cape Ltd © 1916, 1923
by Holt, Reinhart and Winston and renewed 1944, 1951 by Robert
Frost, by permission of Henry Holt & Company Ltd)

Fuller, John, 1937-
'Living a good way up a mountain' *from* The Grey and the Green
The Grey among the Green Chatto & Windus 1988 (© John Fuller
1988)

The Elms
Cannibals and Missionaries Secker & Warburg 1972 (© John
Fuller 1972)

Ginsberg, Allen, 1926-
'Autumn again, you wouldn't know in the city' *from* Autumn Gold:
New England Fall

Collected Poems 1947-80, Penguin Books 1987 (© Allen Ginsberg 1984; reproduced by permission of Harper & Row Publishers Inc. and Penguin Books Ltd)

Gogarty, O. St.John, 1878-1957
The Crab Tree
Selected Poems Macmillan 1933 (© Gogarty 1933)

Graves, Robert, 1895-1985
An English Wood
The Poems of Robert Graves Doubleday Anchor Books, New York 1958 (© Robert Graves 1958)

The Battle of the Trees
The White Goddess Faber & Faber 1961 (© Robert Graves 1961; with thanks to A.P. Watt Ltd on behalf of the Executors of the Estate of Robert Graves)

Grigson, Geoffrey, 1905-1985
Under Trees
Elms under Cloud
The Collected Works of Geoffrey Grigson 1924-62 Phoenix House 1963 (© Geoffrey Grigson 1963)

Gunn, Thom, 1929-
The Cherry Tree
Jack Straw's Castle: Selected Poems 1950-75 Faber & Faber 1979 (© Thom Gunn 1979; reprinted by permission Faber & Faber Ltd and Farrar, Straus and Giroux, Inc. © 1957, 1958, 1961, 1967, 1971, 1973, 1974, 1975, 1976, 1979 by Thom Gunn)

Gurney, Ivor, 1890-1937
Felling a Tree
Collected Poems of Ivor Gurney O.U.P. 1984

Hamburger, Michael, 1924-
Oak
Trees Embers Handpress, Llangynog 1988 (© Michael Hamburger 1988; thanks to the author and to Embers Handpress)

Hardy, Thomas, 1840-1928
To a Tree in London (Clement's Inn)
Throwing a Tree
In a Wood
The Variorum Edition of the Complete Poems of Thomas Hardy
ed. James Gibson, Macmillan 1979

Harrison, Heather, 1943-
Green Man
Roots Beneath The Pavement (West Midlands Arts and Common Ground) Birmingham Readers & Writers Festival 1987 (© Heather Harrison 1987)

Harrison, Tony, 1937-
Cypress & Cedar
Selected Poems Penguin 1987 (© Tony Harrison 1987)

Heaney, Seamus, 1939-
Bog Oak
Wintering Out Faber & Faber 1972 (© Seamus Heaney 1972; reprinted by permission of the author and Faber & Faber Ltd)

The Plantation
Door Into the Dark Faber & Faber 1969 (© Seamus Heaney 1969; reprinted by permission of the author and Faber & Faber Ltd)

Bog Oak and The Plantation *from*
Poems 1965-1975 by Seamus Heaney (© 1966, 1969, 1972, 1975, 1985 by Seamus Heaney; reprinted by permission of Farrar, Straus and Giroux Inc.)

'The bushy leafy oak tree' *from*
Sweeney Astray: A Version From The Irish translated by Seamus Heaney, A Field Day Publication 1983 (© Seamus Heaney 1983)

Heath-Stubbs, John, 1918-
'This night I walk through a forest in my head' *from* The Heart's Forest
Collected Poems 1943-87 Carcanet Press 1988 (© John Heath-Stubbs 1988)

Herbert, George, 1593-1633
'Now I am here what thou wilt do with me *from* The Temple
(Affliction 1)
The Works of George Herbert O.U.P. 1941

Herrick, Robert, 1591-1674
Ceremonies for Candlemasse Eve
The Poetical Works of Robert Herrick O.U.P. 1915

Heyen, William, 1940-
The Elm's Home
Maple and Starlings
Long Island Light: Poems and A Memoir The Vanguard Press Inc.
New York 1979 (© William Heyen 1979)

Horovitz, Frances, 1938-83
Walking in Autumn
Collected Poems Bloodaxe Books 1985 (© Frances Horovitz 1985;
with thanks to Roger Garfitt and Bloodaxe Books)

Housman, A.E., 1859-1936
'Give me a land of boughs in leaf'
'Loveliest of trees, the cherry now' *from* A Shropshire Lad
The Collected Works of A.E. Housman Jonathan Cape 1939

Hughes, Ted, 1930-
'I see the oak's bride in the oak's grasp' *from* Gaudete
'A Wind Flashes the Grass' *from* Wodwo
Selected Poems 1957-81 Faber & Faber 1982 (© Ted Hughes 1982)

A Tree
Remains of Elmet Faber & Faber 1979 (© Ted Hughes 1979;
reprinted by permission of the author, Faber & Faber Ltd and
Harper & Row Inc.)

Hyland, Paul, 1947-
To Make a Tree
The Stubborn Forest Bloodaxe Books 1984 (© Paul Hyland 1984)

Jennings, Elizabeth, 1926-
Beech
Growing Points, Collected Poems Carcanet Press 1975 (©
Elizabeth Jennings 1975)

Jonson, Ben, 1573-1637
'It is not growing like a tree'
The Complete Works of Ben Jonson ed. William Hunter, New York
University Press 1963

Kavanagh, Patrick, 1904-67
Poplars
Beech Tree
To A Late Poplar
The Complete Poems of Patrick Kavanagh Peter Kavanagh Hand
Press 1977, 250 East 30th Street, New York 10016 (© Peter
Kavanagh 1972)

Kavanagh, P.J., 1931-
A Single Tree
Elder
Presences – New & Selected Poems Chatto & Windus 1987 (© P.J.
Kavanagh 1987)

Kilmer, A. Joyce, 1886-1918
'I think that I shall never see'

Kipling, R., 1865-1936
A Tree Song
The Way Through the Woods
Rudyard Kipling's Verse Definitive Edition Hodder and Stoughton
1912

Kitchener Davies, J., 1902-52
'The Land of Y Llian was on the high marsh' *from* The Sound of
the Wind that is Blowing
The Oxford Book of Welsh Verse in English O.U.P. 1983 (with
thanks to Mrs Mair I. Davies for permission to extract Sion y
Gwynt sy'n Chwytha © J. Kitchener Davies 1983; translated by J.P.
Clancy)

Larkin, Philip, 1922-1985
   The Trees
   High Windows Faber & Faber 1974 (© Philip Larkin 1974; reprinted by permission of Faber & Faber Ltd and Farrar, Straus and Giroux Inc.)

Lawrence, D.H., 1885-1930
   Under The Oak
   Bare Almond-Trees
   Delight Of Being Alone
   The Complete Poems of D.H. Lawrence Penguin 1977

Lear, Edward, 1812-1888
   'There was an old lady whose folly'
   Bosh & Nonsense Allen Lane 1982

   'There was an old man in a tree'
   'Y was a yew'
   The Complete Nonsense of Edward Lear ed. Holbrook Jackson, Faber & Faber Ltd 1947

Levertov, Denise, 1923-
   A Tree Telling of Orpheus
   Poems 1968-72, A New Directions Book (© Denise Levertov Goodman 1968)

Levi, Peter, 1931-
   'The wooden-shouldered tree is wild and high'
   Alcaic
   'In midwinter a wood was'
   Collected Poems 1955-75 Anvil Press Poetry 1976 (© Peter Levi 1976)

Llewellyn-Williams, Hilary, 1951-
   Oak Duir
   Tree Calendar Poetry Wales Press 1987 (© Hilary Llewellyn-Williams 1987)

Lowell, Robert, 1917-1977
   'No weekends for the gods now. Wars' *from* Waking Early Sunday Morning

184

Near the Ocean Faber and Faber 1967 (© Robert Lowell 1967; reprinted by permission of Faber & Faber Ltd and Farrar, Straus and Giroux Inc. © 1963, 1965, 1966, 1967 by Robert Lowell)

MacNeice, Louis, 1907-1963
The Tree of Guilt
Tree Party
The Collected Poems of Louis MacNeice Faber & Faber 1966 (© Louis MacNeice 1966; reprinted by permission Faber & Faber Ltd)

Manley Hopkins, Gerard, 1844-1889
Binsey Poplars
Poems and Prose selected and edited by W.H. Gardner, Penguin 1953/63

Marvell, Andrew, 1621-1678
'When first the Eye this Forrest sees' *from* Upon Appleton House, to my Lord Fairfax
The Poems & Letters of Andrew Marvell Vol. I – Poems O.U.P. 1927

Meredith, George, 1828-1909
'Enter these enchanted woods' *from* The Woods of Westermain
Poems and Lyrics of the Joy of the Earth
Poems Volume II The Times Book Club 1912

Meredith, William, 1919-
Two Japanese Maples
The Wreck of the Thresher and Other Poems Alfred A. Knopf, New York 1964 (© William Meredith 1964)

Mew, Charlotte, 1869-1928
Domus Caedet Arborem
Afternoon Tea
Collected Poems & Prose Carcanet Press 1981

Milligan, Spike, 1918-
Tree-kill
Unspun Socks From a Children's Laundry & Other Children's Verse

M & J. Hobbs in assoc. with Michael Joseph 1981 (© Spike
Milligan 1981)

Morrison, Blake, 1950
Pine
Dark Glasses Chatto & Windus 1984 (© Blake Morrison 1984)

Motion, Andrew, 1952-
Wooding
Dangerous Play Poems 1974-1984 Penguin 1984 (© Andrew
Motion 1984)

Muldoon, Paul, 1951-
Wind and Tree
New Weather Faber & Faber 1973 (© Paul Muldoon 1973;
reprinted by permission Faber & Faber Ltd and the Wake Forest
University Press)

Nash, Ogden, 1902-1971
Song of the Open Road
Collected Verse from 1929 on J.M. Dent 1966 (© Ogden Nash 1966;
reproduced by permission of Curtis Brown, London)

Nicholson, Norman, 1914-1987
The Elm Decline
A Local Habitation Faber & Faber 1972 (© Norman Nicholson
1972)

The Wood of the Self-Murdered
Five Rivers Faber & Faber 1944 (© Norman Nicholson 1944;
reprinted by permission of Faber & Faber Ltd)

Pitter, Ruth, 1897-
The Cedar
The Tall Fruit-Trees
Poems 1926-66 Cressof Press 1968 (© Ruth Pitter 1968; reprinted
by permission Parrott & Coales)

Plath, Sylvia, 1932-1963
Virgin in a Tree

Collected Poems ed. Ted Hughes, Faber & Faber 1981 (© Sylvia Plath 1981)

Winter Trees
Winter Trees Faber & Faber 1971 (© Sylvia Plath 1971)

Porteous, Katrina, 1960-
Tree of Heaven
previously unpublished (© Katrina Porteous 1989)

Pound, Ezra, 1885-1972
The Tree
Collected Shorter Poems by Ezra Pound Faber & Faber 1949 (© Ezra Pound 1949; reprinted by permission Faber & Faber Ltd)

Raine, Craig, 1944-
In The Woods
The Onion, Memory O.U.P. 1978 (© Craig Raine 1978; by permission of the author and Oxford University Press)

Raine, Kathleen, 1908-
The Trees in Tubs
London Trees
Collected Poems Hamish Hamilton 1956 (© Kathleen Raine 1956)

The Leaf
'The very leaves of the acacia tree are London'
Poems from *The Oval Portrait* Hamish Hamilton 1977 (© Kathleen Raine 1977)

Salzman, Eva, 1960-
Ending Up in Kent
Poetry Review New British Poets Vol. 77 No. 4 Winter 87/88 (© Eva Salzman 1987)

Sassoon, Siegfried, 1886-1967
Blunden's Beech
South Wind
Collected Poems 1908-56 Faber & Faber 1984 (© Siegfried Sassoon 1984; by permission of George Sassoon)

Scannell, Vernon, 1922-
   Apple Poem
   Funeral Games Robson Books 1987 (© Vernon Scannell 1987;
   with thanks to the author & Robson Books Ltd)

Shakespeare, William, 1564-1616
   'Now, my co mates and brothers-in-exile'
   'O Rosalind'
   As You Like It

   'There is an old tale goes that Herne the Hunter'
   The Merry Wives of Windsor

Sitwell, Osbert, 1892-1969
   from Winter The Huntsman
   Selected Poems Old & New Duckworth 1943 (© Osbert Sitwell
   1943)

Smith, Stevie, 1902-1971
   Alone in the Woods
   The Collected Poems of Stevie Smith Penguin Modern Classics
   1985 (© Stevie Smith 1985; with thanks to James MacGibbon, ©
   Stevie Smith 1972; reproduced by permission New Directions
   Publishing Corp.)

Snyder, Gary, 1930-
   'The groves are down' *from* Logging
   Myths & Texts Totem Books in association with Corinth Books
   1960
   (© Gary Snyder 1960)

   Fence Posts
   Axe Handles North Point Press 1983 (© Gary Snyder 1983)

   Stovewood
   Regarding Wave Fulcrum Press 1967 (© Gary Snyder 1967)

Spenser, Edmund, 1552-99
   'There grew a goodly tree him faire beside' *from* The Faerie
   Queene
   Spenser's Poetical Works O.U.P. 1912

Stallworthy, Jon, 1935-
A Barbican Ash
Root & Branch Chatto & Windus 1969 (© Jon Stallworthy 1969)

Szirtes, George, 1948-
The Silver Tree
November & May Secker & Warburg 1981 (© George Szirtes 1981)

Taplin, Kim, 1943-
The May Tree
First published in Peace News (© Kim Taplin 1987)

Tennyson, Alfred Lord, 1809-92
Amphion
'Old Yew, which graspeth at the stones' *from* In Memoriam A.H.H.
The Poems of Tennyson Longman 1969

Thomas, Dylan, 1914-1953
'Shut, too, in a tower of words, I mark' *from* Especially when the October wind
Collected Poems 1934-52 J.M. Dent 1952 (© Dylan Thomas 1952)
Poems of Dylan Thomas (copyright 1939 by New Directions Publishing Corporation, reprinted by permission)

Thomas, Edward, 1878-1917
The Combe
The Cherry Trees
Fifty Faggots
The Chalk Pit
The Collected Poems of Edward Thomas O.U.P. 1978

Thomas, R.S., 1913-
Afforestation
The Bread of Truth Rupert Hart-Davis 1964 (© R.S. Thomas 1964; reproduced by permission from Grafton Books, a division of the Collins Publishing Group)

The Wood
Experimenting with an Amen Macmillan 1986 (© R.S. Thomas 1986)

Thomson, James, 1700-1748
'Bear me, Pomona! to thy citron groves'
'A waste of time! Till Industry approached'
The Seasons (extracts from Summer & Autumn)

Thwaite, Anthony, 1930-
Dead Wood
Poems 1953-83 Secker & Warburg 1984 (© Anthony Thwaite 1984)

Tomlinson, Charles, 1927-
The Tree
Charles Tomlinson's Collected Poems O.U.P. 1985 (© Charles Tomlinson 1985; by permission of the author and Oxford University Press)

Vince, Michael, 1947-
The Memorial Trees
The Orchard Well Carcanet Press 1978 (© Michael Vince 1978)

The Thicket
In the New District Carcanet Press 1982 (© Michael Vince 1982)

Virgil, 70-19 BC
'Come, farmers, then, and learn the form of tendance' *from*
The Georgics Book II
Translated by L.P. Wilkinson, Penguin Classics 1982 (© L.P. Wilkinson 1982; reproduced by permission of Penguin Books Ltd)

Walcott, Derek, 1930-
The Almond Trees
The Gulf (© 1963, 1964, 1965, 1969, 1970 by Derek Walcott; reprinted by permission of Farrar, Straus and Giroux Inc.)

'The oak inns creak in their joints as light declines' *from*
Midsummer
Collected Poems 1948-84 Farrar, Straus & Giroux, New York 1986

Watkins, Vernon, 1906-67
Trees in a Town
The Collected Poems of Vernon Watkins Golgonooza Press 1986
(© Golgonooza Press 1986)

Whitman, Walt, 1819-1892
'I Saw in Louisiana a Live-Oak Growing'
'You Lingering Sparse Leaves of Me'
The Complete Poems ed. Francis Murphy, Penguin 1975

Wingfield, Sheila, 1906-
Winter
Urgent
Collected Poems 1938-83 Enitharmon Press 1983
(© Sheila Wingfield 1983; thanks to the author, Enitharmon Press, and Hill & Wang)

Wordsworth, William, 1777-1850
'There is a thorn it looks so old' *from* The Thorn
The Tables Turned
Wordsworth & Coleridge Lyrical Ballads ed. H. Littledale, O.U.P. 1959

Young, Andrew, 1885-1971
The Long-Tailed Tits
In Westerham Woods
The Tree-Trunks
The Tree
The Elm Beetle
Complete Poems Secker & Warburg 1974 (© the Estate of the late Andrew Young 1960 & 1974)

Publications by Common Ground

Trees be Company an anthology edited by Angela King and Susan Clifford for Common Ground, Bristol Classical Press 1989, £5.95

In a Nutshell: A manifesto for trees and a guide to growing and protecting them by Neil Sinden with drawings by David Nash, Common Ground 1989, £5.95

Pity the Tree – a teachers' guide through woods in children's literature by Kim Taplin, Common Ground 1989, £3.75

Holding Your Ground – an action guide to local conservation by Angela King and Sue Clifford, Wildwood House 1987, £6.95

Parish Maps and The Parish Boundary by Tom Greeves, Common Ground 1987, each £1.25

New Milestones – Sculpture, Community and the Land by Joanna Morland, Common Ground 1988, £4.95

Mayday, Mayday: 101 Ways to answer Nature's Call For Help (poster/broadsheet), Common Ground, £2.50

Second Nature – a verbal and visual exploration by 42 writers and artists of the idea that our relationship with the land and the natural world is a vital part of our imaginative, cultural and social life. Edited by Richard Mabey, Susan Clifford and Angela King, Jonathan Cape 1984; reprinted in paperback 1989, £7.95

We also produce practical action and arts postcards.

If you order any of these direct please add 33% or more for postage and packing.

Common Ground (charity no. 326335)
45, Shelton Street, London WC2 9HJ, England

Leadership,
Management &
Team Working
in Nursing

Sara Miller McCune founded SAGE Publishing in 1965 to support the dissemination of usable knowledge and educate a global community. SAGE publishes more than 1000 journals and over 800 new books each year, spanning a wide range of subject areas. Our growing selection of library products includes archives, data, case studies and video. SAGE remains majority owned by our founder and after her lifetime will become owned by a charitable trust that secures the company's continued independence.

Los Angeles | London | New Delhi | Singapore | Washington DC | Melbourne

3rd Edition

Leadership, Management & Team Working in Nursing

Peter Ellis

Learning Matters
An imprint of SAGE Publications Ltd
1 Oliver's Yard
55 City Road
London EC1Y 1SP

SAGE Publications Inc.
2455 Teller Road
Thousand Oaks, California 91320

SAGE Publications India Pvt Ltd
B 1/I 1 Mohan Cooperative Industrial Area
Mathura Road
New Delhi 110 044

SAGE Publications Asia-Pacific Pte Ltd
3 Church Street
#10-04 Samsung Hub
Singapore 049483

Editor: Donna Goddard
Development editor: Richenda Milton-Daws
Senior project editor: Chris Marke
Project management: Swales & Willis Ltd, Exeter, Devon
Marketing manager: Tamara Navaratnam
Cover design: Wendy Scott
Typeset by: C&M Digitals (P) Ltd, Chennai, India
Printed in the UK

First published 2011
Second edition 2015
Third edition 2019

Library of Congress Control Number: 2018933058

British Library Cataloguing in Publication data

A catalogue record for this book is available from the British Library

ISBN 978-1-4739-9790-5
ISBN 978-1-4739-9791-2 (pbk)

At SAGE we take sustainability seriously. Most of our products are printed in the UK using responsibly sourced papers and boards. When we print overseas we ensure sustainable papers are used as measured by the PREPS grading system. We undertake an annual audit to monitor our sustainability.

Contents

TRANSFORMING NURSING PRACTICE

Transforming Nursing Practice is a series tailor made for pre-registration students nurses. Each book in the series is:

 Affordable

 Full of active learning features

 Mapped to the NMC Standards of proficiency for registered nurses

 Focused on applying theory to practice

Each book addresses a core topic and they have been carefully developed to be simple to use, quick to read and written in clear language.

An invaluable series of books that explicitly relates to the NMC standards. Each book covers a different topic that students need to explore in order to develop into a qualified nurse... I would recommend this series to all Pre-Registered nursing students whatever their field or year of study.

LINDA ROBSON,
Senior Lecturer at Edge Hill University

Many titles in the series are on our recommended reading list and for good reason - the content is up to date and easy to read. These are the books that actually get used beyond training and into your nursing career.

EMMA LYDON,
Adult Student Nursing

ABOUT THE SERIES EDITORS

DR MOOI STANDING is an Independent Nursing Consultant (UK and International) and is responsible for the core knowledge, adult nursing and personal and professional learning skills titles. She is an experienced NMC Quality Assurance Reviewer of educational programmes and a Professional Regulator Panellist on the NMC Practice Committee. Mooi is also Board member of Special Olympics Malaysia, enabling people with intellectual disabilities to participate in sports and athletics nationally and internationally.

DR SANDRA WALKER is a Clinical Academic in Mental Health working between Southern Health Trust and the University of Southampton and responsible for the mental health nursing titles. She is a Qualified Mental Health Nurse with a wide range of clinical experience spanning more than 25 years.

BESTSELLING TEXTBOOKS

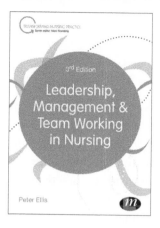

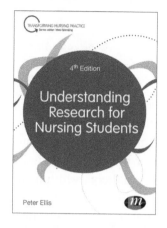

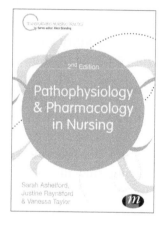

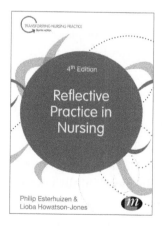

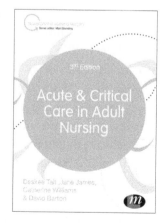

You can find a full list of textbooks in the
Transforming Nursing Practice series at

https://uk.sagepub.com

Foreword

Leadership, Management and Team Working in Nursing engages readers in a step by step exploration ranging from reflecting on how they like to be managed, to understanding how they can be more effective team players, coordinators and leaders in person-centred care. One of the main strengths of the book is the way in which it succinctly integrates relevant management and leadership theory with nursing values and the practicalities of delivering high standards of care within complex multidisciplinary healthcare organisations. It does so by continually drawing parallels between the qualities of a good nurse and a good leader. For example: being self aware of one's own development needs; accepting and respecting individual differences and cultural diversity; creating a collaborative, nurturing culture which maximises the contribution and development of all parties; listening to, negotiating with and caring for colleagues as well as patients; developing emotional intelligence and resilience in managing stressful events; and, inspiring trust in others through one's competence, values and professional commitment. This is very helpful in enabling readers to integrate their understanding of themselves as individual nurses, as members of a multidisciplinary team, and as employees of organisations responsible for providing safe and effective healthcare. As such, it is essential reading for all nursing students so they can understand where they 'fit in' and the important contribution they can make to the healthcare team in delivering care. I also recommend the book to all registered nurses as it will be an invaluable resource when reflecting upon their care management and leadership skills for NMC revalidation purposes.

The third edition has been updated to include the revised standards of proficiency for nurses (NMC, 2018) which future pre-registration nursing curricula have to address. These include: *1. Being an accountable professional, 5. Leading and managing nursing care and working in teams, 6. Improving safety and quality of care,* and *7. Coordinating care.* Hence, the book informs and supports nurses in achieving required NMC standards regarding leadership, management and team working. It also provides informative and practical guidance in how to demonstrate compliance with *The Code*, especially in relation to: *25. Provide leadership to make sure people's wellbeing is protected and to improve their experiences of the healthcare system* (NMC, 2015). Peter Ellis has skillfully combined his nursing, educational and managerial expertise in an excellent book, packed with real life case studies and stimulating activities, enabling nursing students and registered nurses to apply relevant management theory to enhance their nursing practice. I hope you enjoy reading it as much as I did.

Dr Mooi Standing, Series Editor

About the author

Peter Ellis is Registered Manager at Whitepost Healthcare and a freelance nursing consultant, writer and educator. Peter was previously a nursing director in the hospice sector and a senior lecturer and programme director at Canterbury Christ Church University. Peter has degrees in Nursing, Ethics and Medical Epidemiology and has been writing for nurses for nearly 30 years, including three other books in the Transforming Nursing Practice series.

Acknowledgements

This book is dedicated to the many people I have worked with, and taught, over the years and from whom I have learnt so much. Most especially to JEA who is a constant support and inspiration.

Introduction

Leadership is a key feature of twenty-first century nursing. The interdisciplinary requirements of modern healthcare, the multiplicity of nursing, and nursing support, roles and increasing demands of an ageing population all mean the coordination of care is more complex now than it was at any time in the past.

In this book we explore many facets of the leadership role and what these mean for nurses. With the necessity for training to become competent in the delivery of nursing care, the need to train to understand and be able to function as a leader is fundamental to the identity of the twenty-first century nurse. You are encouraged therefore to engage with not only the written content of the book, but also to undertake the activities (described in more detail below). The activities are integral to the learning from this book and you should keep a written record of what you do to engage with them and what you found out as a result.

Who should read the book?

You should read this book if you have, or aspire to have, some element of leadership in the workplace. This applies equally to student nurses, trained nurses, associate nurses and other professionals working in the health and social care arena.

What is it about?

This book focuses on the attitudes, values and practices which serve to make for good leadership and management. Throughout the book the focus is on challenging the reader to adopt an approach to leadership and management which is focused on the human elements of the role. Readers are prompted to think about the ideal which brought them into nursing practice in the first place and consider how these might apply to what they do as potential and actual leaders or managers of people.

Why is it important?

This book is important for you because it brings together many of the elements of nursing leadership which you need to understand both now, as you lead other less experienced students, associate nurses and healthcare support workers and in the future as you become responsible for managing shifts, teams and organisations. Like nursing, leadership is both an art and a science and like nursing, leadership requires you to engage with some learning in order to develop your abilities to practise it.

The special importance of this book is that it is grounded in the learning and development of the author who has been a practising nurse and a leader. The book itself contains case studies and anecdotes from practice which identify and demystify nurse leadership.

How is it structured?

The format of the book reflects the way in which students are encouraged to think about what it means to be led, to work in a team and to lead and manage developing. The individual chapters can be read and understood on their own, but read together they help form a coherent picture of what good leadership and management practice look like.

Chapter 1, *Experience of management and leadership*, highlights the importance of remembering and understanding what it means to be led and what this might mean for the way in which you subsequently choose to lead.

Chapter 2, *Teams and team work*, identifies what teams are, why they exist and how they can work better towards their common goals. The following chapter, Chapter 3, *Working with individuals in teams*, introduces the roles and responsibilities of individuals within teams and issues such as recruitment and delegation. In Chapter 4, *Conflict management and negotiation skills*, the different personality types that may operate within teams are described, and ways of managing conflict within the team and other settings are explored.

Chapter 5, *Coaching, mentoring and clinical supervision*, investigates the role of the leader or manager in supporting team members. The use of the term mentor here refers to the relationship between a leader and someone who is guiding their development, and not the relationship between a student and their practice supervisor or assessor. This is followed by Chapter 6 on *Frameworks for management and leadership*, which identifies and examines some theories of leadership and management and their interconnectedness.

Chapter 7, *Improving care and change management*, presents theories which may underpin leadership practice in relationship to the instigation and management of change, while Chapter 8, *Creating a learning environment*, considers the value of understanding the culture within which teams work and the impact this may have on the successful working of the team.

In Chapter 9, *Developing confidence as a manager and leader*, some of the tasks and roles undertaken by the leader or manager are laid bare. The chapter goes on to look at how these might be used to develop certainty in what they do for the developing leader.

NMC Standards of Proficiency

This third edition refers to the Nursing and Midwifery Council's *Future Nurse: Standards of Proficiency for Registered Nurses* (NMC, 2018), although its content is not narrowly defined by these standards.

Activities

The activities contained within each chapter form an integral part of the learning and development strategy for each chapter. You will get the most benefit from each chapter if you engage fully with the activities and in the order they are presented. The activities are designed to help illustrate the nature and reality of some of the theory presented and to bring to life some of the situations, scenarios and associated skills and competencies described. Some of the activities require you to seek out new information and new experiences; engagement with this process adds not only to you developing your understanding of the theory underpinning good leadership and management practice, but also to begin developing the skills and competences to apply them in practice.

Reflection on the chapter content and on the activities is an important and integral part of the process of the student nurse's development as a leader of people. Some activities require you to come to a decision or understanding for yourself, while others have suggested answers presented at the end of the chapter. You should consider each activity for yourself before reading the suggested answers so that you can come to an appreciation of your own level of understanding of the content of the chapter, as well as your own personal and professional development.

Other features

The text also includes case studies and scenarios, research summaries and the necessary theory. There is also a glossary of terms at the end of the book. Glossary entries are in bold type the first time they appear.

Chapter 1 Experience of management and leadership

NMC Standards of Proficiency for Registered Nurses

This chapter will address the following platforms and proficiencies:

Platform 1: Being an accountable professional

Registered nurses act in the best interests of people, putting them first and providing nursing care that is person-centred, safe and compassionate. They act professionally at all times and use their knowledge and experience to make evidence-based decisions about care. They communicate effectively, are role models for others, and are accountable for their actions. Registered nurses continually reflect on their practice and keep abreast of new and emerging developments in nursing, health and care.

At the point of registration, the registered nurse will be able to:

1.1 understand and act in accordance with the Code (2015): Professional standards of practice and behaviour for nurses and midwives, and fulfil all registration requirements.

1.2 understand and apply relevant legal, regulatory and governance requirements, policies, and ethical frameworks, including any mandatory reporting duties, to all areas of practice, differentiating where appropriate between the devolved legislatures of the United Kingdom.

1.5 understand the demands of professional practice and demonstrate how to recognise signs of vulnerability in themselves or their colleagues and the action required to minimise risks to health.

1.10 demonstrate resilience and emotional intelligence and be capable of explaining the rationale that influences their judgments and decisions in routine, complex and challenging situations.

1.19 act as an ambassador, upholding the reputation of their profession and promoting public confidence in nursing, health and care services.

Platform 5: Leading and managing nursing care and working in teams

Registered nurses provide leadership by acting as a role model for best practice in the delivery of nursing care. They are responsible for managing nursing care and are accountable for the appropriate delegation and supervision of care provided by others in the team including lay carers. They play an active and equal role in the interdisciplinary team, collaborating and communicating effectively with a range of colleagues.

At the point of registration, the registered nurse will be able to:

5.4 demonstrate an understanding of the roles, responsibilities and scope of practice of all members of the nursing and interdisciplinary team and how to make best use of the contributions of others involved in providing care.

Platform 7: Coordinating care

Registered nurses play a leadership role in coordinating and managing the complex nursing and integrated care needs of people at any stage of their lives, across a range of organisations and settings. They contribute to processes of organisational change through an awareness of local and national policies.

At the point of registration, the registered nurse will be able to:

7.7 understand how to monitor and evaluate the quality of people's experience of complex care.

Chapter aims

After reading this chapter, you will be able to:

- identify some of the values which underpin both nursing and nurse leadership and management;
- understand how reflecting on the experience of being led affects the ways in which we choose to lead and manage in nursing;
- comment on the importance of leadership and management in nursing;
- begin to create a coherent picture of what leadership and management structures in nursing look like.

Introduction

The purpose of this chapter is to increase your awareness of the personal and professional values that influence the ways in which managers and leaders should behave. The chapter will both challenge and reinforce some of the assumptions you hold about the ways in which leaders and managers function.

Our **values** and assumptions about leadership and management are largely derived from our experiences of leading and managing, and of being led and managed. This means they will reflect our personal interpretation of what happened during the process. It is important that, at the start of any quest to understand leadership and management, we should first understand ourselves and our motivations. Only in this way can we hope to understand the context of leadership and management and the behaviours and motivations of those we seek to lead.

As well as exploring the context of values in relation to leadership and management, this chapter will explore some of the characteristics of leaders and managers. These descriptions will reflect the characteristics leadership and management theorists believe good managers and leaders should portray, including their personality traits. After examining these characteristics, you will be encouraged to formulate a picture of how you believe good leaders or managers should behave, and the essential qualities they should exhibit within the nursing context.

(For more detailed discussion of theories and frameworks for leadership and management, and how they can be adopted and adapted to help meet the challenges of nurse leadership in the twenty-first century, see Chapter 6.)

Another important theme of this chapter is why leadership and management matter to nursing practice now and in the future, as well as how an understanding of them can contribute to your personal and professional development. We will examine this issue at least in part by discussing the some of the findings of the Francis report (2013), which examined serious failures in care.

Towards the end of the chapter, some of the reasons for the existence of different leadership and management roles in nursing are introduced and discussed. You are invited to collect some data on the nursing structures where you work and consider how these impact on the work you and your colleagues do.

Understanding context and values

Our ideas and opinions about good leadership and management are coloured to a great extent by personal experiences of leadership and management, whether we are managers, leaders or team members. The assumptions we have about management and leadership styles and behaviours are also affected by our understanding of what is going on and the motivations behind the management and leadership styles we adopt or see adopted. The inability to understand why a certain approach to management or leadership has been adopted can lead to misconceptions and misunderstandings; this is something an understanding of the context of nurse leadership and management allows us to see beyond. Sometimes this context is better developed as we gain more experience as nurses and reflect thoughtfully on what these experiences actually mean.

Activity 1.1 Reflection

When you first came into nursing and went into practice for the first time, how did you feel about the efforts made by the staff to get frail, elderly patients to engage in self-care (for example, encouraging elderly patients to get out of bed in the morning and to get washed and dressed)? Now you understand a bit more about the purpose and nature of nursing, have you changed your view? Why?

There are some possible answers and thoughts at the end of the chapter.

Understanding why something is done in a particular way in a given situation allows us to understand the context of an action in the clinical setting. As shown in Activity 1.1, a developing understanding of the nature of nursing and what it means to nurse helps us to make sense of the world of work and the roles in which we find ourselves. The same is true of leadership and management, where actions taken out of context may appear to be wrong.

One of the enduring difficulties for student nurses can be to understand the provision of care beyond the individual. Often the context of nursing management and leadership is about achieving the best outcomes on a regular, recurring and equitable basis for the many. The need to achieve good outcomes for the many rather than the few may help us to understand the context of a management or leadership style we see before us. This view is one which can only develop if we are willing and able to question the leadership and management practices we see around us and are then willing and able to reflect on the answers we find.

Case study: The newly qualified nurse

Julius is a newly qualified staff nurse working on a busy cardiology ward. Julius is irritated by the apparent inactivity of the ward sister Deirdre, who spends vast amounts of time in the office doing what to him appears to be endless and pointless paperwork instead of providing patient care. Julius confronts Deirdre about the lack of time she spends on the ward and suggests much of the time she is doing nothing of value while she is 'hiding away' in her office.

Deirdre understands the point Julius is making and is wise enough to appreciate that his frustrations arise not out of malice towards her but as a result of his inexperience and lack of understanding of what it takes to keep a busy ward functioning smoothly. Deirdre takes Julius into her office and shows him some of the tasks she has to perform on a regular basis, which include writing the duty roster, completing staff appraisals, entering patient dependency scores on to a monitoring database, ordering stock and overseeing staff development planning.

Deirdre explains to Julius she too is frustrated by the lack of time she has to provide care on a daily basis: that, she explains, is after all why she came into nursing. But she

(Continued)

(Continued)

also understands her role now is less about providing care and more about facilitating the delivery of care. Deirdre explains she achieves this through supporting the staff on the ward to improve, using appraisals and accessing appropriate education and development; rostering to allow for a good work–life balance; and managing the budget while ensuring the hospital administrators know what the needs of the ward are by recording the level of dependency of the patients and the stock requirements. She explains she sees her role as supporting the staff to care for the patients, and if she did not do the necessary tasks then there would be chaos.

Julius concedes he had not looked at things in this way and he needed to understand the wider context before criticising.

Clearly, from this example we can see that one of the necessary qualities of a good manager or leader is the ability to see the bigger picture and anticipate and plan what the team will be doing and how they will do it. Leadership and management are therefore as much a forward-looking activity as about managing what is happening in the here and now. One of the characteristics of good managers or leaders is understanding what it is they want to achieve and being able to communicate this, and perhaps effectively delegating associated tasks, to the team. This relates quite well to Platform 5 'Leading and managing nursing care and working in teams', outcome 5.4, stated at the start of the chapter as: 'demonstrate an understanding of the roles, responsibilities and scope of practice of all members of the nursing and interdisciplinary team and how to make best use of the contributions of others involved in providing care'. Julius has some work to do in order to be able to meet this outcome.

What we should remember at this stage is that one of the most important things that motivates us as nurses to achieve the goals we do is our values. Before we explore more about the context of nursing leadership and management, let's stop for a moment to reflect on the values we have as humans, nurses, leaders or managers and see what impact they might have on leadership and management in nursing.

It is not at all easy to state exactly what values are. A cursory search on the internet for values of caring throws up scores of words, all of which may have relevance to nursing, but none of which explain what they are. Various descriptions include reference to best interests, moral duties, likes and preferences.

Concept summary: Human values

One of the widest-cited definitions of values, and one which has resonance with nurse leadership, is the definition by Schwartz (1994, p20), who says that a value is '*a belief pertaining to desirable end states or modes of conduct that transcends specific situations; guides selection or evaluation of behavior, people, and events; and is ordered by the importance relative to other values to form a system of value priorities'.*

The notable elements of the definition by Schwartz are that values relate to:

- achieving a good outcome
- something more important than individual situations
- how we ought to behave
- what we ought to look for in the behaviour of others
- how events ought to be managed
- ways in which we might prioritise how we use our time and effort.

In essence the suggestion here is that our values should be at the centre of everything we do, both as a guide to how we act as well as what it is we act upon. The additional issue for leaders and managers is of course that they need to role model these values to those they lead.

Evidently, within the case study above, Deirdre had not forgotten the values that took her into nursing in the first place. What had changed then for Deirdre as she moved from a clinical role to a more managerial post was simply the way in which these values were allowed to express themselves. In order to develop continually as nurses, leaders and managers, it is important not only that we question our values from time to time, but that we are also able to express what these values are and refine them in discussion with our colleagues.

Activity 1.2   Decision-making

Take some time to think about the values you have as a nurse. Now think about how these values show themselves in the ways in which you act when in the clinical setting. Next time you are in practice, ask your team leader or ward manager what values s/he holds and how s/he thinks s/he expresses them in practice. Now compare the lists, looking for areas of overlap and areas of difference. What do you notice about the similarities and differences between your list of values and corresponding actions and the leader's values and actions?

There are some possible answers and thoughts at the end of the chapter.

What is clear about the values of practising nurses, ward managers and more senior nursing staff is they should, and to a great extent do, share similar values and goals. The role of the leader or manager should be to facilitate the team in the achievement of these goals. Evidently, where there are differences in the values and goals of the team and the team leader, then difficulties will arise. When nurses or nurse leaders forget what their values are, then they will lose sight of what it is they are trying to achieve.

Sometimes it is hard to know what exactly our values are or the limits to which they can be stretched. One method for understanding our values as potential leaders or managers is to ask ourselves hypothetical questions, the answers to which can be searching and difficult for us. The answers to these difficult questions enable us, however, to understand what sort of person we are and what motivates us as humans, nurses and managers. Understanding our own values and underlying motivations will then tell us something about what is likely to motivate and guide the actions of those that may be called upon to lead.

Scenario 1.1: Doing the right thing

Imagine you are working in a nursing home on nights. You are tired, having already worked six shifts in a row. One of the residents, Jane, who is in her late 80s, has been in the home for some time as a result of having had a stroke. Jane needs to be turned 2-hourly to avoid her developing pressure sores, but you and the nurse you are working with decide to turn her just occasionally. You justify this to yourselves by saying this avoids disturbing her sleep and it also protects your backs. At the end of the shift you turn her and record in her notes that you have done so 2-hourly throughout the night. She has not developed a pressure sore, so what is the harm?

Now consider this: you turn her at the end of the night and discover that a small area has broken down on her left hip. Is this your fault? If the matron asks if you have turned her 2-hourly, as stated in the care plan, what will you say? You could say you turned her 2-hourly – this would not change anything for Jane, but would make your life easier.

Alternatively you go to turn her at the end of the night shift only to discover that she has died some time during the night. She has been dead for a while judging from how cold she is and the blood that is pooling on the side she was lying on. You know you can just claim that you found her earlier in the night and prepare her body quickly before the day staff come in to work. Surely this will not change anything; no one will be hurt, will they?

Which, if any, of these scenarios are acceptable? Does the blame attached to any of them change because of the outcome? What does your choice of actions say about you? What values are being displayed here? How do they compare with the values you expressed in Activity 1.2?

There are some possible answers and thoughts at the end of the chapter.

Examining examples such as this enable us to see the bigger picture. They also help us to increase our awareness of our own values as they relate to being led and managed and then, conversely, to us leading or managing. In part our values will be mirrored in the sort of person we are and how we see the world in general, but they will also shape the way in which the world sees us. Of course it might be equally bad if a nurse were to follow policy and procedure blindly, with no thought about the consequences. In this scenario, as in many leadership and management situations, deviating from what we know to be right (i.e. ignoring our values) can have dire consequences for those we care for and for us, both as nurses and humans, as well as for the people we work with.

Scenario 1.2: Being clear

You are working on a medical admissions unit and have asked a colleague, Emma, to go round and do the observations. She takes the temperature, pulse and blood pressure of every patient on the unit, as asked. About an hour later you ask if all the observations were OK. Emma replies that the woman in the first bed had a temperature of 39°C. You ask why she had not informed you of this immediately. She replies that it was her job to do all of the observations as you asked, and that is what she has done.

What does this scenario tell you about managing and leading people in the clinical setting? What does this tell you about the need to understand what we do and why? Is there a place for understanding values of care in this scenario?

There are some possible answers and thoughts at the end of the chapter.

By now you should have developed a fairly clear picture of the values that you believe underpin what you do as a student nurse or nurse. You may also have some insight into the values of those around you and the impact that working among other nurses has on the development of your own value set. It is important to understand that, for leaders or managers to be effective, there is a requirement for there to be some degree of overlap between their values and the values of their team, and the team must be aware of this (Grivas and Puccio, 2012). Put simply, to lead you need people to follow and followers need to want to follow; people will more readily follow those they identify with.

What happens when values are forgotten?

Hospitals, care homes, clinics and community teams are made up of collections of people working together to achieve a common task. This common task requires that the values of the individuals involved in the care align to some extent; otherwise they would be working in opposition to, rather than with, each other. One of the challenges of modern healthcare is that our values can get lost among all the tasks we have to undertake and our attention may be drawn to achieving goals and targets, rather than remembering the values which bring us into nursing in the first place.

When nurses, or indeed any care staff, forget the values that should be driving their work, this has an impact on the culture they work in and this culture ultimately impacts on the care they give.

The following extract is taken from the Francis *Report of the Mid Staffordshire NHS Foundation Trust Public Inquiry (2013)*:

> *The negative aspects of culture in the system were identified as including:*
>
> - *a lack of openness to criticism*
> - *a lack of consideration for patients*
> - *defensiveness*
> - *looking inwards, not outwards*
> - *secrecy*
> - *misplaced assumptions about the judgements and actions of others*
> - *an acceptance of poor standards*
> - *a failure to put the patient first in everything that is done.*
>
> *It cannot be suggested that all these characteristics are present everywhere in the system all of the time, far from it, but their existence anywhere means that there is an insufficiently shared positive culture.*
>
> (Francis, 2013, p65)

What is being identified here is not a list of issues with the organisation, but a list of issues which arise as a result of the collective values of the people in the organisation becoming secondary to other issues. If we take each of the bullet points in turn, we can see each one represents a *value* which is not being exercised:

- competence
- compassion
- thankfulness
- mindfulness
- openness
- trust
- principles
- care.

The report continues:

> *To change that, there needs to be a relentless focus on the patient's interests and the obligation to keep patients safe and protected from substandard care. This means that the patient must be first in everything that is done: there must be no tolerance of substandard care; frontline staff must be empowered with responsibility and freedom to act in this way under strong and stable leadership in stable organisations.*
>
> *To achieve this does not require radical reorganisation but re-emphasis of what is truly important:*
>
> - *Emphasis on and commitment to common values throughout the system by all within it.*
>
> (Francis, 2013, p66)

The Francis report had a major impact on the way in which care is delivered in the UK, not because what happened at Mid Staffordshire was unique (it probably wasn't), but because it reminded care professionals and politicians alike that, once managers impose the wrong sorts of *values* and *targets* on care professionals, then values of care can easily be forgotten. Again the message is about having values which are common to leaders, managers and staff.

In order to become an effective leader or manager of people, we first must know ourselves and our values as well as having some insight into how others see us and how they interpret the way in which we display our values. Part of leadership or management is presentation of self to others and encouraging others to follow our lead by behaving in ways and displaying values that others admire and can identify with – creating a situation where others wish to follow. When you think about it, a leader without followers is just a person working alone!

How we see ourselves and others see us

To understand how we see ourselves and how this compares to how others see us, it is worth looking at the work of Joseph Luft and Harry Ingham, whose Johari window illustrates the point about what we know about ourselves and what others know about us.

What the Johari window allows us to see is how much of the perceptions and knowledge we have about ourselves is also seen and shared by others:

- The open/free area refers to what we know about ourselves and what is also known by other people – it is our public face.
- The blind area is the area of our personality we are blind to but which others can see – our blind spot.
- The hidden area is what we know about ourselves but we keep hidden from others, sometimes called the 'avoided self' or 'facade'.
- The unknown area refers to what is unknown both to ourselves and to others (which can be regarded as an area for potential development and self-exploration).

What is interesting about this model is it shows us there is great potential for us as individuals to lack understanding of ourselves as much as there is potential for other

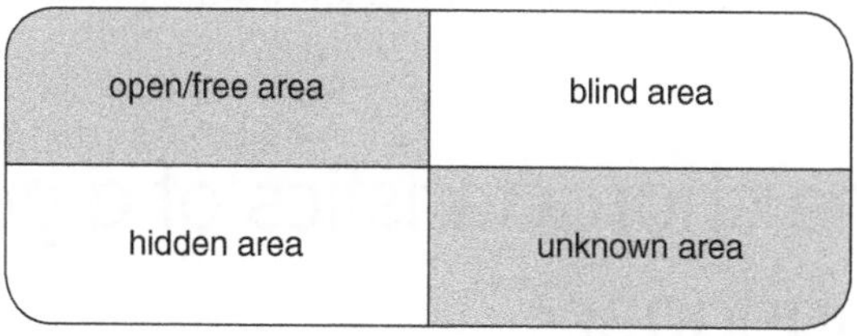

open/free area	blind area
hidden area	unknown area

Figure 1.1   The Johari window

Source: Adapted from Luft and Ingham (1955), p10.

people not to understand us. To some extent we can manage the view others have of us as individuals by allowing them to see what we want them to see and by managing our behaviours at work and in our private lives. On the other hand, people are often aware of issues with our values and personality that we are sometimes aware of and sometimes not.

Being able to adapt who we are and how we behave at work is part of the process of socialising to be both a nurse and a member of society at large. By being aware of our values and acting upon them we allow ourselves the ability to become someone we want to become and potentially to develop the traits that will help us to develop as a person, a nurse and over time as a manager or leader.

Activity 1.3   Communication

In order to get some idea of how your view of yourself is similar to, or differs from, that of other people, undertake the following exercise which may tell you something about how you communicate with and are perceived by other people: Choose five words to describe what sort of person you believe yourself to be and write these down. Ask a number of people who you know to choose five words which describe what sort of person you are and write these down. Include fellow students, lecturers, practice assessors and other people you work with. Examine the lists for similarities and differences and assign the responses to the various boxes of the Johari window and consider what this says about how your perception of self concurs or contrasts with the views of others. You might ask some people to explain their answers and take the time to explore what this means for what you know about yourself and what you do not!

Since this is based on your own thoughts and reflections, there is no specimen answer at the end of the chapter.

Activity 1.3 will help you to see that sometimes people see good and sometimes bad things about us which we may or may not see for ourselves. The lesson for the would-be leader is to learn to change the negatives that we can change and to manage the areas of our personality that we cannot. You should also be prepared to take on board positive insights and use these to continue to improve your relationships with others. One of the main functions of a leader and manager is the development of others; however the failure to develop oneself does not create the confidence in others that you know what you are doing in this regard.

What are the characteristics of a good leader or manager?

What makes a good leader or manager has been explored by many theorists and academics over the years. Some of the early theorists identified characteristics such as physical size, strength and 'presence' (Wright, 1996). Other characteristics and traits that have been favoured include intelligence, personality type such as extroversion, and **charisma** and other interpersonal skills.

Certainly, it is true that being **charismatic** and intelligent helps with the processing of ideas and when communicating with others. But, as we have seen above, there must be more to being a good nurse, good leader or good manager than these superficial qualities alone. Sometimes extreme examples allow us to see things that are perhaps not clear to us in the day-to-day process of being managed or led.

Activity 1.4　Reflection

Reflect on some of the well-known and successful leaders you know from history, perhaps Winston Churchill, Nelson Mandela, Martin Luther King or Florence Nightingale. What characteristics do they share that makes them great leaders? Why are they thought of as great individuals as well as successful leaders?

Next think about some of the other successful leaders from history, like Adolf Hitler, Napoleon Bonaparte, Joseph Stalin or Saddam Hussein. What characteristics made them successful leaders? Why are they thought of as immoral leaders?

There are some possible answers and thoughts at the end of the chapter.

Interestingly, from the examples of good leaders given above, none of them was particularly impressive physically, so their ability to lead and inspire has to be explained in some other way. Certainly this observation calls into question some of the early physical appearance theories of what makes a good leader. Clearly there may be issues relating to their charisma and intellect that attracted other people to them.

What we can see about the leaders in Activity 1.4, and what perhaps others know about some of them that they do not see for themselves, is the leaders we admire have a vision of something better for the people they lead. In the case of Mandela and Luther King, this was freedom from oppression and the achievement of equality of status and human rights. The pursuit of these values and the veracity with which they pursued them give us a clue as to one other quality we might admire in a leader: **integrity** (Frankel, 2008). In this sense integrity may be understood as acting in a manner that reflects the values, ethics and morals that an individual believes to be important.

Integrity alone is not enough, however. Hitler, Stalin and Saddam Hussein all perhaps believed in what they were doing; in that sense they had integrity. What is interesting about what they believed and what they set out to achieve was that it was often more about achieving power for themselves than it was about achieving what was right or something that benefits others.

What is missing therefore is an understanding about what this integrity and leadership should be aimed at achieving. Leaders and managers are the figureheads of teams (Mintzberg, 1975) and teams exist to get a job done (Ward, 2003). In nursing this job is about providing care for others in a manner that reflects the positive values we hold as humans and as nurses. For a nurse leader or manager, therefore, integrity of action means leading and managing in a manner that reflects the values of care which are part of what being a nurse is about and which you have identified for yourself in Activity 1.2.

Activity 1.5　Reflection

Take the time now to reflect on the people you have been led by in your life and consider what was either good or bad about their behaviours and way of interacting with you and others. What values did they show and what caused you to either admire or disapprove of them. Common examples might be a teacher, a youth group or church leader.

Since this is based on your own observations there is no specimen answer at the end of the chapter.

So far in this chapter we have seen that being a good leader or manager in nursing is about the expression of the same values of care being a good nurse requires. What changes when one moves from being a nurse to a nurse leader or manager is the way in which these values are expressed through what we do and how we behave towards others. The consistency of the values between nursing and nurse leadership/management demonstrates integrity – especially when these are expressed in the same individual on their journey from team worker to team leader and beyond. It is a sad fact that those nurse leaders and managers who we see losing sight of their values are the ones we least admire. The report into the failings at the Mid Staffordshire Hospital identified poor leadership coupled with clinical staff *accepting standards of care ... that should not have been tolerated* (Clews, 2010). The collective failing here was that clinically trained managers did not support their staff as well as they might have and the managers and leaders, as well as their staff, allowed the standards of care to slip below a level reflective of the true *values* of nursing.

One of the challenges of this book is for you to recognise and acknowledge the values that you have as a nursing student and to think about how you will continue to exercise these values throughout your nursing career.

Structures of nurse leadership

What we have not discussed so far are the structures that relate to the exercise of leadership and management. Clearly a manager occupies a formal role. The role of the manager is conferred upon the individual by an organisation and its staff are responsible to the manager by virtue of their contract of employment with the organisation – often called **legitimate power** (first identified by French and Raven in 1960). How these lines of responsibility are created and what they mean in practice should be clearer after the next activity.

Activity 1.6   Reflection

To understand the lines of responsibility that form part of a contract, look at the programme handbook for the programme you are on. There will be clear guidelines about some things you can and cannot do as a university student. There will be identified individuals to whom you would have to answer if you break these rules. This forms part of your contract with the university and ultimately with the Nursing and Midwifery Council (NMC) in relation to the fitness to practise criteria.

Alternatively, if you have a contract of employment you may notice it identifies the person to whom you are responsible, usually a line manager (like the ward sister) and to whom you are accountable within the organisation (often the Nursing Director).

As this is based on your own observations there is no specimen answer at the end of the chapter.

Managerial power and responsibility, as you can see from Activity 1.6, are therefore formalised within the contract of employment or training. They are validated by the fact that we choose to submit to these contracts of our own free will, usually because they will confer some benefit on us (in the case of a job, through being paid and in the case of being a student nurse, in gaining a qualification). Similarly, as nurses we agree to be bound by *The Code* and other regulations pertaining to nursing (NMC, 2015).

Within most organisations there are a number of managers at different levels who have different responsibilities for different organisational activities. These managers report to a more senior manager who in turn reports to more senior management. Such structures are formalised and are usually created in order to allow for the overseeing of the functions of the organisation. Each tier within the system of management should be aware of their responsibilities and the limits of their powers in fulfilling the tasks associated with these roles. It is often helpful for novice nurses to have some idea of what the structure of the organisation they work in looks like.

In Chapter 8 we discuss a little about cultures of care and you may find it useful to look up Charles Handy's work (1994) on cultures in order to inform your thinking about the formal and informal management structures which can exist in health and social care.

Activity 1.7   Evidence-based practice and research

Try to find out something about the management structure in the hospital in which you are placed. There may be a diagram that shows the relative management positions (sometimes called an organogram); then try to find out what the main responsibilities are of the people in the various roles you have identified. You might also like to do something similar for a ward or other practice area you work in so you can get an overview of who is responsible for what.

As this is based on your own observation there is no specimen answer at the end of the chapter.

So we can see that being a manager is a formalised position that is conferred by position within an organisation. Being a leader, on the other hand, may or may not be the result of position within a team or organisation. How can this be?

As we will see elsewhere in the book, leadership is in many instances one of the roles of a manager. Think about the ward managers in the areas where you have worked who as well as managing the ward also lead the team. Think also about the areas where you have worked where individuals occupying junior roles in a team exercise leadership. Sometimes then the leadership function is one of the roles of the manager, while on other occasions something else is happening.

How then do some non-managers function as leaders? Essentially there are three answers to this question. First, some leaders, such as team leaders at the ward level, are designated leaders because they are more experienced than the other staff or they hold a higher, non-management grade. They exercise the power of leadership also through virtue of the formal position they hold and the delegation of certain duties from their line manager. In this respect the power they exercise comes from the person who has delegated it to them and is legitimate power. Legitimate power, within society and organisations, arises out of the fact that people vote for their leaders (in the societal sense) or they enter into contracts of work whereby they agree to be subject to the power of others within an organisation. The leadership roles within such arrangement are therefore legitimised by virtue of the fact that they represent a choice on the part of the people who are led by these elected, or contractual, leaders.

Second, other leaders exercise leadership in relation to specific projects or responsibilities within the team. For example, in many clinical areas there are link nurses with responsibility for areas such as diabetes care, wound management or infection control. Again their power to act as leaders is in part conferred by the position they are asked to play in the team and is delegated from the team manager. The other reason they are a leader in their particular area is because they have specialist knowledge of the practice, procedures and guidelines that relate to whatever it is they are responsible for. In this situation a good leader will share the information the team needs to know to get the job done – a bad leader will not! Clearly, then, one of the characteristics of a leader is information management and good communication.

Third, there are those people who lead by virtue of their character. These charismatic individuals are the sort of people others like and respond to. They are able to motivate others and to get the team to follow them by virtue of who they are. They have a compelling vision of what should be done and how, and have a conviction and surety about them which encourage others to follow their lead (Mahoney, 2001). They may not be in positions of formal power, but perhaps they have knowledge or good communication skills that single them out as people others like to follow.

Case study: The new nursing sister

Eileen is a newly appointed sister on the dialysis unit of a busy general hospital. Eileen is liked by all of the staff, but has rapidly built up a reputation for being quite disorganised. When she is in charge of the shift, things go wrong. She gets side-tracked by small details and disappears for long periods of time to sort out seemingly minor issues.

Karen is a healthcare assistant who has worked in the dialysis unit for many years. Karen is familiar with the routine and is able to cope with most situations that arise. Karen often takes charge of the unit, even when Eileen is there. She co-ordinates the workload, makes telephone calls and arranges transport. Karen uses her connections and the relationships she has built up over the years to get things done.

What we can see in this case study is that, even within an essentially quite hierarchical structure, leadership can be found at all levels of the team. In this example there is a real danger that Eileen will lose control of the unit and Karen might overstep her own competence, role and responsibilities. One of the issues that arises out of this scenario is accountability. Eileen as a registered nurse is accountable for what she does as well as the actions of her team, especially the untrained members. Karen as a care assistant is not accountable for her actions in the same way, but is responsible to her employer (actually, Eileen) for what she does.

In this scenario the power which Karen exercises is not strictly speaking legitimate. As with all members of the team, she has roles and responsibilities for which she may need to exercise the power given to her by virtue of her position. It may be that Karen has the power to order stores and perhaps organise transport, but these are subject to the need to recognise the roles and responsibilities of other members of the team, who may need support in developing the skills necessary for them to operate effectively within their identified role.

It may be argued therefore that the leadership that Karen exercises is in this instance a bad thing. Karen is perhaps motivated to get the immediate job done, but perhaps misses some of the bigger-picture issues, such as the quality of the dialysis, that she is not trained in and not in a position to understand. Because Karen takes over the day-to-day running of the unit, she is also both undermining Eileen and preventing her from developing into her new role. While in the short term this might appear to work, it is not a long-term solution.

Activity 1.8   Reflection

Take some time to think about the implications of this case study. Have you seen similar situations? If so, what were the positives aspects for the team and what were the negative ones? How did the role reversal affect you and other members of the immediate team?

There are some possible answers and thoughts at the end of the chapter.

So we have seen that leadership and management within nursing can be broken down into many levels, from the most senior member of the nursing team right through to the most junior, and the qualities that make a good leader can be present at all levels. We have also seen that some managers fail to lead and that some leaders do not really have the formal position or power to do so.

Leading and managing: the policy context

Nursing is not undertaken in a vacuum. What we do as nurses and what nurse managers and leaders do occurs within a healthcare context and is subject to policy, procedure and guidelines. If leadership or management is about leading or managing a team to achieve certain outcomes, and within healthcare these outcomes are derived from policy and guidelines, then there is a need for nurse leaders and managers not only to be aware of what the guidelines are but also to act on them and ensure their team acts on them too.

Historically the caring professions had a great deal of autonomy over the ways in which they worked. In the past they set the standards by which their work was to be measured and audited and decided on clinical and non-clinical priorities. More recently, most notably following the policies of the Thatcher government and subsequently New Labour, clinical priority setting and the standards for care have been determined more centrally through government policy via agencies such as the National Institute for Health and Care Excellence (NICE) or via nationally drawn-up structures for care, such as the National Service Frameworks. So part of the role of nurse leaders or managers will be having the ability to lead or manage their team through the change process to achieve the outcomes of care determined from outside the team (see Chapter 8).

As well as general policy and guidelines in the area of health, as nurses we are subject to policy and guidance from our professional body, the NMC. In order to understand the context of leadership and management in nursing from the point of view of the NMC, it is worth familiarising yourself with the standards and educational outcomes identified at the start of each chapter and asking yourself how these apply within the context of each chapter. You may also wish to look at and reflect on how these ideas reflect the issues identified within other NMC documentation, including *The Code* (NMC, 2015). Most especially, this chapter has highlighted the need for nurse leaders to be 'an accountable professional' as demonstrated in Platform 1 where the nurse has to: 'understand and act in accordance with the Code (2015): Professional standards of practice and behaviour for nurses and midwives, and fulfil all registration requirements'.

For example, in this chapter we have discussed some of the values that underpin nursing practice, as well as leadership and management characteristics of the nurse leader/manager which may contribute to how we choose to behave as good leaders and managers. These characteristics translate well from both the code of professional conduct and the education proficiencies identified at the start of the chapter. What they validate is perhaps the most important message of the chapter: in order to become a good leader or manager of nurses it is important to remain grounded in the values, beliefs and behaviours that guide professional nursing practice.

Think of the leadership function this way: policy and guidelines determine what we do, at a local level these may be seen as mission or vision statements, while how we deliver care and how we behave generally is an expression of our values. Policy and guidelines provide the what, values provide the how.

Chapter summary

Rather than launch straight into a discussion about the nature of leadership and management in nursing, this chapter has sought to identify some of the values, beliefs and behaviours that might be associated with becoming a good nurse leader or manager. These characteristics have been compared and contrasted with some of the values that underpin being a good nurse. There is an explicit challenge here for you to identify and confront the values you have as a nurse, a nursing student, a team member and a leader.

In some part this challenge has been posed by reference to some of the shortcomings identified in the Francis report. While the failings at Mid Staffordshire NHS Trust are useful as a benchmark of what can go wrong, they are exactly that, a benchmark. They should not be considered as merely a footnote in history, but should be seen as a salutary lesson in what could easily happen anywhere when nurses and other care professionals neglect their values.

(Continued)

> (Continued)
>
> An understanding of the context of care and of ourselves is an important first step on the road to becoming a competent leader of nurses; failure to understand what motivates us as individuals lays us open to external criticism. Furthermore, some of the skills and values we develop as nurses in clinical practice will translate well into leadership and management roles. It is never too soon for student nurses to think about what type of leader/manager they want to be and to look around them for suitable role models to guide their development.

Activities: Brief outline answers

Activity 1.1 Reflection (p7)

This reflection is not about understanding the rehabilitation of the elderly as such; it is about understanding context. As a new nurse you may consider asking people to undertake their own care as lazy nursing, because you consider nursing as a caring profession that does things for people. As you understand the nature of care better, you will see the same scenario in a different light, or context, as you understand that encouraging self-care is about helping people address their care deficits and achieve the activities of daily living for themselves.

Activity 1.2 Decision-making (p9)

What you will notice is that the basic values of caring, moral behaviour, putting others before self, protection of rights, autonomy and dignity are common to both lists. What will be different is that the leader will attempt to achieve these aims through the way in which s/he leads. This will include acting as a role model and promoting the welfare of the team who in turn are expected to support these values one to one with patients and clients (Bondas, 2006). If you are still struggling to think about what your values are, try some of the words above or choose some from this list: accountability, accuracy, calm, committed, decisive, fair, honesty, integrity, justice, openness, reliable, team worker or truthfulness.

Scenario 1.1 Doing the right thing (p10)

We hope you found none of these scenarios acceptable. On each occasion, regardless of the outcome, the choice being made was to avoid your duty to Jane to protect her from potential further physical harm. The values displayed here are self-regarding and not other-regarding and are against everything that is to be found in *The Code* (NMC, 2015). At best, the scenario demonstrates lies being told and at worst a dereliction of the duty of care, leading to harm to the patient. Some people might argue that, as no harm ensued, the first scenario might be all right, but the consequences that *could* accrue (as seen later in the scenario) show this to be wrong, regardless of any arguments about duty and outcomes. Of course the precedent in your behaviour and that of the colleague involved may well lead to further harm being done to other patients at a later date, even if you 'got away with it' this time.

Scenario 1.2 Being clear (p11)

This scenario suggests that as a manager or leader it is important not only to have team members who do what they are asked, but also that they understand the purpose of what they are doing. There is a clear need here for the nurse to understand that doing observations is not enough in itself; it is acting on what is found that is important. The values which should drive the undertaking of such tasks is **person-centred** care, which requires that nurses not only undertake a task, but that they think about what it means for the patient or client.

Activity 1.4 Reflection (p15)

Clearly one of the characteristics of good leaders is that people want to follow them. In many of the cases mentioned as potential positive role models, people choose to follow the leader because they believe in what the person is doing. This is also the case for some of the examples of negative leadership role models given, so what is the difference? Some people would not choose to follow the likes of Hitler or Hussein, and although many did, many more were forced to do so. Other people follow bad leaders because they generate a sense of belonging and solidarity, perhaps at a time when there is uncertainty in the world. The integrity and ethicality of the examples of bad leaders are questionable at best and evil at worst. So perhaps integrity and morality are two of the things that we admire in good leaders?

Activity 1.8 Reflection (p20)

While Karen does a good day-to-day job in making the dialysis unit function, there may be longer-term considerations to take into account. As we saw earlier in the chapter, one of the roles of a leader is operating within the bigger picture. This also resonates with the role of the trained nurse, who has to account not only for the day-to-day running of the dialysis unit but also for the long-term health of the patients. So while it may be all right for the leader to allow someone else to take charge of some of the activities of the team, it is better if s/he is selective about who takes over what tasks and what they do. The staff in a scenario where it is uncertain who the real leader is will be confused, and may even be slightly angry as they see someone without genuine authority taking control. When you see this in real life it is confusing for patients, staff and students and in the long term demoralises and destabilises the team.

Further reading

Aldgate, J and Dimmock, B (2003) Managing to care. In: Henderson, J and Atkinson, D (eds) *Managing Care in Context.* London: Routledge.

This chapter explores the values of care as well as social inclusion.

Handy, C (1994) *Understanding Organisations* (4th edition). London: Penguin.

The classic text on organisational culture.

Scott, J, Gill, A and Crowhurst, K (2008) *Effective Management in Long-Term Care Organisations.* Exeter: Reflect Press.

See especially Chapter 4 on Leadership.

Useful websites

www.businessballs.com

An interesting and quirky leadership and management resources website.

www.kingsfund.org.uk/topics/leadership_and_management/index.html

Perhaps the leading UK healthcare think tank.

http://webarchive.nationalarchives.gov.uk/20150407084231/http://www.midstaffspublicinquiry.com/report

The Francis report: *Report of the Mid Staffordshire NHS Foundation Trust Public Inquiry.*

Chapter 2   Teams and team work

Introduction

This chapter will begin by reflecting on your experiences of working in teams and progress to exploring how you can develop the skills to manage and lead a team. Nurses learn through experience and education to make autonomous and independent professional decisions when managing patient care. At the same time, in health and social care environments, there is an expectation for nurses to:

- work within teams of other nurses (e.g. in wards or units);
- work with interdisciplinary teams (e.g. specialist teams, including doctors and other allied healthcare professionals);
- manage and direct teams with specific specialties (e.g. infection control);
- lead teams to introduce new ways of working or maintain high standards of care (e.g. audit, clinical improvement and task and finish groups).

The chapter will examine how teams work and how to evaluate the effectiveness of teams. The different roles team members assume in teams are covered next as are skills for improving team working, dealing with difficulties with team members and team communication are explored. In this section we also explore some of the theoretical positions that have helped to explain team members' behaviour based upon social psychology. The practicalities of leading team meetings are described and finally the role of interdisciplinary team working is discussed.

How teams work

Understanding group dynamics is the starting point for recognising how teams are formed and how they work at their most productive. It may seem some groups work well together as if by magic, but in reality it often needs a deeper understanding of the nature of individuals and how they interact with them in groups to create and sustain useful teams.

Tuckman (1965) is the most often quoted commentator on how groups come together in Tuckman's view there are five stages to the creation of groups:

1. Forming: the group comes together and the task identified and allocated. At this stage the group may not know each other, but may share similar goals.

2. Storming: the group starts to explore how to tackle the allocated task. Relationships in the group start to build, although in some cases this never happens and the group gets stuck in this phase.

3. Norming: the group has moved through storming and working practices start to emerge.

4. Performing: not all groups get to this stage. Groups that get to this stage are highly independent and motivated.

5. Adjourning: once the project, the reason for forming the group, is completed, the group has no further reason to meet and will adjourn.

Activity 2.1   Reflection

Think of the current, or last, team or group in which you worked. Think about the key activities of the group or team and make a list of what they did together. Would you describe the experience as one where individuals came together for personally focused but unifying relationships, such as found in families, religious groups, political affiliations or students studying the same module? Or did the experience involve a number of persons associated together in specific work, activity or task, perhaps working towards a common goal or with a set of particular aim and objectives?

If it was the former, this would be described as a group activity. If it was the latter, it would be described as a team. A well functioning team has:

- defined objectives
- positive relationships
- a supportive environment
- a spirit of co-operation and collaboration.

Since this is based on your own thoughts and reflections, there is no specimen answer at the end of the chapter.

In summary, a team is created from a number of people who are all organised to function co-operatively as a unit. By contrast, a group is deemed to be a number of people sharing something in common, such as an interest, belief or political aim. In common with wider organisations, teams exist to get a job of work done (Ward, 2003) and, like organisations, the purpose of teams is to get the job done efficiently and effectively.

Activity 2.2   Critical thinking

Think about a time when you were involved in working in a team. This could be the experience you thought of in Activity 2.1 if it fits the definition of a team. Write down the main aim or purpose of the team. Find out if the team/organisation has a values and vision statement or area philosophy (e.g. a ward philosophy). Consider the behaviours in the team that reflect these values/vision/philosophy and therefore if the statement contributed to the success or otherwise of the team.

There are some possible answers and thoughts at the end of the chapter.

It is often said of teams that the team as a whole is more effective than the sum of its parts (Wuchty, Jones and Uzzi, 2007); that is to say, a team can get more done and get it done effectively than the same number of individuals undertaking the task alone or in an uncoordinated fashion. What do you think it is about teams that makes them more efficient and effective?

Team effectiveness

When a team works well together this is reflected in the culture and atmosphere of the workplace. This is noticeable in several different ways, for example when team members:

- have a shared understanding of team goals and tasks
- are willing to listen to each other
- feel comfortable discussing their work with each other
- handle disagreements positively and openly
- demonstrate the team values in their day to day work activities
- give and receive feedback with respect for each other's feelings.

Activity 2.3   Reflection

Compare the list of issue of attributes of an effective team, listed above, to the list of problems which Francis (2013) identified in the *Report of the Mid Staffordshire NHS Foundation Trust Public Inquiry*, discussed in Chapter 1.

Reflect on what this means for the role of values in the creation and effective working of teams.

There are some possible answers and thoughts at the end of the chapter.

In contrast to effective teams, an ineffective team can be dominated by a few members with strong views, opinions and characters. This can mean other members feel isolated from the main purpose of the team, which in turn can lead to feelings such as disenfranchisement, boredom and a lack of engagement and commitment.

An overuse of rules and regulations can lead to a stifling of informal relationship building, a process necessary to achieve team harmony and a supportive atmosphere. For example, each team will have a set of norms to guide it on how each person should be addressed – whether by organisational title and family name, or by first name. Another example might occur when a team has devised a specific method of dealing with patients' personal effects that fits fundamentally with the principles of the organisation's policy but which has been tested and proven to be less than practical given the nature of the unit – such as an emergency care unit, where people are constantly being moved around. On the other hand, a leader needs to know which institutional or legal regulations have to be followed for procedures and patient safety to be maintained. Individual team members should also be aware of their own professional responsibilities and accountability, guided by professional codes of conduct such as the Nursing and Midwifery Council (NMC) *Code* (NMC, 2015). Acknowledging individuals' responsibility also reinforces a sense of professional autonomy that can contribute positively to (or indeed detract from) team working.

Conflicts and disagreements are uncomfortable situations to deal with in a team. However, if not dealt with, these situations can lead to team members avoiding each other and suppressing negative feelings. This, in turn, can lead to resentment and frustration. So it is important to look at disagreements as opportunities for improving team relationships, by talking through differences and discussing alternative ways of working together. Team leaders can facilitate these discussions or they can be between the individuals provided ground rules are established and resolution of the differences is made a focal objective. A helpful team activity for dealing with differences is for the team to develop a team code of co-operation. (See the useful websites section at the end of this chapter, as well as Chapter 4, for further information on dealing with conflict.)

In some situations where issues arise between team members, the manager may need to mediate. Ideally in a team of adults working together team members who have issues with each other they will address these themselves first and managers should encourage staff to do so before being draw into inter-staff issues. That said where team effectiveness is impacted by issues between staff members it is the role of the manager to make sure these are sorted out.

Giving feedback on performance to team members (whether you are a leader or from one co-worker to another) is an activity that, for an effective team, needs to be integrated into discussions about work. Effective feedback can enhance performance and improve the outcomes for the team. Done badly, or too infrequently, feedback can come across as negative criticism. This is especially so when it may be about the work or behaviours of someone of a different grade, be that more senior or more junior. Chapter 3 looks more closely at working with individuals within teams, and Chapter 5 at issues around coaching and practice assessing colleagues.

Negative or destructive criticism that is personal and hurtful has the potential to erupt and create discordant relationships that in turn lead to resentment which can lead to a lack of co-operation between individuals. One way for a team to learn to work with constructive feedback is to practise, or role play, in a simulated situation by giving feedback to one another to experience what it feels like; and to generate or become accustomed to phrases that are acceptable to convey feedback to one another in a respectful manner, as shown in Table 2.1.

Team dynamics and processes

The manner in which team members engage with each other and the factors that affect the team functioning well together are crucial aspects of effective team working. It is customary for there to be a designated team leader who will guide the team's performance and set the tone for how a team will work together. There are occasions, however, when a team will be self-directed and led jointly by members who have similar status or responsibilities, such as in a multidisciplinary group.

Characteristic	Effective	Ineffective
Leadership	Has a clear idea of what the team needs to do to achieve its goals, facilitates team working in a supportive atmosphere and uses team skills wisely	Unclear idea of direction, does not allow team members to express ideas, does not capitalise on individual strengths in the team, overly autocratic
Environment	Informal, open, based on mutual learning	Indifferent, tense, strained, unable to learn
Discussion	Shared, focused on getting the job done and making improvements, actively listening to each other	Unfocused, dominated by a few strong characters, no active listening
Response to points of view	Respectful, encouraging, trusting each other's judgement	Patronising and judgemental, overly critical, mistrustful
Decision-making	Reached by consensus, general agreement acceptable, dissenters tolerated, diverse views accepted guided by mission and vision	Lack of consensus and discussion, lack of flexibility or appreciation of differing perceptions, reliance on only majority acceptance as basis for agreement
Feedback	Constructive, honest, directed towards problem solving	Personal, destructive, aimed at creating embarrassment
Tasks, responsibilities	Clear, agreed by all despite some disagreement	Unclear, resented by dissenting members
Feelings	Open for discussion, exploration and support	Hidden, potentially explosive

Table 2.1 Summary of effective and ineffective team characteristics

Source: Adapted from Yoder-Wise (2007), p345.

Norms

Most teams develop norms, which are the informal rules of behaviour shared and enforced by team members. These norms are developed by the team as a form of self-regulation to enable stable team functioning and survival. Norms are often linked to expected contributions from individual performances. For example, a student nurse's contribution to the team will be bounded by him or her being supernumerary, what they are allowed to do and by how far s/he is into training. A healthcare assistant will have expectations of the role of a qualified nurse and will support the qualified nurse with agreed activities or parameters.

However, these parameters may vary from unit to unit and ward to ward, depending on local policy, the nature of the work or the experience of the team members. Trying to adapt to these different parameters can sometimes lead to misunderstandings because of the variations between teams, and student nurses, or new team members, will need to find out the norms of any group by discussion and reference to unit protocols. Examples of norms may include when breaks are taken, how shifts are negotiated, how to prevent embarrassment by being loyal to the team, and how collectively held values or principles are best expressed.

Roles

A role is an expected set of behaviours which are characteristic of a specific function in the team. Individuals may have an inherent tendency to perform a role, such as a nurturing role; alternatively, roles may be informally ascribed by the group or formally designated by the leader. Sullivan and Decker (2009, p152) suggest roles can be divided into either task roles or nurturing roles and they are set out in Tables 2.2 and 2.3.

Initiator	Redefines problems and offers solutions, clarifies objectives
Contributor	Suggests agenda items and maintains time limits
Information seeker	Pursues descriptive baseline information for the team's work
Information giver	Expands information given by sharing experiences and making inferences
Opinion seeker	Explores viewpoints that clarify or reflect the values of other members' suggestions
Opinion giver	Conveys to group members what their essential values should be
Elaborator	Predicts outcomes and provides illustrations or expands suggestions, clarifying how they could work

Initiator	**Redefines problems and offers solutions, clarifies objectives**
Co-ordinator	Links ideas or suggestions offered by others
Orienter	Summarises the group's discussions and actions
Evaluator critic	Appraises the quantity and quality of the team's accomplishments against set standards
Energiser	Motivates the group to accomplish, qualitatively and quantitatively, the team's goals
Procedural technician	Supports team activity by arranging the environment and providing necessary equipment
Recorder	Documents the team's progress, actions and achievements

Table 2.2   Task roles

Encourager	**Compliments members for their opinions and contributions to the team**
Harmoniser	Relieves tensions and conflicts
Compromiser	Sets aside own position or views to maintain team harmony
Gate keeper	Stimulates discussion to enable all team members to communicate and participate, without allowing any one member to dominate
Group observer	Notices team processes and dynamics and informs the team of them
Follower	Passively attends meetings, listens to discussions and accepts the team's decisions

Table 2.3   Nurturing roles

Task roles keep the team focused on their objectives or functions, whereas nurturing roles are facilitative or concerned with meeting interpersonal needs. Team members may adopt more than one role. A team leader may wish to accentuate one role in place of another to improve team functioning or alternatively to suppress a role that becomes over-emphasised. This is where the team leader assumes the nature of a conductor of an orchestra to utilise the different talents of the team, possibly at different times, to achieve a successful performance.

Meredith Belbin (2010) continues to be one of the major contributors to team role theory. Based on research into dysfunctional teams in the 1970s, Belbin found that effective teams were founded upon individual behaviours. The research was originally contrived to examine ways to control team dynamics; however, the researchers found that the difference between success and failure in a team was not based on intellect but on separate clusters of behaviour, each behaviour making a specific contribution to effective team working.

Belbin went on to identify nine team roles, each equally essential to the team and necessary to create a balance of roles. Of note, each identified role also displays some potential weaknesses which can interfere with team productivity but which are tolerated because of the positives that role also brings to the team. (See the useful websites at the end of the chapter for more information on Belbin's work.)

Influence of social systems on teams

Teams do not work in isolation. In healthcare they are often located in organisations or as subsets of other larger team structures such as departments or divisions. These background factors need to be taken into consideration for a full analysis of team dynamics (personal relationships) and processes (actions directed towards a specific aim). The sociologist George Homans (1961) used a systemic model to describe what he determined as the *internal systems* facing *external systems* and the impact of systems or feedback loops on team dynamics and consequently the effectiveness of teams.

An example of a system is the water cycle. Water vapour is condensed from the atmosphere into clouds. It falls on to the earth as rain or snow and is collected into some form of reservoir. Humans channel the water into homes, factories and buildings. It is then utilised and transformed into waste water, which travels into rivers and seas to be evaporated back into the clouds, thus beginning the cycle all over again. At each stage, there are factors that influence the system, such as drought, over-usage and contamination. Equally, social systems can be affected by political, economic, social, technological, legislative or environmental factors and therefore indicate the complexity and vulnerability of any system, as well as an ability to adapt to change. Understanding systems and how they work can have an impact on problem solving, team working and the management of change (see useful websites for more information on management application of systems thinking and PESTLE analyses).

While the importance of Homans' focus on individuals in small groups is now quoted less often, the fundamental findings of his work help to illuminate the factors that influence small-group functioning as a system and the consequences of those interactions, such as the impact of the manager's leadership style and external organisational infrastructures. Homans considered the essential elements of a group system to be the activities, processes, interactions, interpersonal relationships and attitudes of team members towards the goals of the team. See Figure 2.1 for a contemporary version of Homans' conceptual scheme.

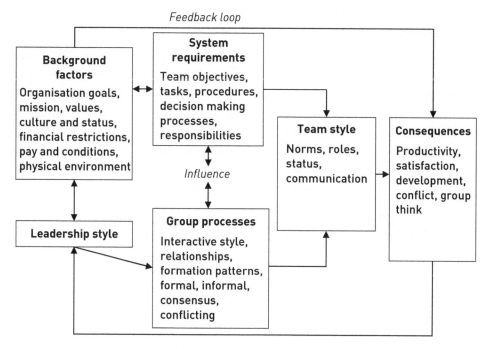

Figure 2.1 Homans' (1961) conceptual scheme of a small social system modified to reflect external and internal influences on consequences or effective outputs of a team in the twenty-first century

The conceptual feedback loop scheme Homans designed can help us to analyse groups and pinpoint problem areas when teams are ineffective. The importance of this work is to acknowledge that each action has an effect on another part of the process in a system, which is a major characteristic of general systems theory (von Bertalanffy, 1968) and also of any small-group interaction. Homans' studies led to the development of social exchange theory and the premise that social interaction is based on the exchange of rewards.

Theory summary: Social exchange theory

This theory is predicated on establishing and sustaining reciprocity (equal exchange) in social relationships, or mutual gratification between individuals, and the comparison of alternatives. The theory relies on the assumption that humans are rational and willing to exchange items, material or emotional, that are important to them for the benefit of other people. Integral concepts of the theory are the notions of justice and fairness. If the perceived costs of a relationship outweigh the benefits, the theory predicts that a person will leave the relationship. However, criticisms of the theory are that it favours an economic model, whereby all human interaction is likened to a process of cost–benefit analysis. Furthermore, there are opportunities for coercion

(Continued)

(Continued)

and power tactics through the use of punishments and rewards if benefits are withdrawn. This is particularly evident in hierarchical or highly structured environments and groupings. The perceived effect of social obligations versus the amount of freedom of choice to exchange commodities can also negatively affect relationships. Understanding the intricacies of social exchange theory can help you understand social relationships in a team, when some people are more willing to help others, for example. (See the useful websites listed at the end of the chapter for further information.)

Creating effective team working

There has been much emphasis in the management literature on team-building activities to enhance team effectiveness by focusing on both task and relationship aspects of team working. The aims of team building are generally to:

- establish goals or specific objectives
- clarify the values, purpose and functions of the team
- allocate or re-allocate work roles and responsibilities
- establish or revive communication patterns
- clarify the group norms or expected behaviours of the team
- complete a job of work
- identify the decision-making processes, responsibilities and hierarchies to define interteam relationships.

Team building starts at recruitment. Identifying the skills, both essential and desirable, which are needed when recruiting to a team create the opportunity for the manager, or leader, to complement and strengthen those skills already available to them and to fill skills gaps which will be of benefit to the team. This team building continues at short listing and interviewing when the manager has the opportunity to first sift applicants for talent and then interview them to ensure their values are a good fit for the existing team (Foster, 2017).

Team-building strategies can be used to help integrate individuals into teams, for example at induction, thereby creating effectiveness from the beginning of a team's lifetime. This may require funding and time away from the work situation. Alternatively, the team leader can undertake an analysis of the team's functioning if the team only needs fine tuning (see the useful websites at the end of the chapter for team-building ideas). Team leaders can undertake an objective observation of team activities and then take this to team meetings for an open and self-aware evaluation and discussion. The team leader will need to take the emotional temperature of the team to decide if this will be appropriate.

Where the leader has to intervene because a team is not functioning effectively, there will need to be preliminary preparation aimed at analysing and defining the problems. This involves four steps:

1. Gathering information through different means, such as:

    (a) informal and formal discussions with individuals

    (b) surveying the work done and comparing it to that which should be done

    (c) reviewing notes from one-to-one sessions and personal development reviews/appraisals

    (d) team meetings

    (e) team supervision.

2. Identifying the team's, and individuals within the team's, strengths and areas for development.

3. Creating a plan of action with the team.

4. Identifying time to work on the issues identified in steps 1 and 2 above and in implementing the plan.

Background information can also be gathered about the structures of the organisation in which the team works. This includes the current work climate and culture (e.g. financial constraints), team goals, and the professional setting (e.g. mental health, community nursing, interdisciplinary, stroke rehabilitation, infection control). It is important to consider the extent to which members work as autonomous individuals within the team, whether they are based in a unit or spread out over a geographical area, the complexity of roles and responsibilities, problem-solving styles, interpersonal relationships and relations with other groups in the organisation.

Sullivan and Decker (2009) suggest the following eight questions should be asked:

1. To what extent does the team accept the goals of the organisation?

2. What, if any, hidden agendas interfere with the team's performance?

3. How effective is the team leadership?

4. To what extent do team members understand and accept their roles and responsibilities?

5. How does the team make a decision?

6. How does the team handle conflict? Are conflicts dealt with through avoidance or denial, force, accommodation, compromise, competition or collaboration?

7. What personal feelings do members have about each other?

8. To what extent do members trust and respect each other?

All this takes time and the leader will need to exercise diplomacy and tact when seeking answers to these questions. The leader also needs to be aware that the process of asking these questions may uncover some difficult truths about the team, or individuals within the team, which they will not be able to ignore.

Strategies for managing team problems

We have discussed how to create effective team working, and we go into more detail by studying different styles of leadership and management elsewhere in this text. However, a few pointers from Antai-Otong (1997) are worth considering at this stage. These are aimed at specific team problems in nursing that a team leader will need to consider.

If the member is not a team player:

- consider carefully whether or not you want the person on the team
- interact with the member assertively
- give the person an opportunity to provide feedback on problematic situations.

If communication with other team members is part of the problem:

- speak to the person one-to-one
- listen actively when the person speaks, assessing verbal and non-verbal messages to identify any underlying issues or anxieties
- avoid blaming and shaming, which tends to create defensiveness and arguments.

If the member seems to lack a sense of personal accountability:

- explain how failure to take responsibility affects the whole team (and give an example)
- without blaming or shaming, provide feedback from all team members.

If the team lacks clear goals:

- brainstorm activity to clarify short-term goals and develop an action plan with the team
- strive for consensus regarding mission and goals
- define member responsibilities
- determine resources to accomplish goals (e.g. staffing expertise, financial, administrator support, time and equipment)
- periodically review team progress and achievements.

If team roles and boundaries are unclear:

- clarify role boundaries with the team's input
- define all roles in the team, including the leader's
- periodically review the team's staff or professional development needs.

Communication within the team

One of the most frequent causes of poor team work is inadequate or failing communication. A major problem in busy units, wards and departments is dealing with distractions if essential information is to be communicated. Most distractions are through sensory perceptions, such as poor lighting or background noise, talking, music, ringing phones and interruptions. Moving to a quieter environment or agreeing a time to speak when all parties can concentrate will help to minimise distractions. Anxieties around reporting, heavy workloads and keeping up to date can also be distracting.

Different levels of knowledge can create frustration between staff and misunderstandings over expectations if a standard of knowledge is not met. This requires a culture of openness in the team so that members feel free to ask questions and are not embarrassed to admit to not having specific information. It also requires the leader to act as the conductor employing the different and varying skills of the team members in different ways, ensuring they understand their contribution and appreciate the contribution of others towards getting the job of work done.

Good communication in teams needs to be frequent and involve all staff members. When spontaneous decisions have to be made, individuals can feel left out of the loop. All organisational and planning decisions should be agreed by consensus. However, an understanding that in exceptional circumstances there may be no time to communicate should also be agreed. Building in protected time or a mechanism to debrief the team on situations that fall outside the usual can help.

Differences in perception can misrepresent messages. The same message can be distorted through a lens of individual biases and preconceptions, sociocultural, ethnic and educational differences. Teams need to develop tolerance and awareness of individual perceptual filters – that is, how various team members see the world. This is best achieved through team meetings and encouraging team members to work in the same space where possible.

Distress, anxiety, heightened emotional states and certain personality traits, such as neuroticism, which is one of five key personality traits typified by excessive anxiety or indecision, can interfere with message communications. As all members of any team are only human, home life stresses may be brought to the workplace. Team members need to feel safe to express their anxieties and have support from colleagues and the leader. However, if the stresses are interfering with effective working, occupational health support should be sought.

Dealing with meetings and committees

When you have a busy day ahead with many things on your to-do list, the last thing you may feel like spending time on is either going to a meeting or leading one. Meetings have a reputation for being boring and ineffective. But a well-led meeting can produce some very satisfying results and ensure everyone uses their time efficiently and purposively. Meetings are the processes by which organisations conduct their business through committee structures. There are different types of committees with distinct responsibilities and decision-making powers. Formal committees are part of the governance structures of an organisation and have different levels of authority and scope to make decisions. The highest level of committee structure within an organisation is board level (see useful websites for further information). The responsibilities and functions of any committee are outlined in their **terms of reference** along with the membership, frequency and **quorate** requirements (minimum numbers attending allowing for decisions to be made). Very often committees have subcommittees that are convened to deal with specific tasks or matters that need specialist and focused attention.

Other committees may have an advisory remit but no authority or power, although they may have a strong influence on decisions. Committees are also set up to undertake specific tasks to be completed in a defined time span. An example is to develop a proposal for service development. The committee may then be tasked with implementing the developments (often called a task and finish group) or alternatively charged with investigating problems that require recommendations to be sent to a formal committee for action. Another form of committee will monitor activities such as standards or quality enhancement (for example an audit or service improvement committee).

At ward or unit level the team meetings, where staff get together to discuss issues and problems and formulate local policies and procedures, are the focal point of work life. These meetings need to be seen as the pivotal place for decisions, discussions and forward planning to enhance the work environment and service delivery. It is the team leader's responsibility to ensure that the relevance and role of the meetings are understood and valued by team members. It should also be a time to enjoy being with colleagues who have a shared vision of their working lives.

Preparation, place and time, participation

The key to successful meetings is to follow the three Ps: preparation, place and time, and participation.

- *Preparation* is about clearly identifying the *purpose* of the meeting. Even if it is a short meeting, there should be an agenda with items to be discussed plainly stated and an indication as to whether the item is for discussion, decision or information. The leader needs to think ahead about the agenda items and undertake pre-reading, so that s/he is ready to respond to questions and has potential solutions to problems ready as well as an idea of delegated responsibilities if this is required.
- *Place and time*: advance information about venue and duration is vital. Meetings are work and not social gatherings, so an emphasis on getting things done and an action-oriented approach are needed to encourage effective use of time. Members will also think it worthwhile attending if their time is not wasted.
- *Participation*: your knowledge of team dynamics and the roles your team members play, whether nurturing or task-oriented, will be valuable in understanding how team members participate in the meeting. Their ability to contribute will also depend on their level of skills and knowledge. However, this could be detrimentally affected by the phenomenon known as **group think**, which is a particular concern if you have a philosophy of self-directedness in a group of experienced professionals.

The ability to chair meetings, take notes if necessary, delegate activities and follow up on actions are key elements of an effective meeting.

Theory summary: From group think to team think

In the 1970s social psychologist Irving Janis identified the phenomenon of group think that happens when a group makes faulty decisions (Janis, 1972, 1982). This is due to pressures from within the group whose members ignore alternatives and make irrational decisions that ignore the humanising factors present in other groups or sections of an organisation or community. When group members are from the same background, are insulated from outside influences and there are no clear decision-making structures, they are particularly susceptible to group think. There are eight documented symptoms of group think:

1. An illusion of invulnerability creates excessive optimism that encourages taking extreme risks.
2. Belief in collective rationalisation – members discount warnings and do not reconsider their assumptions.
3. Belief in inherent morality – members believe in the rightness of their cause and therefore ignore the ethical or moral consequences of their decisions.
4. Stereotyped views of other groups lead to negative views of 'the enemy', which make effective responses to conflict seem unnecessary.
5. Direct pressure on dissenters involves putting members under pressure to avoid expressing arguments against any of the group's views.
6. Self-censorship means that doubts and deviations from the perceived group consensus are not expressed.
7. Illusion of unanimity – the majority view and judgements are assumed to be unanimous.
8. Self-appointed 'mind guards' involve members protecting the group and the leader from information that is problematic or contradictory to the group's cohesiveness, view and/or decisions.

When groups are tightly knit and under pressure to make decisions, irrational decisions are likely as alternatives are not considered. Failure to discuss options and potential outcomes leads to carelessness and a need to achieve unanimity. The overall outcome is groups that have a low probability of successful decision making.

To move towards 'team think', team leaders need to facilitate discussions in teams that are not reliant only on members of the team, by introducing observers to the team or other specialists to give a point of view. Dealing with dominant members, as discussed previously, and not putting the team under pressure will also offset these effects. One of the main factors is always to consider alternative perspectives and the viewpoints or goals of other teams or activities in the organisation to gain a wider viewpoint of how decisions fit into the whole picture before making final decisions.

Interdisciplinary team working

Up until now this chapter has focused on team working within a professional group or disciplinary area, although it is acknowledged that there are many different types of teams working within nursing. In healthcare today there is an increasing need for professionals from different disciplines to work together to improve patient services for seamless care. Nurses, physicians, dieticians, social workers, pharmacists, physiotherapists, administrators and technicians, among others, may all find themselves working together with a common aim but a different perspective on how to achieve this aim.

Activity 2.4 Evidence-based practice and research

In your most recent practice placement, were you aware of any interdisciplinary teams functioning in the organisation? Next time you are in practice ask your practice assessor if there are any interdisciplinary teams and find out what the objectives are for these teams. You might like to ask your practice assessor if you can sit in on an interprofessional meeting so that you can listen to the ways in which the professions interact.

At the start of the chapter, outcome 5.4 requires the registered nurse to: 'demonstrate an understanding of the roles, responsibilities and scope of practice of all members of the nursing and interdisciplinary team and how to make best use of the contributions of others involved in providing care'. Analyse one interdisciplinary team's activity in your placement area, note the role of each member of the team and discuss with your practice assessor how each person contributes to the holistic care of patients. You may want to make notes for your assessment portfolio.

There is no right or wrong answer to this activity.

According to Hewison and Sim (1998), interprofessional working requires co-operation and mutual understanding, yet there are many barriers that can prevent this from happening. They explored the role of professional codes of ethics and the potential to foster professional distinctiveness and exclusivity. By identifying areas of common ground, in particular around **whistle blowing**, they felt multidisciplinary working could develop. To achieve effective interprofessional working they argued that the role of management was crucial in leading teams in order to minimise professional rivalries and retain a central focus on patient need.

In common with all elements of good leadership, working with other professions requires that the leader is clear about the values of the team. In the care setting this will mean a desire to achieve positive outcomes for patients or clients; what different professionals view as a positive outcome and how this is achieved is not as important as the fact that they all support achieving a positive outcome, as described by the patient.

The following is an account of a study to examine the effectiveness of a team and the multidisciplinary working processes.

Research summary: The impact of team processes on psychiatric case management

This is a study undertaken to identify the structures and interactions within community mental health teams that facilitate or impede effective teamwork and psychiatric case management. The view of the researchers was that effective case management requires close collaboration between case managers or care co-ordinators and other members of the multidisciplinary mental health team, yet there has been little research into this relationship. A multiple case study of seven UK community mental health teams was conducted between 1999 and 2001, using qualitative methods of participant observation, semi-structured interviews and document review. Factors were identified from the study that impacted on the ability of care co-ordinators to act effectively. These were *structure and procedures; disrespect and withdrawal; humour and undermining; safety and disclosure.*

Care co-ordination was enhanced when team structures and policies were in place and where team interactions were respectful. Where members felt disrespected or undermined, communication, information sharing and collaboration were impaired, with a negative impact on the care provided to service users. The researchers concluded that teams require clear operating procedures alongside trust and respect across the professions if there is to be open, safe and reflective participation.

Chapter summary

This chapter has given you an overview of how teams work and how you might better understand the way in which individuals in teams work together. There are strategies in the chapter to help you work more effectively with others in a leadership capacity or collegiate manner in teams. The chapter has only touched the surface and you are strongly recommended to access the useful websites or further reading to provide you with more detailed guidance.

Activities: Brief outline answers

Activity 2.2 Critical thinking (p27)

Teams utilise all of the skills of the people in the team and, because these skills complement each other and one person can pick up where another person's skills end, teams can solve more complex problems than individuals can manage alone. Because people have different skills, then the breadth of work they can achieve in teams is increased, as is the complexity of the task which may be undertaken.

Activity 2.3 Reflection (p27)

Teams are not effective just because they are; rather they are effective because the people within the teams want them to be, share common goals and values and put these into practice. When values are relegated to second place after targets, then the quality of the work of the team is affected, as described in the Francis report.

Further reading

Grant, A and Goodman, B (2018) *Communication and Interpersonal Skills in Nursing* (4th edition). London: SAGE.

Two chapters deal with effective team working and the working environment – Chapter 5: Understanding Potential Barriers, and Chapter 7: The Environmental Context.

Goodman, B and Clemow, R (2010) *Nursing and Collaborative Practice* (2nd edition). Exeter: Learning Matters.

Chapter 6: Teamwork is about interdisciplinary team work.

Useful websites

www.acas.org.uk/index.aspx?articleid=1218

Advisory, Conciliation and Arbitration Service (ACAS), dealing with conflict at work.

www.managementhelp.org/grp_skll/meetings/meetings.htm

Free Management Library information on preparing, planning, leading and evaluating meetings.

http://managementhelp.org/systems/systems.htm#anchor6759

Free Management Library on the development and application of systems theory to analyse problems and influence change management.

www.businessballs.com/teambuilding.htm

This site provides ideas for team building, organisational structures and also discussion around corporate social responsibility and ethical organisations.

www.belbin.com

Home page for Belbin's team role theory, role descriptors and explanations of the theory.

www.infed.org/thinkers/george_homans.htm

www.angelfire.com/bug/theory_project/Exchange_Theory.htm

These two websites both provide background to the work of the sociologist George Homans and the development of social exchange theory.

www.the-happy-manager.com/tips/pestle-analysis

A short and clear overview of the PESTLE analysis tool.

Chapter 3 — Working with individuals in teams

(Continued)

and sleep can be met, acting as a role model for others in providing evidence based person-centred care.

Platform 5: Leading and managing nursing care and working in teams

Registered nurses provide leadership by acting as a role model for best practice in the delivery of nursing care. They are responsible for managing nursing care and are accountable for the appropriate delegation and supervision of care provided by others in the team including lay carers. They play an active and equal role in the interdisciplinary team, collaborating and communicating effectively with a range of colleagues.

At the point of registration, the registered nurse will be able to:

5.4 demonstrate an understanding of the roles, responsibilities and scope of practice of all members of the nursing and interdisciplinary team and how to make best use of the contributions of others involved in providing care.

5.6 exhibit leadership potential by demonstrating an ability to guide, support and motivate individuals and interact confidently with other members of the care team.

5.7 demonstrate the ability to monitor and evaluate the quality of care delivered by others in the team and lay carers.

5.9 demonstrate the ability to challenge and provide constructive feedback about care delivered by others in the team, and support them to identify and agree individual learning needs.

Platform 6: Improving safety and quality of care

Registered nurses make a key contribution to the continuous monitoring and quality improvement of care and treatment in order to enhance health outcomes and people's experience of nursing and related care. They assess risks to safety or experience and take appropriate action to manage those, putting the best interests, needs and preferences of people first.

At the point of registration, the registered nurse will be able to:

6.8 demonstrate an understanding of how to identify, report and critically reflect on near misses, critical incidents, major incidents and serious adverse events in order to learn from them and influence their future practice.

Chapter aims

After reading this chapter, you will be able to:

- understand the significance of the concepts 'responsibility' and 'accountability' in relation to individuals in teams;
- evaluate the factors affecting the delegation of work to others in a team;

- evaluate the role of personal development plans (PDPs) for an individual in a team;
- understand the relevance of individual, organisational, generational and cultural differences to team working.

Introduction

In this chapter topics such as individual roles, responsibility and accountability with reference to the Nursing and Midwifery Council (NMC) *Code* (NMC, 2015) will be discussed along with techniques for delegating. PDPs, performance appraisal and staff development principles will be explored. Cultural and generational differences will be discussed. Employment issues such as health and safety legislation and risk management will be included in this chapter. How to recruit, select and retain staff to work in teams will be covered briefly in Chapter 7. In addition, you will find it helpful to look at the NMC (2015) *Code*, which has specific guidance for nurses and midwives working with others. A number of key areas are covered in this guidance, including:

1. Communicate clearly.

2. Work cooperatively.

3. Share your skills, knowledge and experience for the benefit of people receiving care and your colleagues.

4. Be accountable for your decisions to delegate tasks and duties to other people.

Activity 3.1 Evidence-based practice and research

Go to the NMC web page (**http://www.nmc-uk.org**) and review the underpinning principles of these themes proposed by the NMC.

These principles and themes are further discussed throughout this chapter.

The *2018 Future Nurse: Standards of Proficiency for Registered Nurses* and *The Code* (2015) place considerable emphasis on team working and the responsibility of both the individual in the team and the team leader. In this chapter we will be focusing on the leadership role in supporting, developing and challenging individuals in the team.

Individual roles, responsibility and accountability

In the previous chapter we looked at the many different forms and types of team and the ways in which teams can work together. In this chapter we will be concentrating

on the individuals in the team and begin by looking at roles and responsibilities. Each team will have a defined purpose, indicated in the two scenarios below.

Scenarios: Different examples of teams

Team A is brought together for a short-term activity such as the length of a shift. This could be a band 5 nurse caring for six patients in a section of a ward with possibly, and depending on the acuity of the needs of the patients or the seriousness of the illnesses, another band 5 colleague and two healthcare assistants (HCAs) from 7 a.m. to 3 p.m.

Team B is a multidisciplinary team convened to work together for a longer duration to implement a new service initiative to improve patient care. In this example it is a project group to ensure patients receive dignified care.

Within each of these teams an individual team member will have a role or a part to play in completing a task and in the overall remit of the team and be responsible for various actions. It is worth reminding ourselves of the meaning of the word 'responsible' and how that relates to the concept of accountability.

Activity 3.2   Critical thinking

Write out your definitions of 'responsible' and 'accountable' without referring to a dictionary. Think about the differences between the two concepts.

Then think about what the difference is for those who are leading teams and for those who are being led. The exercise should be about leadership styles and priorities, not accountability.

Further guidance is given on this activity at the end of the chapter.

The next step is to ensure that team members understand their responsibilities in relation to a task. A team leader is expected to assign responsibility for activities and this can become a minefield of emotions and hurt feelings if communicated inappropriately or to a person with the wrong skill set or knowledge. We will discuss this in more detail later in the chapter under the heading of delegation, but in this discussion we are focusing on conveying a sense of responsibility to complete team work successfully. This is not achieved by magic or guesswork or estimates of a team member's capabilities. It requires clear thinking about what is expected and clear communication as well as checking progress throughout the task. If this is not done, leaders are responsible for less than satisfactory results and cannot hold team members accountable for any shortfalls. To ensure responsibilities are understood and carried out:

- identify the appropriate team member with the skills and knowledge to carry out the task

- ensure resources are available for the task to be completed or advise the team member how to obtain resources
- explain and assign the task
- identify the level of support to be given to the team member (e.g. is the person novice or experienced?)
- set the standards
- check progress
- make sure the standards are met and the task completed.

At team level the same rules apply. The team needs to be put together so that the skills and abilities needed to undertake the task are all collected in one place. Team members need an understanding of the task and the resources to do it and they will need support and their progress checking by the manager.

Delegation

As a team leader you can only delegate those tasks for which you are responsible. As we have seen in the discussion above and in the activity, the delegator remains accountable for the task, whereas the delegate is accountable to the delegator and has responsibilities for the task being assigned.

Delegation is a means of dividing up the workload in a team. It is also a way for leaders to help team members develop or enhance their abilities and skills. It can promote team working, foster collaboration and increase the amount of work achievable in a given time when compared with a person working alone. Delegation is also a good tool for preparing people for the next step in their career; in this sense it can prove to be very motivational (Curtis and O'Connell, 2011).

Delegation is not a means of escaping tasks or responsibilities that you do not want. Nor is it work or task allocation. Allocating tasks is to transfer a task from one person to another, whereas delegation gives someone the authority to carry out a task in place of the person who would normally undertake that task. By transferring authority, the person has the right to act and is empowered to undertake the task (i.e. this could be to ask others to undertake subtasks as part of the overall activity). This difference should be made explicit to the delegatee when a task is delegated.

Scenarios

Let's return to the scenario of Team B. Within this group there are representatives from different wards in a hospital as the initiative is to be undertaken across the organisation. The team also includes representatives of different disciplines. Once a plan of action has been agreed, to ensure dignity is implemented on the wards, the

(Continued)

(Continued)

representatives will go back to their bases and initiate changes in the ward to bring about a successful outcome. They will need the collaboration of their peers, subordinates and, possibly, seniors to carry out subtasks. They may be experts in change management strategies and be able to charm the birds from the trees, but they will also need the authority to undertake this task and have that recognised by the teams they are going to be working with. Multidisciplinary workers may have to work with professions other than their own. To be successful, they will also need their personal skills and the support of the authority invested in the group to bring about these changes. The authority invested in the project group, probably by a senior member of the directorate or division, will provide the legitimate authority for the project to carry out adjustments in the wards.

In the case of Team A, where tasks are being divided amongst the team, the aim is to assign relevant activities to the appropriately qualified or grade of staff. The team leader will have the authority to assign the tasks and the responsibility to match activities to grade or competence. However, the team member has the responsibility for his or her own activities and the care of the patient.

Delegation decisions

Who to delegate to and how to delegate are, for the novice, quite daunting decisions. There are several potential competing thoughts and feelings impacting these decisions, such as:

- guilt in asking someone else to do a job that you are well qualified or competent to undertake
- reluctance to delegate if you think you can do a task better or quicker
- having to ask someone you are equal to in grade or who you haven't worked with before.

Activity 3.3   Reflection

Consider the last time someone delegated responsibility to you. How did you feel? What reasons might you have had for wanting to do the task? What reasons might you have had for not wanting to undertake the task? Did you feel you had the authority to see the task through? Did the person delegating the task make you feel they still had some accountability for how the task turned out?

Further guidance is given on this activity at the end of the chapter.

Working with skill mix

Changing care needs and priorities mean care leaders have to get used to thinking about and adapting to the changing **skill mix** in their teams. In NHS acute care settings, increasing numbers of HCAs will be working alongside qualified nurses undertaking whole-patient care and not just tasks such as observations of temperature, pulse and respirations (Gainsborough, 2009). The majority of HCAs are employed on band 3 grades and you may want to request a copy of the generic job description for this grade to understand the scope of practice for this grade. The job description should link to the NHS Agenda for Change band and the NHS Knowledge and Skills Framework national clinical grading criteria. Some HCAs will take up assistant or associate practitioner roles, with many having completed a specialised Foundation degree in healthcare. These were introduced by the Skills for Health organisation in 2000. HCAs with this specialist qualification can move from the Agenda for Change band 3 grade to band 4. It would be worth your while looking at the difference between these two grades and the difference in the roles and responsibilities of an associate practitioner and a registered practitioner. Each band has a corresponding list of likely responsibilities and roles (**www. NHSemployers.org**).

In addition, some HCAs will have achieved National Vocational Qualifications (NVQs) at level 3 or 4. NVQs are a competency-based qualification and there are five levels. Although NVQs are not usually compared directly to conventional academic qualifications, approximate equivalences have been established. Additionally, NVQs are currently in the process of being replaced by the new Qualifications Credit Framework. See the useful websites at the end of the chapter for more information.

In mixed teams providing acute care to adult patients, qualified nurses will need to delegate care to HCAs and other non-professionally registered staff such as domestic or ancillary personnel. In community settings health visitors delegate care to nursery nurses and band 5 nurses (staff nurses) who undertake some developmental screening. In some teams, such as intermediate care in the community, community practitioners are band 5 staff nurses working with specialist community practice home nurses. In acute mental health settings assistant practitioners work with registered mental health nurses. In child care nursery nurses work with staff nurses and in learning disability settings registered learning disability nurses work with nursing assistants.

All this points to the fact that the leader has to be aware not only of the work which needs to be done by the team, but also the skills sets available from within the team. Knowing the team and the skill mix within the team will enable the leader to make appropriate decisions about task delegation and will help to promote effective care provision.

Enabling staff development through delegation

By delegating tasks and responsibilities to other members of the team, opportunities can be provided for staff development, increased job satisfaction and promotion. It has been understood for some considerable time that one of the key motivators of people in the workplace lies in giving them responsibility to undertake tasks which stretch them professionally (Herzberg, 1959). People also have a need to undertake tasks which they see as worthwhile and which might contribute to their advancement both personally and professionally (Herzberg, 1959). It should be clear by now that one of the criteria for role satisfaction for all team members has to be that they are doing something which aligns with their values. Factors such as a positive organisational culture encourage delegation, as well as the expression of personal qualities that engender co-operation and a willingness to collaborate, the appropriate use of resources (equipment and learning environment) and appropriate supervision or guidance for the task.

Selecting the right person to delegate to requires a corresponding leadership style. It is often assumed that delegation is a management role; however, recognising the talents and strengths of individuals and working to meet their developmental stages require leadership qualities. Kotter (1990) recognised this and developed a scheme for matching the appropriate leadership style to the individual's levels of commitment and competence. This enables leaders to draw out the best in their team members and identify where development needs to take place. Table 3.1 outlines an adaptation of Kotter's ideas. We discuss coaching in Chapter 5.

The rules for delegation are the same no matter what the task or the grade of the person being delegated to:

1.   Identify the task to be delegated.

2.   Identify the person(s) to be delegated to.

3.   Ensure that the person(s) being delegated to have the ability to undertake the task.

Developmental level of individuals	Appropriate leadership style
Low competence – high commitment	Directing
Some competence – low commitment	Coaching
High competence – variable commitment	Supporting
High competence – high commitment	Delegating

Table 3.1 Matching individual levels of competence and motivation for tasks with leadership style

Source: Adapted from Kotter (1990).

4. Ensure the reasons for the delegation are understood.

5. Ensure the expected outcome and time frame are understood.

6. Ensure resources and authority to see through task are in place.

7. Ensure the recipient(s) of the delegated task are supported.

8. Give feedback on the results of the delegation.

(Ellis, 2015, p71)

Personal development plans

We have just talked about developing staff, so it would seem timely to introduce the topic of development planning. The PDP (sometimes called individual development plan or staff review) is intended to help employees enhance existing skills or knowledge and develop new skills to fulfil an existing role. If responsibilities have increased, the PDP may be utilised to identify a level that requires a regrading to a higher grade. Alternatively, it can be used to identify a role at a grade equivalent to a previous role. In NHS settings the PDP should be carried out annually and is a method of ensuring staff maintain their skills and knowledge to perform their roles.

The PDP provides a framework for:

*   prioritising developmental support
*   planning related activities, such as attending study days, seminars or courses, in an appropriate sequence and within agreed timescales
*   monitoring progress within those timescales
*   evaluating outcomes in terms of skills, knowledge and expertise
*   developing individual career plans and identifying organisational succession plans.

A specifically designed e-platform for working with PDPs in healthcare settings can be found on the Knowledge Skills Framework website (see the useful websites at the end of the chapter). As a student you may have completed a PDP that looks at your personal growth and development during your course. As a newly qualified nurse you will be expected to follow a period of preceptorship which will give you the opportunity to identify areas you want to concentrate on during your preceptorship to extend your confidence in specific skills and knowledge. As you progress in experience and seniority you may be involved in undertaking PDPs for HCAs and you would be advised to look out for any training being offered, as all organisations have a slightly different emphasis on how they conduct the PDP process. As a registered practitioner you will be required to maintain your professional knowledge to remain on the NMC register. In order to meet the criteria for revalidation, as a registered nurse you will have to demonstrate that you have undertaken (NMC, 2017):

- 450 practice hours, or 900 if renewing as both a nurse and midwife
- 35 hours of CPD including 20 hours of participatory learning
- Five pieces of practice-related feedback
- Five written reflective accounts
- Reflective discussion
- Health and character declaration
- Professional indemnity arrangement
- Confirmation.

The practice element can be met through administrative, supervisory, teaching, research and managerial roles as well as providing direct patient care.

Activity 3.5   Reflection

Look at the learning objectives you set with your practice assessor at the start of your last placement. Consider how the allocation of work which you undertook allowed you to meet the targets for development which you set. If you are newly qualified you might like to do this activity with your preceptor or line manager, considering how your skills sets are growing to help meet the needs of the service in which you are working. These reflections are good practice for reflective discussions and accounts you will need to undertake for revalidation.

As this answer is based on your own observation, there is no outline answer at the end of the chapter.

Performance appraisal

Redshaw (2008) investigated the role and extent of appraisal in nursing. At the time, only six out of ten staff in the NHS received a formal appraisal. There is a distinction between appraisal – the judgement and assessment of the worth or value of an employee's performance at work – and personal development – a process of mutually planning (between staff member and senior staff in the organisation) supporting activities for individuals to undertake their role in the workplace. Appraisal does not always have a good press as staff can feel that it is a waste of time or does not measure accurately their contribution to the work. Alternatively, some staff want to know how they are performing and have some measure of performance as a yardstick to improve, for their own satisfaction or to progress in their career or work roles. Chapter 7 gives more information about performance appraisal.

There are different forms of appraisal scheme: top-down (the most common), self-appraisal and peer appraisal, upward appraisal where appraiser reports on management's performance (the least common) and multi-rater appraisal, which is usually in the form of 360-degree feedback about an individual from a variety of peers, subordinates, external and internal appraisers and superiors – that is everyone within the sphere of influence of an individual staff member.

There are difficulties with performance appraisal both in the implementation and management of appraisal schemes. Some appraisal systems can be time consuming both in terms of the interview and form completion. The objective of appraisal is to identify and reward performance. If this is not achieved in practice, the scheme will lack merit. If there is an appraisal system alongside a development-planning scheme, often known as personal development planning, the allocation of rewards can undermine the personal developmental aspects as the emphasis will be on organisational aims and outputs. There are also concerns about the subjectivity of making appraisals that can be influenced by personal attributes of the appraiser or employee and environmental or situational factors such as individual health or organisational changes.

Support for staff – including performance review – can raise standards in the workplace. However, the quest for better performance has not always been accompanied by a better system of appraisal. According to Redshaw (2008), the most important process for improved performance is not to set goals and order staff to achieve them, but to improve relationships so that staff feel highly valued and have a sense of belonging. So, the development of positive manager–employee relationships is an effective way of improving the appraisals process. Conflicts, lack of understanding of the aims of the process and mutual distrust will have a negative effect, resulting in staff finding it difficult to accept criticism and feedback. This in turn will have a wider impact on staff performance. This is especially relevant in team-based work where the style of the leader can influence colleagues' performance and attitudes towards appraisal. Another factor is the way in which feedback is handed to employees. Giving feedback can be challenging and managers need good communication skills to ensure feedback is constructive and helpful. Feedback that is focused on blame damages self-confidence, whereas constructive criticism to recognise and improve poor performance is appropriate.

One way to think about the distinction between performance and appraisal, and the call from Redshaw to improve relationships, is to take the view that as appraisal only happens once a year, it may be too late, or too slow, in addressing issues in the workplace. A good relationship with staff is an ongoing thing and will reap rewards for the manager, and the staff member, throughout the whole of the year.

Case study: Ensuring adequate nutrition

The setting is a busy acute female medical ward. In a six-bedded bay, Mary, a slight 72-year-old who was originally admitted with unstable type 2 diabetes, is waiting to be discharged home. Although the ward staff have told her she won't be leaving until after lunch, Mary has had her bags packed since 7 a.m. as she is keen to leave the ward. Mary is a quiet and undemanding person who rarely complains. The band 5 team leader for the shift, Sandy, passes by the bed and sees that Mary has been provided with her lunch of soup and a sandwich. Nutrition is an important part of Mary's recovery plan to treat her diabetes and also to help her restore her body mass index to within normal limits. Mary should be having fortified soups and not the usual soup, as she has been given in this instance, from the hospital menu. Fortified soups are available for patients in the ward kitchen. Sandy has spoken to the HCAs and ward hostess before about ensuring that Mary has fortified soups and that she receives reinforcing messages when she has her meals of the relevance and importance of maintaining her nutrition once she is at home. Sandy believes the HCAs are capable of giving health education as well as ensuring patients receive the appropriate nutrition. This would be in line with the NHS Knowledge and Skills Framework section on health and well-being and appropriate for an HCA to undertake. She also believes that the HCA, Joanna in this case, should have responsibility for ensuring the ward hostess provides the correct soup and that Joanna should monitor this. Sandy resolves to speak to the HCA to provide feedback on her performance and what she expects the HCA's role to be in this respect.

Fowler (1996) suggests the following principles when giving feedback:

1. Be specific and give examples.
2. Be constructive and focus on what can be learnt from the event.
3. Avoid comments about attitude or personality that cannot realistically be changed and concentrate on behaviour and how it affects performance.
4. Give feedback regularly and do not wait for annual reviews; it should be timely and as close to the event as possible.
5. Encourage self-reflection – feedback is not just about telling.
6. Avoid argument – a practical discussion about differences of opinion on performance is much more helpful. Listen to the other person's point of view.
7. Explain the reasons for the request for a change that may be needed and encourage the development of an action plan.
8. Take feedback yourself – the discussion should be two-way and there may be lessons to learn from your own performance.
9. Encourage openness and this will lead to the other person seeking regular feedback as part of the culture of the unit/department and your leadership style.

Activity 3.6   Decision-making

Imagine that you are Sandy, the band 5 staff nurse on this shift, who is leading the team. Make a draft plan of how you would give feedback to Joanna. What points would you make? What would be the principles upon which you would base your feedback for Joanna? When would you go about giving the feedback?

Further guidance is given on this activity at the end of the chapter.

Individual, cultural and generational differences

Working with individuals in teams, the team leader will encounter individual differences in the team members that have to be acknowledged and worked with to ensure effective working relationships. In Chapter 1, we examined different roles that individuals assume in a team by individual differences. The chapter concentrates on the individual traits and personality that a person has. In Chapter 2, we had a brief look at these characteristics and now we can further explore personal characteristics that fall within the 'big five personality theory'.

Research summary: Five-factor model of personality

In 1991 Barrick and Mount reported on a study that they undertook to examine the relationships between workplace roles and individual personality characteristics, defined in the 'big five personality theory' or 'five-factor model of personality', as it is known theoretically. The personality dimensions are:

1. extroversion
2. emotional stability
3. agreeableness
4. conscientiousness
5. openness to experience.

These were matched to three job performance criteria (job proficiency, training proficiency and personnel data – i.e. age, time in occupation) for five occupational groups (professionals such as teachers, nurses and doctors; police; managers; sales; skilled/semi-skilled occupations).

The results of their analysis indicated that one dimension of personality, conscientiousness, showed consistent relations with all job performance criteria for all

(Continued)

(Continued)

occupational groups. For the remaining personality dimensions, the correlations varied by occupational group and professional criteria.

Extroversion was a valid predictor for two occupations involving social interaction: managers and sales (across criterion types). Also, both openness to experience and extroversion were valid predictors of the training proficiency criterion (i.e. those persons who had a role as educators and this was across all professions in the study). Other personality dimensions were also found to be valid predictors for some occupations and some criterion types, but the correlation between the occupation and criterion was small.

Overall, the results illustrated the benefits of using the five-factor model of personality to predict suitability for job performance. The findings were thought to have numerous implications for research and practice, especially in the subfields of personnel selection, training and development, and performance appraisal. This means that there is some substance to the theory that certain personal characteristics are better suited to certain occupational roles.

Organisational culture

Another factor to influence individual behaviour in teams is cultural mores. Culture is not so much about what an organisation does; rather, in the sense we are thinking about it in this book, culture is about how staff experience their place of work (Kohn and O'Connell, 2005). The philosophies, social and historical background to an organisation all shape the prevailing culture. In addition, practices within an organisation that are derived from leadership or management style have an impact. Examples include whether an organisation is people- or task-oriented; if there is an emphasis on control and command; the extent of tolerance to risk taking; if there is a reward culture or a blame culture; the manner in which an organisation responds to change – rapidly or at snail's pace – and finally, the extent to which an individual willingly signs up to the philosophy of the organisation.

Activity 3.7   Reflection

Take a moment to reflect on the culture of the organisation you have worked in, or had practice experience in, most recently. Can you recognise any of the characteristics mentioned above? How do they relate to the culture of the organisation? Then think about what kind of culture you would want to foster if you were leading a team.

As this answer is based on your own observation, there is no outline answer at the end of the chapter.

Cultural diversity

The other aspect of culture is the sociological phenomenon of culture, which affects our lives in a complex and multifaceted manner in our culturally diverse society. To work collaboratively in teams, nurses have to understand and respect unfamiliar behaviour patterns and attitudes without dismissing or devaluing them. Yet, this diversity needs to be harnessed to be effective and to meet patients' needs. Grant and Goodman (2018) consider the relevance of focusing on cultural diversity and communication, as this is often the first barrier to overcome.

There are thought to be four cultural dimensions along which cultures differ in the workplace:

1. directness – getting to the point ↔ implying the messages
2. hierarchy – following orders ↔ engaging in debate
3. consensus – dissenting is accepted ↔ unanimity is needed
4. individualism – individual winners are acceptable ↔ team effectiveness is paramount.

Different attitudes to authority, culturally embedded notions of authority and power, perceptions of gender stereotypes and acceptance of directness or expectations of hidden meanings in communications all influence these cultural dimensions. A team leader will need to be observant to recognise at which point of these dimensions individuals are expected to behave in the team and how each individual will be interpreting these dimensions, depending on their social and cultural background and the norms they are accustomed to. In addition, the philosophy of the organisation and the nature of the tasks undertaken (e.g. the perceived status of those tasks) will have an influence.

Generational differences

Every generation is affected by the time in which they are growing up. Influences such as economic (e.g. post World War II thriftiness), political (e.g. Thatcherism and individualistic political policies), social events (Bob Geldof Live Aid concerts), feminist ideology and technological advances will play a significant part in forming the context for attitudes to be formed about work. While the cusp years can vary depending on the individual, here's how the generations are typically described:

- traditionalists or veterans: born before 1946
- baby boomers: born between 1946 and 1964
- generation X: born between 1965 and 1980
- generation Y or millennials: born after 1980.

Patterson (2005) has gathered together observations from her work as an organisational psychologist and the business management literature to assemble impressions of the main characteristics associated with generations since the early part of the last century (Table 3.2).

Traditionalists (1925–1945)	Baby boomers (1946–1964)	Generation X (1965–1980)	Millennials (1981 to present)
Practical	Optimistic	Sceptical	Hopeful
Patient, loyal and hardworking	Teamwork and co-operation	Self-reliant	Meaningful work
Respectful of authority	Ambitious	Risk taking	Diversity and change valued
Rule followers	Workaholic	Balances work and personal life	Technology-savvy

Table 3.2   Defining work characteristics

Source: Adapted from Patterson (2005).

While not everyone will fall into a defined category, taking note of generational diversity is important as intergenerational conflict, or lack of understanding of different generational mores, can impede plans, team work and ideas for service improvement. For example, a baby boomer manager may not be familiar with social networking and the impact technologies have had on social relationships. The manager's ideas on how relationships are communicated and sustained might involve paper notices on notice boards, whereas the millennial team members will be likely to expect messages to be posted on a social networking site.

Research summary: Generational differences

Smola and Sutton (2002) surveyed 350 baby boomers and generation Xers in 1974 and 1999 and found an overall change in work values as generations matured, such as giving work a lower priority in life and placing less value on feeling a sense of pride at work. In particular, the younger women tend to question workplace expectations more often, such as long work hours or taking work home, and they are often more open about their parenting obligations and commitments. The study also found generational differences, for example, generation Xers report less loyalty to their companies, wanting to be promoted more quickly and being more 'me-oriented' than baby boomers. It is suggested that such differences are, in part, accounted for by workers' values shifting as they age.

Working in teams can cause clashes between individuals in the workplace. Baby boomers, traditionalists, generation Xers and millennials all represent different cultural norms as far as respecting tradition, social manners, speaking frankly about personal issues and attitudes to hierarchy are concerned. The generations will respond to change in different ways – fear of change can be expressed in one way if it results from being too used to certain ways of doing things, and in another way completely if it results from immaturity and insecurity. Baby boomers may find traditionalists inflexible, and themselves be perceived as self-absorbed in return. Generation Xers, on the other hand, may find themselves criticised for being cynical and negative while seeing baby boomers as having their own conventional rigidity, and millennials as spoiled upstarts. Such clashes may be reduced if there are opportunities for facilitated discussion in team meetings, helping the various participants to explore the benefits and disadvantages of different approaches to working methods. A team leader will have the role of encouraging effective listening between team members, reducing ambiguity and misunderstandings, supporting the sharing of expertise and recognition of individuals' contributions to the team. It is helpful if the various generational groups can be encouraged to understand why each might respond in a particular fashion, and how patients might benefit in each case.

This approach is even more useful in interdisciplinary teams if misunderstandings are to be avoided. Team members can then work towards seeking a balance between building on traditional procedures and supporting newer ideas to blend the different work ethics of the generational groups.

According to Patterson (2005), effective, or similar, messages are for:

- traditionalists: 'Your experience is respected' or 'It is valuable to hear what has worked in the past'
- baby boomers: 'You are valuable, worthy' or 'Your contribution is unique and important to our success'
- generation Xers: 'Let's explore some options outside of the box' or 'Your technical expertise is a big asset'
- millennials: 'You will have an opportunity to collaborate with other bright, creative people' or 'You have really rescued this situation with your commitment'.

What this research shows, and the important message for the leader, is that different people view the world in different ways. This will mean that differing members of a team will have different needs and wants, as well as different abilities, and being aware of, and responding to, this in an appropriate way will mean the manager will get the most from individual team members and as a result from the team as a whole.

This might remind you of the Johari window (Luft and Ingham, 1955) in Chapter 1 which presents to us some thoughts about the correlation between how we see ourselves and how other people see us. We said on p13 that 'there is great potential for us as individuals to lack understanding of ourselves as much as there is potential for other people not to understand us'. The message for the manager is that a good part of their role is learning to understand people and learning to use that understanding to get the best from them.

> ### Chapter summary
>
> This chapter has given you an overview of how teams work and how you might better understand the way in which individuals in teams work together. There are strategies to help you work more effectively with others in a leadership capacity or collegiate manner in teams. The chapter has only touched the surface and you are strongly recommended to access the useful websites or further reading for more detailed guidance.

Activities: Brief outline answers

Activity 3.2 Critical thinking (p46)

The term 'responsible' can be understood from two perspectives:

1.   being the cause of something, usually something wrong or disapproved of;

2.   being answerable to someone for an action or the successful carrying out of a duty.

In a team, the team member has responsibility for carrying out an activity to the standard required by the team leader. To avoid perspective number 1 above, where misunderstandings, inaccuracies and disappointments may have occurred, the required standard should be explained to the person who is responsible for the task. In this situation it is the team leader's responsibility to be clear about what is expected in a task and the team member's responsibility to accomplish the task. Spending time explaining to a team member what is required can save time later and also enables the team member to carry out the task up to the level required. It may be a peer who is in the team and in this case it would be helpful to clarify that both of you are working towards the same goal or outcome. If it is a subordinate or someone with untested skills or knowledge of the situation, an example or demonstration may be necessary to indicate the standard required for the task.

The term 'accountable' can be understood from two perspectives:

1.   The obligations to report, explain or justify a behaviour or activity that has taken place and take responsibility for this activity. In this sense a person is answerable to, or responsible to, another person, organisation or professional body for the manner in which an activity has been undertaken. A key factor here is the word obligation, which can be interpreted as the legal responsibility or employment responsibility of the grade in which a person is employed. In this sense it is accepting ownership for the results, or lack thereof.

2.   The capability of explaining why something has taken place (i.e. to give an account of something with reasons and/or evidence). In nursing, we more often use the first perspective rather than the second perspective as the concept of accountability is blended with responsibility. Therefore, the team leader is both accountable to the employer with the responsibility for carrying out the task through the activities of the team members. The team members are accountable to the team leader and have responsibility to the team leader to carry out the required activity. However, the second perspective may be drawn upon if a person is required to give an account of the failure or success of a task.

Activity 3.3 Reflection (p48)

You may have wanted to do the task because it made you feel special, it may have been a good learning opportunity or because you just wanted to be helpful. Reasons you might not have wanted to undertake the task include a lack of confidence, fear of failure or a dislike of taking responsibility. As a student you may have felt that you did not have the skills to do what is asked, but you should be learning them. Again as a student delegated a task, the registered nurse should make it plain that they are accountable for the outcome, while you remain responsible for what you are doing.

Activity 3.6 Decision-making (p55)

The points you make may include the following:

1. Importance and rationale for nutrition in:

    (a) treatment of type 2 diabetes

    (b) weight maintenance.

2. Importance of health education information about maintaining diet when patient goes home.

3. Ensure the ward hostess gives the correct type of soup to Mary by monitoring delivery.

4. Ensure Mary drinks the soup, even though she is keen to go home and not make a fuss.

5. Has Joanna had any additional training in diet and nutrition, and in particular with type 2 diabetes? If not, is there a training day coming up soon that she could attend?

6. Is Joanna comfortable monitoring the ward hostess? Does she see this as part of her role and her work in the team on this section of the ward? If not, explain that you have this expectation and you will support Joanna to do this by mentioning this as the expectation for all HCAs in the next team meeting.

When giving Joanna feedback, what principles would you be thinking of, drawn from Fowler's (1996) list in the section on giving feedback in the text above?

When would you go about giving the feedback? It is suggested that feedback should be given at a time close to the event occurring. You will have to balance this decision with an evaluation of the suitability of the time available during a shift, at the end of the shift or at a pre-arranged time other than during the day of the shift. It depends on how busy you are and any other situational factors. However, do not let these factors obstruct you from your task. If this is the first time you are to give feedback you may want to let your ward manager know and practise how you are going to handle the situation with her/him. S/he can also give you support when the issue is raised in the team meeting.

Further reading

Grant, A and Goodman, B (2018) *Communication and Interpersonal Skills in Nursing* (4th edition). London: SAGE.

An accessible introduction to the subject.

Sullivan, EJ and Decker, PJ (2009) *Effective Leadership and Management in Nursing* (7th edition). Harlow: Pearson International Edition. Chapter 10, Delegating successfully.

Although this book is written for the USA, the principles are transferable and this chapter provides some in-depth analysis of the difficulties and methods to overcome the art of delegation.

Useful websites

http://www.nhsemployers.org/~/media/Employers/Publications/NHS_Job_Evaluation_Handbook.pdf

Provides information on the Agenda for Change bands – see especially Chapter 6.

http://www.nhsemployers.org/PayAndContracts/AgendaForChange/KSF/Simplified-KSF/Pages/SimplifiedKSF.aspx

Introduction to the NHS Knowledge and Skills Framework and its links to the NHS Agenda for Change National Pay Agreement.

http://rapidbi.com/created/personaldevelopmentplan.html# formonthejobdevelopmentrecord

Link to an example of a personal development plan from a commercial organisation.

http://revalidation.nmc.org.uk/welcome-to-revalidation

The Nursing and Midwifery Council's webpages dedicated to the requirements for revalidation.

http://www.qca.org.uk

Website of the Qualifications and Curriculum Authority.

http://www.skillsforhealth.org.uk/standards/item/216-the-care-certificate

Skills for Health website giving information on the Care Certificate.

http://www.nhsemployers.org/your-workforce/retain-and-improve/managing-your-workforce/appraisals/appraisal-tools-and-tips

NHS Employers appraisal tools and tips.

Chapter 4 Conflict management and negotiation skills

(Continued)

work in partnership with people to develop person-centred care plans that take into account their circumstances, characteristics and preferences.

At the point of registration, the registered nurse will be able to:

3.10 demonstrate the skills and abilities required to recognise and assess people who show signs of self-harm and/or suicidal ideation.

3.11 undertake routine investigations, interpreting and sharing findings as appropriate.

Chapter aims

After reading this chapter, you will be able to:

- identify situations during which conflict might arise;
- discuss strategies for preventing conflict arising;
- demonstrate awareness of methods of managing conflict;
- comment on your own ability to understand and manage yourself in difficult situations involving interpersonal conflict.

Introduction

Nursing involves caring for people during some of the most emotionally difficult times of their lives. As well as patients, nurses come into contact with relatives, friends and carers of patients who are themselves distressed and anxious. In some circumstances, nurses and other care staff can become upset or angry themselves.

Within any clinical setting there is the potential for anxiety, confusion, distress, hurt and pain to erupt into conflict. Sometimes distress arises as a result of a patient's physical, psychological or spiritual condition.

At other times, frustration may surface as a result of apparent failures within systems, poor communication or lack of understanding.

Conflict may arise between patients and care staff; between patients; between care staff; between patients and significant others; or between staff and patients' significant others. Recognising the potential for conflict and learning how to prevent and manage conflict are all key skills in leadership and management. Perhaps the most important skill aspiring nurse leaders can have however is the ability to understand and manage themselves in such situations.

The purpose of this chapter is to enable you to explore some of the issues that contribute to the development of conflict in the clinical setting, and to examine strategies to prevent these occurring or to defuse such situations when they do occur.

What is conflict?

Understanding what conflict is and why it arises is fundamentally important in understanding both how to prevent it from occurring and how to manage it once it has arisen. Conflict is the expression of a disagreement between two or more parties that arises out of a difference in opinion, needs or desires. It is important to recognise that conflict is not usually about the individual; it is more likely to arise as a response to an individual's perception of a situation or circumstance. The prevention of conflict, therefore, has as much, if not more, to do with the management of perception as with anything else.

Not all conflict is physical in nature, although what started as a disagreement, a heated discussion or an argument can soon escalate to violence if it is not handled well. The following example encourages you to think through an everyday situation in a hospital to increase your understanding of how easily a confrontational situation can develop.

Case study: The protracted wait

Stan is a busy man who has to attend hospital regularly for monitoring of his emphysema. The hospital is quite old and Stan is forced to wait in the corridor along with the rest of the people attending the clinic because there is no waiting room. The corridor is cold and draughty, and has a constant stream of people through it. Stan has waited over an hour past his allotted appointment time and is fed up, not only with the hanging around but with having to sit in the corridor. Stan approaches the receptionist and demands to know how much longer he will have to wait. The receptionist's response, while polite, is not helpful as she does not know why the appointments are running so far behind. Stan is upset by the lack of information he is given and the seemingly poor communication within the team. He shouts at the receptionist for being 'incompetent'.

This case study illustrates how perception and the physical environment can contribute to bad feeling. Stan is aggrieved at having to wait in an environment that is not designed for the purpose for which it is being used. He is forced to wait for a protracted period of time but does not know why. When Stan tries to find out why he is waiting, he does not get what he considers to be a reasonable response. The receptionist is not being rude, but Stan's perception of the fact she is unable to give him a reason for the delay is that his needs are not being met. He finds this unacceptable.

We can imagine the same scenario acted out in various different ways which may lead to different outcomes. The receptionist might tell Stan to sit down and wait, thus escalating the situation to one of open conflict. She might apologise for the delay and say that she will find out what is happening and come back to him, thus meeting his need to feel that he is being taken seriously. She might empathise with Stan about his situation and say how bad it is for her as well; while this may distract Stan from shouting at her, it may lead to his anger being focused at other staff in the hospital. Evidently there may be little that she, or indeed many leaders or managers, can do about the physical surroundings (since this may require a considerable investment of money) but they can and must exercise control over the psychosocial, interpersonal environment of care. This is a reflection of values in action and demonstrates the leader's compassion, respect for people and person-centredness.

What is also clear from this scenario is that prevention of conflict is everyone's business. It may seem to some that it is the role of managers, senior staff and security to deal with issues of conflict when they arise. What the protracted-wait scenario shows is this perception is wrong. Being polite and appearing to be helpful is the role of all staff, whether they be care professionals, students or support workers. Clearly, and as is explored later in the chapter, one of the roles of the manager in this sort of scenario is to look for ways in which such situations can be managed better in the future to achieve better **outcomes** (that is experiences of care) for patients.

Why managing conflict is important

The need to manage conflict effectively may seem obvious: conflict is just not nice. There are good reasons why managing conflict is important in the context of leadership and management, and these go beyond merely preventing an unpleasant situation.

The first reason that conflict management in care environments is important is it can negatively affect the experiences of patients and clients (Northam, 2009a). This applies equally to those involved in the conflict and those forced to witness it. The same is true of the staff in a department or team when conflict occurs regularly. The negative experiences of staff will almost certainly affect their ability to care and may give rise to absence through sickness associated with stress. Continued poor management of conflict may cause some staff to leave their posts, creating recruitment and retention issues.

Managing complaints and conflicts properly can lead to benefits for the team and the organisation. Recurrent complaints arising from the provision of care may be turned around to create opportunities for development. If conflict and complaints arise out of people's perceptions of the care they receive then these can be used to help redesign both the ways in which care is delivered and the nature of the care itself. A key message for leaders and managers in the management of conflict is therefore about learning from it. Properly managed, perhaps through the use of **clinical supervision** (see Chapter 5) and individual reflection (Hocking, 2006), conflict may prove to be a catalyst for innovation and creativity. **Total quality management** requires nurse leaders and managers to recognise and engage in practices which improve both the processes and practices of healthcare; this includes responding to complaints, criticism and compliments from clients.

The best leaders, teams and organisations don't ignore adverse comments, they use them to redesign the delivery of care thereby preventing issues mounting up so that they become complaints. Teams which learn from their mistakes, grow and develop and are often said to have a learning culture (see Chapter 8).

While there is no specific legislation in the UK covering workplace conflict or bullying, the Health and Safety at Work Act (1974) makes it plain that employers are responsible for the health of their employees – this includes their mental well-being. Legislation against discrimination on the grounds of age, sex, disability or ethnicity does exist and requires that managers behave in an equitable manner towards all of their employees, as required in the Equality Act (HM Government, 2010), and that they protect employees from harassment in the workplace. This requires managers, leaders and all care staff to be aware of situations which might lead to conflict and to manage them and the behaviour of staff effectively.

Consider the following case study, where conflict arising out of the way in which a service is provided is reflected on and used to develop a better way of working with potential to improve patients' experience.

Case study: The pain clinic

The pain clinic in the local district general hospital provides many services to local people, one of which is minor pain-relieving procedures requiring a short period of sedation. Each morning ten people are admitted to the clinic to undergo procedures such as facet joint injections and selective nerve root blocks. Each procedure is quite short but requires a small amount of sedation so it usually takes about 3 hours to get through the whole procedures list.

Tom is asked to attend the clinic at 8 a.m. in order to have an injection to help manage his back pain. Tom duly arrives at 8 a.m. and sits in a waiting room along with the other nine people. By 9.30 a.m. Tom is still waiting to be admitted as he is the last on the procedures list for that day. Tom is irritated by the wait as he is in pain and the chairs in the waiting area are uncomfortable. He asks Emma, the nurse admitting the patients, why he has been brought in so early when it is clear he will not need to be in a bed until about 11 a.m. Emma responds that it is just the way the clinic runs. Tom protests loudly that this is silly and that there has to be a better way of running things.

(Continued)

(Continued)

Another patient joins in, saying he feels as if they are being treated like cattle, being forced to wait for no apparent good reason. Both Tom and the other patient become quite excited and start to talk loudly about how ridiculous it all is until they are both called in to be admitted.

Emma is quite intimidated by what has happened. She reflects that this is a regular occurrence and perhaps the patients have a point about the way in which the clinic is run. She decides to talk to Hamida, the clinical nurse manager, about the complaints.

Hamida points out that the orthopaedic day unit in the same hospital sends out different appointments for admissions on surgery days, with an hour between patients. The staggered admission times mean one nurse can comfortably admit and prepare three or four people for surgery on the same day and no one is kept waiting unnecessarily. Emma reflects on this and decides she should go and see what the orthopaedic unit are doing to understand the pros and cons of their approach with a view to adopting the practice in the pain clinic.

What we can see in this case study is that patients have a real issue with being kept waiting, especially if they are in pain. Rather than ignoring this, hiding away or perhaps leaving the clinic, Emma takes on a leadership role and seeks to turn a problem into something that works for everyone's benefit. She reflects on the situation and then seeks help and support from a more experienced member of the team.

Perhaps the second key message of managing potential conflict is to listen to what is being said, rather than just to how it is being said. A third lesson might be to seek help in understanding and solving potential issues.

Again, this case study shows the value of learning from and acting upon complaints, or adverse comments, to improve the quality of care provision. If we can do this, we demonstrate our engagement, both as nurses and as leaders, with improving the lives of our patients.

Identifying potential sources of conflict

Conflict is a constant possibility in any organisation where there are human interactions (Johnson, 1994). The potential for conflict to arise in the hospital or other clinical setting is compounded by the type of work that occurs there (Kim et al., 2016). People visiting hospitals or other healthcare facilities, either as patients or visitors, are in physical and psychological distress. This means they are vulnerable, particularly if they do not understand what is happening. The fact that healthcare is often delivered in an autocratic manner also makes people feel vulnerable.

This vulnerability is perhaps not, in itself, something which nurses can eliminate. However, recognising it and doing something about it may make the difference between conflict arising or not. What is clear is that feeling vulnerable makes some people defensive and aggressive (Kim et al., 2016) and in identifying this nurses, along with all care professionals, can do a lot to avert conflict.

Taking a leadership role in the management of conflict is every nurse's role. As we saw in Chapter 1 on the experience of leadership, this involves seeing the bigger picture and understanding how the structures within which we work affect both us and the people we work with. In good part these sentiments are reflected in the increasing importance of user consultation and patient involvement forums. Clearly the best way to understand how care is experienced is to ask the people experiencing it and the best way to improve how care is experienced is again to involve those in receipt of care.

It is worth reflecting on the effect a lack of understanding can have on how we feel about ourselves and others around us, and how this lack of understanding can create a real sense of vulnerability.

Activity 4.1 Reflection

Cast your mind back to your first day on your most recent clinical placement. Think about the feelings that you had about working in a team of people you did not know, in an area with which you were unfamiliar and with patients whose conditions you perhaps did not fully understand. Think about how all these unknowns made you feel. How did you react? Who made you feel less at ease? Who made you feel more at ease? What did people do that made you feel more or less at ease? What lessons can you draw from this experience to help you to understand how patients might feel and behave in unfamiliar circumstances?

There are some possible answers and thoughts at the end of the chapter.

This activity emphasises that fear is a natural response to the unknown, and what people do and say can have a great impact. Understanding what may create feelings of vulnerability in ourselves can help us to understand which issues might create vulnerability in others. Managing our encounters with others and recognising the potential for conflict that arises out of our interactions allows us to demonstrate the important, people-centred aspects of leadership.

The potential for conflict can be heightened by the amount of specialisation and organisational hierarchy that is present in many clinical teams (Swansburg and Swansburg, 2002) (for more on managing conflict in teams, see Chapter 2). The manner in which we choose to present ourselves to others can heighten feelings of inadequacy and fear. The specialist knowledge we have in an area and the position we hold can be used to create barriers between us, our team and our patients. The idea of separation created by titles and roles is well demonstrated in the theory of **binary thinking** which demonstrates how we can create our own identities by comparing and contrasting ourselves with others (Davies, 2004).

We like to identify ourselves in various different ways as perhaps a parent, a partner, a nurse or a student. While these identities mean that we can explain who we are and what we do, they can also create a sense of difference between us and other people.

Concept summary: Binary thinking

Exploring the notion of binary identity and how this might apply in the clinical setting may help us to understand some of the ways in which conflict might arise. Within binary logic, 'A' is 'A' and anything that is not 'A' is 'something else'. Translated into the nursing workplace this may be seen as operating as: 'I am a nurse; you are not'; 'I know what is happening here; you do not'; 'I am the powerful professional; you are the compliant patient'; 'I know best; you do not'. You may have experienced this type of feeling yourself perhaps as a student nurse, or in relation to another more 'powerful' professional.

In this sense binary is seen as one of only two options, as in the code used to program computers where the only options available are 0 and 1. This tends to suggest strongly a sense of them and us – when someone is not one of us, they are something else.

In part, the differences expressed here represent some of the more negative aspects of creating for ourselves a professional identity which excludes others who do not share our identity (as a nurse, say) – sometimes called **othering**. This way of looking at ourselves creates a scheme whereby we see patients and non-nursing colleagues as 'other'. It is a small step from seeing ourselves as something different and set apart to the creation of conflict. Acting in ways which can be seen as highlighting and exploiting the differences between us as nurse and 'others' as patients, or us as leaders and 'others' as followers runs counter to everything we identified as important in the way of exercising our common values in Chapter 1.

Conflict often arises because of perceived, if not real, differences between the needs, wants and desires of individuals. When we as nurses, and nurse leaders, remember that we are people first and nurses second it will allow us to start to see something of the nature of the fear that being 'the other' brings. This realisation will help enable us not only to respond to, but to pre-empt, some of the conflict that arises as a result of fear and perceived isolation.

Activity 4.2   Critical thinking

Think about what binary thinking says about professional image and presentation of self to others in the care setting. How is binary identity used in the care setting to advantage the professional? Can you think of times someone has made you feel different or excluded by their behaviour? Have you used binary thinking to your own advantage? What approaches to self-presentation and leadership can stop these sorts of situations arising?

There are some possible answers and thoughts at the end of the chapter.

It is worth thinking critically about binary thinking here, not because it is a clever way of understanding how we create identities but because it reflects a way in which conflict may be generated. Quite clearly, using binary thinking theory, we can see divisions between individuals are readily created when we start to see ourselves as something other than fellow human beings. This idea translates well into how we might think about preventing conflict as well as how we lead others by example in the ways in which we interact with our managers, peers, those who work under our leadership and our patients.

Conflict may also arise in the clinical setting when staff disagree about the care and management of a particular patient. Sometimes conflict may arise because of an ethical dilemma, such as a family requesting that a loved one is not told her diagnosis when it appears she should be (Ellis, 2017). When ethical dilemmas occur, they can give rise to conflict between people with different views about how the issue should be resolved. Differences of views may then arise along professional boundaries, or between professionals and patients. Alternatively, they may result as a consequence of age, gender, status, culture, religion or experience (Northam, 2009a).

Binary theory helps us to understand what is going on in such situations where conflict arises. People who disagree with our point of view, instead of being accepted as people with another viewpoint, are regarded as 'other' and therefore become a legitimate target of attack. The role of the leader or manager in such situations is to focus the discussions back to the issue under dispute and away from the personalities involved.

The Chartered Institute of Personnel and Development (2007) identified general behaviour, disputes about performance, attendance at work and relationships between colleagues as being the main causes of conflict at work. Of note, people in public-sector employment rated relationships, bullying and harassment and all forms of discriminatory behaviour as being among the major causes of conflict at work.

Bullying takes many forms in the healthcare sector and can involve staff bullying other staff, staff bullying patients, patients bullying staff and visitors and relatives bullying staff. In a survey of NHS staff in England, 25 per cent reported having been bullied, harassed or abused in the last year by other NHS staff (NHS Employers, 2016) with 29.9 percent of NHS employees claiming to have experienced psychological stress as a result.

Bullying can take many forms. Some bullying is deliberate, whereas other bullying arises out of differences in perception and poor communication. Gossiping about someone, spreading rumours, ridiculing someone as well as being consistently rude or abusive, all constitute bullying behaviour.

Case study: Bullying

Steve was a newly qualified nurse who prior to becoming a nurse had undertaken a first degree and Master's degree in biology. Steve joined the team in the intensive care unit at his local hospital as a junior staff nurse and greatly enjoyed his job.

Amanda was one of the unit sisters who had been qualified for many years and was a very experienced nurse. When Steve was on shift with Amanda he was often allocated the patient in the isolation room. Steve got the feeling that Amanda did not like him and noticed that he was often overlooked for breaks and was never allowed to look after unusual cases in the main unit when she was on duty.

Steve felt that he was being bullied and started to become very unhappy at work. Steve raised his concerns with one of the unit charge nurses, Des. Des had also noticed the behaviours that Steve described and advised Steve to have a word with Amanda about it. When Steve asked to talk to Amanda, she was dismissive but Steve persisted. In the office Steve raised his concerns, saying he had joined the team to learn how to nurse in the intensive therapy unit and he was keen to be useful. He said he felt excluded by Amanda and that she appeared to have taken a dislike to him for no apparent reason. Amanda started to cry.

Amanda admitted that she felt intimidated by Steve as she had found out he had two degrees and she did not even have a diploma. Amanda admitted she was worried about her position in the team with bright young things threatening her status.

In this real-life case study, we can see that Amanda's behaviour has arisen out of her own fears about her position in the team. It could have all been so different, however; she might have treated Steve in the manner she did because she did not like men, he was gay, from a different ethnic background or she did not like his religious views. Quite clearly, any one of these alternative explanations is unacceptable, as is the fact that she was using her position to bully him because she felt threatened.

As well as understanding that bullying can take many forms, the other message from this scenario is that leaders and managers need also to be careful that their actions are not misinterpreted as bullying. This requires as we have discussed before, that the manager knows their staff group well and acts to develop a positive work place culture.

Activity 4.3   Evidence-based practice and research

Unfortunately, bullying and harassment are common workplace occurrences (see the statistic cited earlier). When you are next at work, find a copy of the local bullying and harassment policy and familiarise yourself with the definitions it contains as well as the local practices in relation to it. Also go on to the internet and find some definitions of bullying and list some of the effects it can have on an individual experiencing it.

As the answers to this activity will depend on the policy available in your own workplace, no outline answer is given.

What all of the examples of how conflict could emerge in the clinical setting have in common is that they all come about as a result of communication issues. Handling communication, perception, relationships and being self-aware are therefore important elements of conflict prevention and management.

Managing to reduce the potential for conflict

What we have seen so far in this chapter points to the fact that much conflict can be avoided. From the leadership and management perspective, as well as from the perspective of individual behaviours, there are a number of strategies which can be used to help prevent conflict. The key to reducing the potential for conflict lies in managing the environment of care in such a way that it is focused on achieving high-quality patient outcomes. Hocking (2006, p250) suggests that the route to achieving this is *through open communication, trust, and accountability.*

There is good reason to think as a leader or manager that treating the staff in our team as people first and as staff second can lead to an increase in the level of trust and reduce the potential for conflict – as well as signposting the values we want the staff to display in their interactions with each other and patients. A meta-analysis by Dirks and Ferrin (2002, p621) demonstrated that when team members trust a leader, they are more likely to work co-operatively and are less likely to act negatively towards each other and those around them: *As predicted, trust in leadership was most strongly related to work attitudes, followed by most of the citizenship behaviors, and finally job performance.*

In his widely cited piece of work, Scholtes (1998) identifies two elements to the generation of trust in leaders: first, that leaders are competent and able to do their job and second, they demonstrate that they care for the staff who work with them (see also p123). It is in the demonstration of caring about the welfare of staff, the exercise of the value of *person-centredness,* that the leader sets the tone for how the team will work with each other and patients.

The strategies for managing to reduce the potential for conflict are, like so many issues and ideas in leadership and management, heavily interlinked. The culture of the organisation, department or team all contribute to the ways in which conflict arises, is prevented, recognised and dealt with. Creating a culture where we learn from our mistakes and environments which allow people to develop and grow as individuals and professionals will have a great impact on reducing the likelihood of conflict arising in a team. While **learning organisations** are explored in more depth in Chapter 8, it is worth noting here that an organisation which allows people to make mistakes, learn from their mistakes and develop is more likely to reduce the likelihood of conflict arising and to handle conflict in a meaningful way. The same message translates well down to team level where a manager who encourages and supports learning enables members of the team to understand the root causes of conflict and how to deal with them.

Managing situations where conflict arises

When conflict does arise, there are a number of approaches that can be taken to manage it. The choice of which approaches to use will depend on the nature of the conflict: who is involved, where it is taking place and whether the conflict is physical or purely verbal in nature. The choice of approach to managing the situation will make a great deal of difference to the potential outcome of the situation. Thought should always be given to what strategy is right in any given situation, but if this is not possible it is always best to start with the minimum intervention required and scale up.

Table 4.1 gives some ideas about general approaches to managing conflict, along with when to use them and their pros and cons.

Collaboration: creates a potential situation where everyone can win and allows for creative solutions. It requires that the situation is worked through and a solution found which addresses concerns. This is useful where the conflict arises between individuals who either trust each other a lot or where there is pre-existing enmity. Collaboration, while it may be an effective means of managing conflict, can be time consuming and is open to abuse if both parties are not really committed to it.

Compromising: leads to a situation where everyone involved has to give a little ground. This may prove beneficial where the parties in the dispute are equally committed to their own point of view and where they are of similar status. It can speed up the process of resolving a dispute, but only when the exact outcome is not too important. Compromise may lead to a solution that is not acceptable to anyone and may not work if the sides are too far apart at the start.

Accommodating: is useful when one side of a conflict realises the issue is more important to the other side, or that s/he is wrong. Accommodating allows for **social capital** to be built up and called upon later and helps maintain relationships which may be more important than the disagreement. The problem with being accommodating is that people may see it as a sign of weakness and take advantage.

Competing: sometimes other avenues of reaching agreement have been exhausted, so when the point being made is correct it is important not to give in easily. On other occasions when someone is trying to forcibly get his or her way it is best to challenge the person. The experienced leader or manager will recognise that competition can escalate some conflicts and it may not be wise when the conflict is or may become physical in nature.

Dodging: is perhaps the best strategy when the conflict is not important, you are too busy to deal with an issue at that time, you need to cool off or there is no chance of winning. Dodging the issue can, however, make matters worse in the long run and may allow a transgressor to win. Dodging can be used as a short-term strategy by the manager but rarely results in a satisfactory solution to the issue of conflict.

Table 4.1   General approaches to managing conflict situations

Source: Adapted from Thomas and Kilmann (1974).

Activity 4.4   Critical thinking

Sue has been admitted to the orthopaedic ward following a fall in which she broke her arm. It is late evening and, just as visiting is about to finish, Dave, Sue's husband, arrives to visit her. You are asked by the ward sister to tell Dave that he must leave in 5 minutes, despite him having just arrived. Dutifully you tell Dave that visiting is nearly over and he must leave. Dave is angered by this and aggressively states that he has only just been able to get there and he should be allowed to see his wife and that the rules are ridiculous.

Use the strategies identified in Table 4.1 to think about the alternative approaches you might use to handle this situation. Which approach(es) best fit this particular scenario? Why?

There are some possible answers and thoughts at the end of the chapter.

What seems clear from the strategies in Table 4.1 is that different approaches will suit different scenarios. Constant use of one strategy will lead people to thinking that you do not have the **emotional intelligence** to work out when to change what you do in response to different situations. Knowing what strategy to employ is not something that is easily taught and, like emotional intelligence, it is something that comes with time, experience and reflection.

This activity, drawn from a real-life experience, demonstrates how rigid adherence to rules can be construed as insensitivity and so inflame what must already be a worrying situation. Clearly the right approach would have been not to provoke conflict in the first place, but to ask whether Dave knew the visiting times and why he had been so late. Perhaps a compromise might then have been reached without the need for generating bad feeling. Always the number one rule of conflict management is to avoid starting it in the first place.

There is a key message for the novice manager – rules need to be interpreted within the context of individual situations and not followed blindly. The emotionally intelligent manager will realise that on occasions breaking the rules is the right thing to do and that in exercising wise choices such as this s/he is demonstrating leadership rather than being weak.

Negotiation

Although it is easy to imagine **negotiation** is the starting point for dealing with all conflicts, in some instances it is not. Negotiation means trying to reach an agreement with another party when both parties share the same overall objective but perhaps differ on how this objective might be achieved. Negotiating is the process that is undertaken in order to reach a compromise solution to an issue. One of the fringe benefits of successful negotiation is that the relationship that builds up in a successful negotiation may lead to future collaboration.

The first rule of negotiation is to know what it is you want to achieve – the outcome that is acceptable to you. Once you know what is acceptable as a solution you know what ground you can give in the process and what you need to defend to achieve your goal. This is also the time to decide what the points of conflict are: why do you and the other party not agree?

The second most important negotiating skill is listening (Northam, 2009b). Listening not only allows you to understand the other person's point of view; it also creates opportunity for you to ask sensible questions about what they are saying.

The third rule of negotiation is to build on small successes, get agreement on small issues and then work up towards the main issue of the conflict. This allows for an environment of collaboration and agreement to be created and built upon. What are you willing to give up, and what is the other party willing to give up as part of the process?

Activity 4.5   Reflection

Taking the idea that negotiation, like most approaches to conflict resolution, requires **active listening**, consider the ways in which you can demonstrate to someone that you are listening to them. Consider your body language, the non-verbal and verbal cues you can give them and the sorts of questions you might ask to demonstrate engagement. Think especially about a recent interaction you have had which could have been tricky had you not used your verbal and non-verbal skills and, as with all reflection, think about what you did well and what you might do next time you encounter a similar situation.

As the answer to this activity is based on your own reflection, there is no specimen answer at the end of the chapter.

Mediation

Sometimes a dispute or conflict between individuals cannot be resolved by the individuals themselves. At this stage there is a need for a third party to help find a resolution to the issue. One approach to conflict resolution is the use of **mediation**. Mediation is not about the settlement of a dispute by the imposition of an agreement; rather, it is a means of facilitating a resolution that both parties can agree to. A mediator's role is that of an impartial third party who helps progress a solution to a problem.

In mediation, the mediator listens to both sides of an issue, sometimes in private, and then brings the two sides together to discuss their grievances. The mediator will try to identify common ground, things the two parties can agree on, and uses these in order to start building a resolution to a problem. Fundamental to the process of mediation is that both sides in a dispute agree to take part in the mediation process and that they are both willing to seek agreement. Reaching agreement is not simply about compromise, or one side backing down; instead, mediation seeks to build on small agreements until a consensus is reached.

Mediation is especially useful where two sides have a history of not working together as it helps to build relationships which allow for future development and joint working. For a leader, this may mean facilitating discussions between two members of a team who do not get on or who are in conflict about some aspect of their working life.

Activity 4.6   Evidence based practice and research

Next time you are in the workplace take the time to find the human resources policy which covers conflict between individuals and read the section about mediation. Also using the link at the end of this chapter go on line and look at what the Advisory, Conciliation and Arbitration Service's description of mediation.

As the answer to this activity is based on what you find, there is no specimen answer at the end of the chapter.

Arbitration

When the processes of negotiation or mediation fail, it may become necessary to look for other ways of resolving a dispute between two parties. Arbitration and conciliation, like mediation, employ the services of a third, impartial individual to help reach a resolution.

In arbitration, the role of the third party is to decide on and impose a final solution to the conflict. The decision that is reached is based on the third party gathering together all of the facts and coming to some conclusion about what should be done to resolve the issue. An arbitrator has the authority to impose the decision on those in dispute – however, there may be instances when one or both sides in a dispute feel unhappy about the result, creating continued tensions in the workplace. Leaders who have to arbitrate will therefore need to stick to their values and demonstrate emotional intelligence in managing such situations.

Case study: The rota

Ann and Claire are junior staff nurses on the same ward. There is a concert by a well-known band in the town in a couple of weekends' time and both Ann and Claire want to go. Both nurses are rostered to be at work at the time of the concert and so both approach the ward sister and ask for an early shift or the day off instead. The sister says that she needs one of them to work and that they must sort it out between them.

Ann and Claire, who aren't the best of friends anyway, soon get into a verbal fight about who should have the opportunity to go to the concert. The argument spills over from the staff room to the ward and the sister has to take them both into her office. Both Ann and Claire claim they need to have the evening off the most and again begin to squabble. The sister has to intervene and suggests that she will have to make the decision and they will have to abide by it as that is what is required. Reluctantly they both agree. The sister says that, as she cannot choose between them, then the original rota which was written without any knowledge of the concert must stand.

Whistle blowing

So far, the examples we have used all have some reasonable explanation and resolving the issues they create is relatively easy. Sadly, this is not always the case. Sometimes there are situations of conflict, bullying or harassment which are not amenable to being dealt with locally. Whistle blowing offers one avenue for people who witness, or who are experiencing, conflict or bullying in the workplace to get help.

Essentially, whistle blowing is the act of bringing an important issue to the attention of someone in authority. Sometimes whistle blowing occurs within a team or organisation. If there are issues with an organisation, however, whistle blowing may need to be external. Within the NHS there are policies in place for both forms of whistle blowing. In certain circumstances, these allow the whistle blower to remain anonymous.

The Public Information Disclosures Act 1998 protects people who blow the whistle about poor practices specifically where the worker has real concerns about any one of a number of issues (**www.legislation.gov.uk/ukpga/1998/23/contents**). Such issues for the manager or leader may include the health and safety of workers. As discussed earlier, this includes protecting staff from abuse and conflict and the subsequent impact of this on their health.

Activity 4.7   Evidence-based practice and research

When you are next at work find a copy of the local whistle-blowing, or raising concerns, policy and familiarise yourself with what it says. You may want to repeat this exercise when you are in university: you may find these policies on the local intranet.

As the answers to this activity will depend on the policy available in your own workplace, no outline answer is given.

Deciding to blow the whistle is a big step for anyone involved in conflict or bullying. In all such situations it is better, if possible, to try to come to some solution more locally. However, there are times, perhaps involving a legal or ethical issue, where whistle blowing may be the right thing to do. One example is to be found within the key findings of the Francis report (2013), which demonstrated too great a degree of tolerance of poor standards and of risk to patients, along with assumptions that monitoring, performance management or intervention was the responsibility of someone else.

These key findings suggest the culture prevented good practice in both care and in the communication of the lack of good care. Good care and intolerance of poor standards and risk to patients is everyone's concern and the need to do something about it, potentially by blowing the whistle, is something all nurse leaders should encourage.

Managing yourself

It may seem strange to say this towards the end of a chapter dealing with conflict, but the first point of reference for anyone involved in conflict is to ask if they, themselves, are the problem. Management of yourself and your relationships with other people is an important step on the road to becoming an effective leader and manager of others. Who wants to be led by a person who cannot manage him- or herself?

If you are not sure if you are the cause of the conflict you are experiencing there are two things you can do to be certain you are not. First ask yourself the question, 'do I have a problem with a lot of the people I work with?' If the answer is yes, then you may well be the person who has the problem, if no then you might not be. Second ask people you trust, perhaps people who are not dependent on you, if they think you are the cause of conflict. Again if they say yes, you are probably the problem, if they say no, you may not be.

Since differences of opinion, perception and power all play a role in creating conflict situations, it is important for prospective leaders and managers to be aware of the influences on their thinking as well as how they come across to others. It may be tempting to think that this can be achieved purely through reflection, but reflection alone is likely to produce a flawed view. Self-management is as much about self-development as it is about being aware of your own opinions, and if you are to develop you need to take on board feedback from other individuals.

It would be easy to say that, in order to avoid unnecessary conflict, you should always follow what you believe to be the moral and ethical thing to do. This over-simplifies the case for self-management, however. Evidently there are some ethical and moral principles which, if you believe in them and act on them, will mean you can usually justify your actions – it is the exercise of the principles that allows others to see the sorts of values we hold dear and what sort of person we therefore are (Ellis, 2017). Such principles might include treating others as equals and always trying to be fair. Rigid adherence to rules, as we saw in Activity 4.4, can lead to problems and so part of managing yourself is to learn when to adapt what you do to the situation. This means being open to the views of others and being able to adapt your behaviours when necessary, while not abandoning important ethical principles.

In essence this is about good communication, awareness of how others see you and how you behave and being aware of the perceptions of others. Mayer and Salovey (1993, p433) termed this ability emotional intelligence and described it as *a type of social intelligence that involves the ability to monitor one's own and others' emotions, to discriminate among them, and to use the information to guide one's thinking and actions.* There are essentially four elements to the Mayer–Salovey model of emotional intelligence: (1) the ability to identify emotions in yourself and others; (2) the ability to use emotion to communicate; (3) the ability to understand how emotional information is used to construct meaning; and (4) the ability to manage your own emotions.

Being able to read and understand the emotions that lie behind your own behaviours and the behaviours of others is helpful in identifying whether conflict is a result of your behaviours or a reasonable response to the behaviours of others. To grow your emotional intelligence, it is important to reflect on your own motivations, to ask others about their motivations, and to put this in the context of the situation in which you find yourself. The essence of conflict management, therefore, is honest communication with yourself and with others.

Chapter summary

In this chapter we have identified some of the causes of conflict which arise in the clinical setting. We have identified that perception plays a large part in how people feel about a situation and that poor management of a situation, often the result of poor or non-existent communication, is often the root cause of conflict.

We have identified that there are a number of strategies that can be employed by the nurse leader to prevent conflict from arising, to identify situations in which conflict may arise and to manage conflict when it does occur. The fundamental messages for the management of conflict appear to lie in the need for good communication, management of self and treating others as equals.

We have seen that not all conflict can be dealt with by the individuals involved in the conflict, and that it is sometimes necessary to involve a third party either to help those in conflict come to a negotiated settlement or to have a settlement imposed. As with all aspects of nursing and interpersonal relationships, the key skill of reflection (both alone and with others) is helpful in resolving situations that arise.

Activities: Brief outline answers

Activity 4.1 Reflection (p69)

Entering a new clinical area for the first time may have made you feel quite unsure about yourself and your own abilities and capacity to fit into the team. You may have been uncertain about where everything is kept and what the routine of the area is, as well as what would be expected of you. Some kind staff would tell you not to worry and might perhaps show you where things were and explain what they expected of you, while others might ignore you or make it quite plain that they were not happy about someone who was unable to pull his or her weight. The people you most admired and who most put you at your ease would probably be the staff who wanted to share their knowledge with you and who reassured you that in time you would understand what was expected of you as well as how to work effectively within the team.

Patients and visitors feel the same emotions. They are worried about what might happen, what is expected of them, who they will meet and how they will be treated. They also have the concerns that accompany being a consumer of healthcare, what the long-term outcomes might be, how they will be treated and who will be caring for them. Unlike the staff, they do not have the luxury of going home at the end of the shift or of having an education and training that prepare them to understand and make sense of their care. Because of this, they may well feel frightened and vulnerable; some may become aggressive or confrontational in order to hide their vulnerability.

Activity 4.2 Critical thinking (p71)

The answers to this issue lie in the way in which we choose to present ourselves to others, as well as the values we hold and the ways in which we choose to express these values. If we are quite clear in our interactions with patients and more junior staff that we are the knowledgeable professional and they are not, we will cause antagonism. If we choose to remember, as nurses and leaders of people, that we too are people and that we are dealing with people, then the ways in which we interact will demonstrate this, and will be less likely to give rise to behaviours that cause conflict to occur.

Avoiding othering is in fact quite simple, treating people as equals, asking their permission to do things 'May I take your blood pressure please?' and 'Would you please take Mrs Smith to the toilet?' demonstrate that we value the people we are interacting with, rather than treating them as in some way inferior.

Activity 4.4 Critical thinking (p75)

- Collaboration will require a discussion to take place about Dave's concerns and that you show understanding in reaching a solution which addresses them.
- Compromising will allow you to reach a mutually agreeable solution with Dave – perhaps allowing him to stay a little longer, but only on this occasion.
- Accommodating: allowing Dave to stay because of the circumstances would perhaps seem reasonable and will defuse the situation, but it may mean he abuses the system in the future.
- Competing would mean demanding Dave leaves and perhaps calling security. This would alienate both Dave and Sue, and may not be a good idea in the long run.
- Dodging: just walking away and hoping Dave will leave is not really an option as other patients in the ward will see what has happened and may choose to do the same with their visitors or may be disturbed by Dave's continued presence.

Further reading

Benson, G, Ploeg, J and Brown, B (2010) A cross-sectional study of emotional intelligence in Baccalaureate nursing students. *Nurse Education Today,* 30 (1): 49–53.

A study of emotional intelligence in nursing students and how it changes across the years of training.

Grant, A and Goodman, B (2018) *Communication and Interpersonal Skills in Nursing* (4th edition). London: SAGE.

See especially Chapter 4 on understanding potential barriers to safe and effective practice.

Hocking, BA (2006) Using reflection to resolve conflict. *Journal of the Association of Operating Room Nurses,* 84 (2): 249–59.

A helpful view of conflict management.

Thomas, J (2006) *Survival Guide for Ward Managers, Sisters and Charge Nurses.* London: Churchill Livingstone, Elsevier.

See especially the chapter on dealing with complaints.

Wedderburn Tate, C (2006) The art of managing difficult people. *Nursing Standard,* 20 (19): 72.

A brief but interesting look at managing difficult people.

Useful websites

www.cipd.co.uk/NR/rdonlyres/1EB2AE66-D1A8-4641-AB8B-B6C67D38E6D9/0/4334Managing conflictWEB.pdf

From the Chartered Institute of Personnel and Development, an easily understood guide to managing conflict at the personal and team level.

www.acas.org.uk/index.aspx?articleid=1364

The Advisory, Conciliation and Arbitration Service's guide to managing conflict at work.

http://www.acas.org.uk/index.aspx?articleid=1680

The Advisory, Conciliation and Arbitration Service's guide to mediation.

www.nmc-uk.org/Nurses-and-midwives/Raising-and-escalating-concerns

The Nursing and Midwifery Council's guidance on raising concerns and whistle blowing.

www.pcaw.co.uk

Public Concern at Work is the independent charitable authority on public-interest whistle blowing.

www.gov.uk/whistleblowing

UK governmental whistle-blowing guidance.

www.danielgoleman.info/topics/emotional-intelligence

The website of the most widely cited writer on emotional intelligence.

Chapter 5　Coaching, mentoring and clinical supervision

person-centred and evidence-based nursing interventions and support. They work in partnership with people to develop person-centred care plans that take into account their circumstances, characteristics and preferences.

At the point of registration, the registered nurse will be able to:

3.4   understand and apply a person-centred approach to nursing care, demonstrating shared assessment, planning, decision making and goal setting when working with people, their families, communities and populations of all ages.

Platform 5: Leading and managing nursing care and working in teams

Registered nurses provide leadership by acting as a role model for best practice in the delivery of nursing care. They are responsible for managing nursing care and are accountable for the appropriate delegation and supervision of care provided by others in the team including lay carers. They play an active and equal role in the interdisciplinary team, collaborating and communicating effectively with a range of colleagues.

At the point of registration, the registered nurse will be able to:

5.7   demonstrate the ability to monitor and evaluate the quality of care delivered by others in the team and lay carers.

5.8   support and supervise students in the delivery of nursing care, promoting reflection and providing constructive feedback, and evaluating and documenting their performance.

5.9   demonstrate the ability to challenge and provide constructive feedback about care delivered by others in the team, and support them to identify and agree individual learning needs.

5.10 contribute to supervision and team reflection activities to promote improvements in practice and services.

Chapter aims

After reading this chapter, you will be able to:

*   identify different methods of coaching;
*   recognise the different ways in which practice assessment and management may be applied;
*   understand the benefits of clinical supervision;
*   recognise the signs of burnout and methods to reduce these effects.

Introduction

The main emphasis in this chapter is on the support of staff through leadership and management techniques such as coaching, mentoring and clinical supervision.

This chapter will investigate when to coach to improve performance or achievements. Different forms of coaching and mentoring, whether in an educational role or as a supporting role model, will be discussed and compared as methods of staff support. Problem-solving and decision-making frameworks are included in the discussion on coaching techniques. Clinical supervision models will also be introduced and discussed. The concept of a **learning culture** will be explored. The detrimental effects of staff burnout will be considered, as will the notion of establishing a workplace environment that embraces the philosophy of work–life balance.

You may feel these roles do not belong to the nurse leader, perhaps fitting better within the development team or perhaps at university but, in reality, the techniques and ideas contained within this chapter can be applied throughout the working day as the nurse leader encounters different situations at work. For example, mentoring or coaching techniques can quite easily be seen in action as the nurse provides direction and support to more junior staff who are providing care, while clinical supervision can happen informally when the team need to debrief following a difficult day at work.

Coaching to improve performance

The term 'coaching' is more often used in the UK when referring to the training of athletes or performers, and may be caricatured by a person with a whistle and clipboard. You do not need to be a coach to provide coaching, as we shall see, but you do need to understand some of the necessary skills and have an understanding of the general approach.

Increasingly the term coaching is seen as referring to an approach used in encouraging the improved performance of skills. Coaching in this sense is based upon an interpersonal relationship between a manager or team leader and a team member; but might equally apply between a team leader and a member of their team, or between a registered nurse and a nursing assistant.

In Chapter 3, we spoke about staff development and touched on performance appraisal as a means of planning and supporting staff to improve their knowledge and skills. Coaching is one method of supporting others to improve in an individually tailored manner. It is based upon a belief that individuals can develop skills and knowledge through frequent interactions (often called one-to-one meetings, 1:1s, or perhaps confusingly supervisions) that are planned and carried out with an agreed outcome in mind.

The notion of coaching in organisations, and mentoring, which we will look at later in the chapter, as a management tool began with the introduction of the people management and development literature. It can be traced back to the situational leadership model developed by Hersey and Blanchard in the 1960s (Hersey et al., 2007). The model is composed of four quadrants (Figure 5.1). Within their model, Hersey and Blanchard's use the term coaching to mean the process by which the leader both leads and persuades followers to adopt a solution to a given situation. In this way the member(s) of staff is/are included both in the decision making and in making suggestions toward the

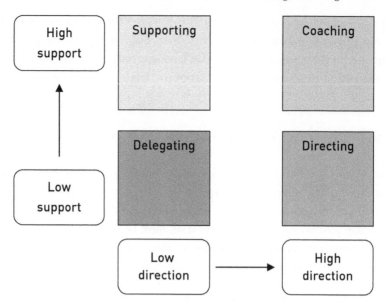

Figure 5.1 Hersey and Blanchard's situational leadership model
Source: Adapted from Hersey et al. (2007).

completion of the task. It is an approach that both motivates and builds team members competence.

In Chapter 3 we explored the work of Kotter (1990), who recognised the importance of matching one's leadership style to the level of commitment and competence of the individual staff member. Kotter's approach identifies to the manager when and how tasks should be passed on to the team member. This enables a leader to draw out the best in team members and identify where development needs to take place. The Hersey and Blanchard model extends this approach and stresses that the leader has to be flexible and have at the forefront the developmental needs of the individual and not only the appropriate delegation method.

The leader needs to select an approach, or combination of approaches, from one of four leadership styles:

1. telling/directing;
2. selling/coaching;
3. participating/supporting;
4. delegating.

These are matched, respectively, with one of four follower styles, or developmental levels of maturity in the individual:

1. high competence/high commitment;
2. high competence/variable commitment;
3. some competence/low commitment;
4. low competence/high commitment.

Depending on the maturational level of the person the leader provides high to low support along an axis of low to high direction. For example, the person with high commitment/high competence requires the least support and direction and can assume delegated tasks with minimal interference from the leader (as can be seen in Figure 5.1).

Case study: Teaching a procedure

David is a band 6 staff nurse, and Jasmine a new healthcare assistant. On Jasmine's second day, David spends 30 minutes telling her how to carry out a procedure to clean and redress a wound with the expectation that she will do this herself once the knowledge and skills required for the task have been thoroughly explained. David gives Jasmine instructions on what to use, why, when, where and to whom. Then he tells her he will come back in 2 hours' time to see how she is getting on.

When David returns, the wound has not been dressed with the appropriate dressing and he has to redo the dressing. This causes unnecessary discomfort to the patient and wastes time.

Although David may feel frustrated about this, questions have to be asked about the process of instruction that took place and whether it can be improved. Hersey and Blanchard maintain that leaders have to match the style of leadership to the maturity (or developmental style) and readiness (i.e. competence and motivation) of the person or team they are leading to perform a task. Thus, a simple telling and instruction session will not be sufficient. There needs to be an assessment of the individual's learning style, level of comprehension, confidence, motivation and a relationship established or developed between the leader and the 'follower'.

This means that David, as the senior, might be advised to take the following steps:

1. Make an overall assessment of Jasmine's scope of current tasks and activities. Determine her current workload and how she is coping with it.

2. Assess Jasmine's development level on the requested task by questioning and/or demonstration.

3. Decide on the leadership style.

4. Discuss with Jasmine the approach to be taken.

5. Follow up and discuss progress; correct where necessary.

Activity 5.1   Critical thinking

Imagine you are the leader of the team on a shift in a busy female medical ward and are asking a junior member of staff to undertake a task similar to the one delegated to Jasmine in the scenario. Write out an imaginary short story of how you would have tackled the five steps above. What factors would you take into account? You may want to revise your knowledge of Mumford's (1999) learning styles to help you consider how individuals learn. A web link is in the useful websites section at the end of the chapter to help you here. Which leadership approach would you take to coach the junior member of staff based upon your version of events? Try to see it from the junior staff's point of view as well as the senior's perspective.

As this answer is based on your own reflection, there is no outline answer at the end of the chapter.

Since the introduction of situational leadership, other approaches have been developed in coaching methods for work improvement. In the UK, the notion of coaching as a metaphor for improving performance came to prominence with the publication of *The Inner Game of Tennis* (1974), by Tim Gallway, who went on to publish *The Inner Game of Work* (2000). The latter drew on a philosophy summarised as *Performance = Potential minus Interference.* Thus the coach's job was to release the self-knowledge and potential that everyone possesses rather than deliberately instructing an individual towards achievements. The key ingredient was to develop greater self-awareness and a sense of responsibility in the performer. Since these early proposals, and a call for more evidence-based approaches utilising such philosophies, a body of literature has grown to support the coaching approach (Grant, 2001).

Activity 5.2   Reflection

Consider the notion that performance = potential minus interference. What does this mean? Have you ever found yourself frustrated because you know what to do and someone else interferes? What impact did interference have on your motivation and your ability to complete the task in hand? What impact did it have on your relationship with your leader? Conversely if you are a leader are you guilty of preventing your staff from reaching their full potential because you interfere too much?

As this answer is based on your own reflection, there is no outline answer at the end of the chapter.

The GROW technique

Developed from the original Gallway texts is a coaching technique that relies on using questions and which follows a structure to involve the person in problem solving as well as learning. Known as the GROW technique, the idea is to use a simple guided set of questions that can form the basis of a discussion in a coaching session or as a means of establishing the developmental level of a person to be supported. The aim is to assist the person to think about the problem/task at hand and identify a solution or range of options.

An easy way to remember the structure of the questions is to refer to the mnemonic that summarises the GROW technique in this way:

- Establish the *goal.*
- Examine the *reality.*
- Consider all *options.*
- Confirm the *will* to act.

This approach has been found to be helpful in improving motivation with a person who has basic knowledge, expertise and enthusiasm. However, with inexperienced learners this can be time consuming and not practical for day-to-day work-based situations (Parsloe and Leedham, 2009). For this approach to be effective the questions need to be expanded, undertaken over a period of time and yet remain focused on the main goal to be achieved. The prominent factor is that the coaching is undertaken as a conversation, with two-way communication between the person and the leader or manager.

The 3 D technique

A more rapid approach is known as the 3 D technique. When time is really short and a solution to a problem has to be identified quickly the technique is to identify elements on three dimensions:

1. The situation – for example timescales, lack of resources, lack of expertise.
2. People involved – for example, unhappy, impatient, unreliable, over-confident.
3. You – for example, lack of knowledge, conflicting priorities, general attitude.

From this analysis it is possible, by using questioning techniques around the dimensions, to draw out potential actions or plans.

Activity 5.3   Reflection

This activity is designed to help you with rapid coaching and skill building.

Practise the 3 D technique on yourself to coach yourself through a problem by following the following steps:

1. Define a current problem in a single sentence.
2. List three general issues relating to the problem situation.
3. List three issues relating to the people involved.

4. List three issues that relate specifically to you and the problem.
5. Choose one issue from each of your three lists of three issues.
6. Now identify one or more actions/options that are most likely to make progress in solving the problem.

As you are going through the steps, imagine you are asking yourself questions and make a note of the coaching questions you ask, to reflect later if they were the right questions to ask.

You may want to gain further skills in this approach by working with a fellow student or friend on a problem either you or s/he wishes to solve. In this way you not only develop your own skills; you can also ask for feedback on the different types of questions you need to ask to elicit answers that are helpful from your colleague or friend.

As this answer is based on your own reflection, there is no outline answer at the end of the chapter.

You may now be thinking that there is an overlap between the role of coach and the practice assessment role you are experiencing in your practice learning and you would be right. However, there are subtle differences, which we will look at in the next section.

Mentoring

Mentor was the name of a character in Greek mythology, the tutor of Odysseus' son Telemachus in Homer's *Odyssey*. So he could hardly be more different from the person with a whistle and clipboard described earlier in this chapter.

The tutoring Mentor offered was not restricted to the giving of information; rather he encouraged the exploration of subjects such as virtue, integrity, responsibility and character development. He was a trusted and wise counsellor. This historical meaning has remained in use over time and is still used today for someone who has acted as a role model or who has had a significant influence on a person's career or professional outlook on life. The term 'coach' is a more recent one and is used specifically to describe the growth in skills and knowledge towards a higher or improved level. More recently the NMC has replaced the term mentor with the terms practice supervisor and practice assessor.

Confusingly, coaching can also be incorporated into a mentoring role. The term mentoring, today, can cover several roles, such as coach, adviser, guide, confidant/e, teacher, role model, counsellor, friend, consultant, critic and advocate. The Nursing and Midwifery Council (NMC) has identified standards for the practice supervisors and assessors (formerly called mentors, although we will use mentoring as a description of a form of management and leadership supporting and developing practice supervision and assessment when referring to the support and development of students) of nursing and midwifery students; these standards apply to already registered nurses who take on this role in addition to their day to day duties.

Activity 5.4   Evidence-based practice and research

Go to the website address in the useful websites section for the NMC *Standards to Support Learning and Assessing in Practice* and review the standards in section 2 for mentoring, in the future to be called practice supervision and assessment. Think about how you will undertake this role when you become a qualified nurse and how you will plan to take a recognised practice supervision and assessment education programme.

This activity aims to help you understand more fully the role of practice supervising and assessing nursing students but also encourages you to think about your own personal development plan as well as your engagement with the notion of lifelong learning.

You may want to discuss with your practice supervisor his or her experience of taking the practice supervision and assessing course and of being a practice supervisor and assessor to students. Reflect on what you can learn from your practice supervisor's experiences.

As a final part of this research activity, ask your practice supervisor if s/he had or has a practice supervisor now that s/he is qualified and, if so, what impact this has had on their working life.

As this answer is based on your own research and reflections, there is no outline answer at the end of the chapter.

Research summary: Multiprofessional views of mentorship

Bray and Nettleton (2007) researched the role of the mentor in nursing, midwifery and medicine using questionnaires and semi-structured telephone interviews with both mentors and mentees. They were interested in any differences in the professional perceptions of the role. They were also interested in the potential dilemma that mentors, who are perceived as wise guides, have to become assessors and make judgements on their mentees' abilities. This could be viewed as a conflict of interest. They found that for nurse mentors the roles of teacher, supporter and role model were most important, with only 5 per cent indicating assessor as part of the role. By contrast, in midwifery the role of facilitator came higher than teacher and similarly few regarded assessor as part of the role. Within medicine, advisor and supporter were regarded as most important, with only 2 per cent regarding assessing as important.

When asked about any aspect of the role they found most difficult, both nurses and midwives reported difficulties in being objective towards their students when they had become 'supportive friends'. In medicine, less difficulty was reported with the assessor role. The biggest difficulty was finding time to commit to the role and all its aspects.

Bray and Nettleton found that across the professions there was a lack of clarity about the combination of the role of assessor with mentor. They admit that they had a small sample and have reservations about the **generalisability** of their findings. Yet, they make an interesting observation that, as we move towards further collaboration within multidisciplinary professional teams, a multiprofessional approach should be adopted towards defining the role and function of mentoring in healthcare professional education.

The confusion about the nature and purpose of mentoring remains a perennial problem within nursing. Nowell et al. (2017) identify that even in academic institutions there is a lack of clarity about what mentorship means and its general purpose in the development of mentees. Benner et al. (2009) describe both the novice and the advanced beginner nurse as requiring a mentor. They see a mentor as someone, perhaps an experienced nurse, whose role it is to assist with defining situations, setting priorities and integrating practical knowledge into working situations. Being in a relationship with a mentor aids nurses in their development from novices to an expert practitioners (Benner, 1984). Certainly, within the trainee model in the UK, the NMC have decided to split the role of the practice supervisor and assessor and stop using the term mentor for pre-registration practice supervisors and assessors.

Mentoring in other contexts

While we may be familiar with mentoring and practice supervision and assessment in healthcare settings, it is worth noting that mentoring takes place in other sectors and organisations outside of healthcare education. We can learn from these relationships as they provide a contrast to the practice supervisor and assessor experienced in healthcare, as well as ideas for opportunities for service development and relationships. This could be to develop entrepreneurial or business skills (see Chapter 7), or alternatively to enhance working in community settings or with third-sector or voluntary services groups in the fields of mental health and learning disabilities. One example can be in business-to-business relationships where a mentor from a large organisation may work with a small organisation to advise on development and growth. In business-to-social-enterprise relationships, organisations like the Prince's Youth Business Trust have mentors to guide young starters who have received grants from the Trust. Similar to this are training schemes supported by the government.

Providing mentoring to special needs or community projects has become an important part of community university engagement schemes, where more personal or individually tailored mentors are matched to individuals (Schuetze and Inman, 2010). Working the other way around, business people can work with education (e.g. head teachers, universities and students) to advise on business skills. There are also 'buddying' schemes between first- and third-year students, which are another version of mentoring.

Broadly speaking there are three main types:

1. The corporate mentor, who is a guide or counsellor in someone's career from orientation into the company to senior management.
2. The qualification mentor, who is required by a professional organisation – such as the NMC – to guide candidates towards achieving a qualification, including NVQs.
3. The community mentor, who acts as a guide or counsellor to individuals who may be disadvantaged, experiencing social inclusion or in a distressing situation (see the Mentoring and Befriending Foundation in the useful websites section at the end of this chapter).

Throughout these discussions there has been a tacit acknowledgement that everyone needs access to guidance or experienced advice at several points in their professional lives. Returning to the model of development associated with the seminal work of Benner (1984) it is clear that even experienced nurses return to the role of the novice when they move to new areas of work or take on new roles.

The notion of lifelong learning, mentioned earlier, is highly relevant in nursing where care may not change but clinical treatments are constantly evolving. Consequently, we need to be prepared to update our practice and ensure our practice is meeting the needs of the client group with whom we work. Gaining experience in a given field is one way to add to our skills and knowledge. Seeking the guidance of a clinically experienced practitioner is another means of reflecting and learning from everyday practice. Often termed clinical supervision, it is the focus of the next section.

Clinical supervision

Thomas (2006) claims some nurses have become too focused on definitions of clinical supervision and that it is simply someone who is more expert than you, with whom you can have regular contact to help reflect and learn (for a more detailed literature review, see Further reading). She suggests this could be a nurse specialist, a consultant doctor, a nurse consultant or another more experienced ward manager. Thomas maintains that all nurses should have access to clinical supervision. A more junior nurse can be matched with a more experienced nurse who is not a direct assessor or appraiser, thus providing a basis for a trusting relationship to develop. The aim is to build up a relationship so that the clinical supervisor can be contacted in times of need, rather than you just meeting them at set times. This model may be suitable for busy acute adult care environments but may not suit all situations, specialties and fields of practice.

Activity 5.5   Critical thinking

Supervision can be on a one-to-one basis or in groups. Think about the advantages and disadvantages of each approach and draw up a list to compare.

Further guidance is given on this activity at the end of the chapter.

There are very specific and different statutory requirements for supervision of midwives and the NMC has standards for the selection and activities of supervisors of midwives. In mental health settings, clinical supervision was introduced into pre-registration education in 1994 and in 1995 the UK Central Council for Nursing and Midwifery (forerunner of the NMC) declared clinical supervision should be in all fields of nursing and midwifery. The literature suggests that the number of nurses receiving clinical supervision varies between regions and specialties. Similarly, the length of time and training for providing supervision is variable.

There do seem to have been technical advances made in the delivery of clinical supervision in community settings using telephone conferencing and similar techniques. However, the majority of research literature concerns the educational provision of clinical supervision in pre-registration nursing courses (Butterworth et al., 2007). Employer organisations and their influence on implementing a culture for clinical supervision are seen as crucial themes in the literature. The factors influencing levels of engagement in organisations appear to be culture, availability of time, supervisor numbers and local factors. The role of the organisation in creating a culture of learning will be discussed next.

The learning organisation

Learning organisations are seen by many as the way in which organisations will have to manage their structures for the twenty-first century. Up until the mid-1980s it was quite possible to have a successful organisation without mentioning the word *learning*. As we move further into the twenty-first century, there is a world of global information and technologically driven organisations. Speed will be important to communicate changes and information management systems are increasingly important, as we see in practice with electronic patient records etc. The importance of information, information management and information sharing means people in healthcare and health and social care organisations need to learn to do things differently and in a more timely manner. New information is constantly becoming available, requiring new ideas to be adopted and skills and knowledge to be continuously updated.

In healthcare we have seen the implementation over the last ten years of developments such as telemedicine, microsurgery, stem cell research, patient-held records, shared patient management systems and many other technological and pharmacological advances. In addition, there are constant pressures to reduce costs and maximise efficiencies, which have led to a short-term focus on immediate results and constant efforts to rationalise the number of employees in organisations.

There is a conflict, therefore, between the organisation's need to manage the learning potential of its employees actively and the pressures to change employment practices and professional roles. Not surprisingly, there is a culture of resistance to change if professional status and roles are eroded or services are seen to be reduced.

Case study: Changing the skill mix

The scene is a community healthcare setting. Two new roles have been introduced into the health visiting team to improve the skill mix. Joan, a nursery nurse, is employed to carry out focused parenting skills training over 6 weeks with families, providing weekly support to learn new skills. Joan is also available for advice at child health clinics. Usha is a staff nurse who used to work on a children's ward. She has a children's nursing qualification and experience, and is now employed to perform 3-month developmental checks in the home. She is also available for pre-school checks to work with the school nurses. This frees up time for Liz, Jamil and Frances (the three health visitors in the team) to deal with complex family cases and public health initiatives. These kinds of cases have become much more prevalent in their caseloads and, while they would like to continue with providing a service to all mothers and their families, they realise that they need to focus their specialist expertise on more complicated cases where they can give extra time. Liz, Jamil and Frances are encouraged to undertake specialist, post-qualifying courses in child protection and public health. Joan (the nursery nurse) and Usha (the staff nurse) are also given the opportunity to go on to further training: Joan to become a registered nurse and Usha to become a registered community health visitor and public health nurse. The team manager and the organisation (as part of its staff development strategy) are prepared to sponsor them for future training for career development. This also supports the organisation's strategy for succession planning and maintaining a learning culture.

This is an example of where new roles have been introduced into the team that are less costly than the health visitors to employ, which means efficiencies have been made. But Joan and Usha have the potential and ability to make a significant contribution to the work of the team as well as supporting the notion of a learning culture. At the same time the experience and skills of the health visitors, Liz, Jamil and Frances, are maximised and not diminished by the inclusion of new roles into the team.

It is always worth your while looking into the staff development strategy of the organisation you will go to work for after you qualify to see what opportunities there are for you to develop promotion opportunities or a career pathway.

The main features of a learning organisation are:

- an increased focus on learning and development to ensure organisational effectiveness and a sustainable future;
- encouraging as many people as possible to become coaches, practice supervisors and assessors or clinical supervisors to ensure learning takes place in the workplace;
- establishing training programmes in coaching, practice supervision and assessment and clinical supervision;
- generating a culture that accepts the need to move from current standards of performance to higher levels to ensure continuous improvements in performance;
- supporting individuals to manage their own learning to develop their skills, maximise potential and enable a satisfactory work–life balance (adapted from Parsloe and Leedham, 2009).

Activity 5.6   Critical thinking

Imagine you are working in a hospice and your manager has asked you to take on responsibility for managing all student placements. This role means you have to think about the learning needs of students from a variety of professional backgrounds, paying special consideration to what they might need to learn while on placement with you. How will you develop the culture of the team so that your hospice becomes a *learning environment?*

Hints

1. Would you first find out what kind of students attend the hospice and who the practice supervisors and assessors are?
2. Would you undertake an informal survey of their views on how to create a learning environment and one that considers, and that would benefit, multidisciplinary team working if more than one profession is represented?
3. Would you draw on any of your positive learning experiences as a student in other settings?
4. Would you look for any evidence in the literature of other initiatives to create learning environments or evidence to support your initiative?
5. Would you draw up your ideas into a proposal, citing the advantages and disadvantages of your ideas and a plan of implementation for discussion in the team meeting?

As this answer is based on your own research and reflections, there is no outline answer at the end of the chapter.

The adoption of a learning culture in the health and social care workplace is in essence a reflection on the values of the workplace. Workplaces which value people, and their development, are likely to be workplaces which attain good standards in patient care, as opposed to workplaces where staff are not valued and therefore the work they do is valueless to them as well. One of the values underpinning nursing is the desire to provide the best care possible, often expressed as the value of *striving for excellence.* This is best achieved by a motivated workforce working in an environment which rapidly adopts improved ways of working and new practices, such as are found in a learning organisation. In this respect, creating a learning organisation as a nurse leader is a reflection of the core values of nursing.

Burnout and work–life balance

Throughout this chapter we have discussed ways that leaders and managers can support team members and colleagues. With increasingly complex workloads and demanding resource pressures we have to consider the effects this can have on the working life of the individual. In extreme cases staff may experience degrees of burnout. It is important to recognise the early signs of burnout before it takes hold and also to look at ways of creating a work setting with a philosophy of encouraging and supporting a healthy work–life balance.

Burnout

Burnout is defined as a prolonged response to chronic emotional and interpersonal stressors on the job and is defined by the three overwhelming dimensions of exhaustion, cynicism and sense of inefficacy (Maslach, 2003). Unlike acute stress reactions, which develop in response to specific situations, burnout is a cumulative reaction to work stressors; that is it tends to be chronic and its onset is low and perhaps, in some cases, hard to detect. The emphasis is on the process of gradual psychological erosion and the social outcomes rather than physical outcomes of this chronic exposure. Burnout is therefore the result of prolonged exposure to chronic interpersonal stressors. Exhaustion, cynicism and a sense of inefficacy are the predictors; however, other workplace factors, such as working in care-giving environments where there is a sense of giving with little regard for self, as well as reduced resources, have been found to compound the likelihood of burnout (Heeb and Haberey-Knuessi, 2014).

Research summary: Burnout

In 2002, as part of a larger survey into the relationship between qualified nursing staff and quality of patient care outcomes, Aiken et al. studied the relationship of burnout to qualified nurse/patient ratios. They found that higher emotional exhaustion and increased job dissatisfaction were strongly and significantly associated with nurse/patient ratios. Their findings indicated that increasing a ratio of patients to nurses by one patient could increase emotional exhaustion. This implied that nurses in hospitals with patient:nurse ratios of 8:1 would be 2.29 times as likely as ratios of 4:1 to show signs of high emotional exhaustion.

In 2006, Edwards and colleagues surveyed community mental health nurses using the Maslach Burnout Inventory (MBI) and the Manchester Clinical Supervision Scale (MCSS) to identify whether effective clinical supervision could have a positive effect on burnout. Their findings indicated on the MBI that 36 per cent of staff had high levels of emotional exhaustion, 12 per cent had high levels of depersonalisation and 10 per cent had low levels of personal accomplishment. Those nurses who had completed six sessions of clinical supervision scored lower MBI scores and higher scores on the MCSS, which indicated effective supervision (Edwards et al., 2006).

These two studies are examples of the extensive research undertaken in this area and which offer means of early detection and solutions to minimise effects in the workplace.

Work–life balance

Linked to the subject of burnout is the more recent concept of work–life balance. This is about people having a measure of control over when, where and how they work. It is achieved when an individual's right to a fulfilled life inside and outside paid work is accepted and respected as the norm, to the mutual benefit of the individual, business and society. Striking a balance between the needs of the individual employee, customer and organisation demands the following:

- For employees: Different individuals will have different expectations and needs at different times in their life.
- For customers: Organisations need to respond to the demands of their customers if they are to continue to be successful.
- For organisations: Organisations need to be able to manage costs, maintain profitability and ensure that teams work effectively together.

In 2010, an estimated one in five UK workers were mothers, 25 per cent of all families were single-parent families, and up to ten million people were caring for elderly relatives. By 2022 there will be one million fewer workers under 50 and three million more over 50. We now live in a 'service' world where customers increasingly expect a personalised, 24/7 service (The Work Foundation, 2008). The demands on workers to juggle home life, health and happiness are even greater in the twenty-first century than ever before.

Case study: Work–life balance

This example is from the Work Foundation, a not-for-profit organisation that has the aim of improving working life. The Good Hope Hospital in Birmingham had a project to improve work–life balance through improving recruitment and retention. The

(Continued)

hospital had 2,841 employees, with 81 per cent women and 14 per cent ethnic minorities. Staff turnover was high, at 18 per cent (this includes 12 per cent voluntary leavers but excludes completed contracts such as doctors on 6 months). Eighty-five per cent of women returned to work after maternity leave.

The NHS in general, including Good Hope Hospital, was facing a recruitment and retention crisis. The response was to introduce a system of self-rostering, whereby nurses choose the shifts they want to work rather than the traditional off-duty system of nurses writing down the shifts they cannot work. The off-duty system, apart from being extremely time consuming, was open to abuse and favouritism and was well recognised as being a cause of friction on wards.

The computerised RosterPro system turned the whole process on its head, and removed the administrative burden from the nurse manager. Once a month nurses simply enter the shifts they want to work on to the computer. As well as identifying their availability, the nurses are able to assign a preference rating to each shift. RosterPro does the rest, with the system allocating shifts on a fair and equitable basis.

Overall benefits were:

- improved staff morale;
- boost in recruitment rates;
- reduction in staff turnover from 14.4 per cent to 9.3 per cent;
- huge administrative burden released from ward managers;
- sickness and absenteeism rates greatly reduced;
- average sickness at Good Hope reduced from 6 per cent to 5 per cent (against an increase on wards with no self-rostering);
- better customer care, due to staff having a better work–life balance;
- 15 per cent increase in staff being able to work the hours of their choosing in the space of 1 year;
- improvement in computer literacy amongst nursing staff in practice.

An example of a nurse who has benefited from the introduction of self-rostering is Auveen, a ward sister and mother. Auveen's story can be found on the Work Foundation website (see the useful websites at the end of this chapter), but in short, the flexibility of self-rostering allows her to manage her work–life balance so she has time for her husband and children, and her work. Auveen works 37½ hours a week and, using RosterPro, chooses her shifts to allow her to make time for activities with her two young children. For example, if her children have after-school activities or an appointment with the dentist, Auveen can work an early shift to accommodate this. The Work Foundation's account quotes her as saying: 'Whether I'm providing an after-school taxi service or spending time doing homework with the children, I love the fact that my job now allows me this flexibility. I firmly believe that young minds need to be nourished and my working pattern allows me to spend quality time with the children that a fixed-hours job just wouldn't allow.'

It may not always be possible to introduce the flexible work scheduling in the example above; however, working creatively with the philosophy of creating a work–life balance in the workplace will go some way to improving difficult working lives. In the useful websites section you will find further ideas which you may wish to take to your workplaces and discuss with your teams.

Chapter summary

In this chapter you have explored three different methods of staff support that can improve staff performance as well as improve work–life balance. Coaching can be used to improve performance and problem solving. It does not have to be undertaken by an expert in the field of practice. Mentoring has many different forms and can include coaching. Clinical supervision is usually undertaken by an expert in the field around a very specific area of knowledge.

It is essential for twenty-first-century organisations to create a learning culture if they are to keep abreast of innovations, support staff morale and encourage personal development options. In addition, the pressures of contemporary life need to be supported by initiatives to bring about a balance between work and personal life. Leaders at all levels in the organisation have a part to play in creating these environments. Environments of care are influenced directly by the way in which leaders exercise their values, which need to remain central to everything they do.

Activities: Brief outline answers

Activity 5.5 Critical thinking (p95)

Clinical supervision	Advantages	Disadvantages
• Group supervision	• More people seen at one time, saving time • A variety of ideas can be offered from different perspectives • Helps with team building	• Takes more people away from the clinical area at one time • Requires an experienced/trained facilitator • May not meet everyone's specific needs
• One-to-one	• More personal and focused • Deeper trusting relationship can be established • Can specifically match specialty advice	• Could become too intense • Personalities may not match • More resources required for time

Further reading

Benner, P (1984) *From Novice to Expert: Excellence and Power in Clinical Nursing Practice.* Menlo Park: Addison-Wesley.

One of the most influential pieces of work on the development of the nursing student.

Cummins, A (2009) Clinical supervision: The way forward? A review of the literature. *Nurse Education in Practice,* 9: 215–20.

This article gives a more recent review of the clinical supervision literature and how it complements mentorship and preceptorship programmes postqualification.

Koy, V, Yunibhand, J, Angsuroch, Y and Fisher, M (2017) Relationship between nursing care quality, nurse staffing, nurse job satisfaction, nurse practice environment, and burnout: literature review. *International Journal of Research in Medical Sciences,* 3 (8): 1825–31.

An interesting review of the causes of burnout in nursing.

Parsloe, E and Leedham, M (2009) *Coaching and Mentoring: Practical Conversations to Improve Learning.* London: Kogan Page.

Gives useful detail on how to conduct the coaching conversation and advice on how to deal with difficult conversations.

Thomas, J (2010) *A Nurse's Survival Guide to Leadership and Management on the Ward* (2nd edition). London: Churchill Livingstone/Elsevier.

A pocket-sized, practically focused guide to surviving in a new managerial role. It does what it says in the title and is a very easy, quick reference guide.

Useful websites

http://rapidbi.com/created/learningstyles.html#honeymumfordlearningstyleslsq

Learning styles review: several learning styles theories are displayed on this url; however, the overview of Honey and Mumford's four learning styles – activist, reflector, theorist and pragmatist – will be particularly helpful for Activity 5.1.

www.nmc-uk.org/Educators/Standards-for-education/Standards-to-support-learning-and-assessment-in-practice

This link will take you to the NMC *Standards to Support Learning and Assessing in Practice.* See section 2.1 for the standards for mentorship.

www.mandbf.org

Website of the Mentoring and Befriending Foundation.

www.princes-trust.org.uk

The Prince's Youth Business Trust, which has mentors to guide young starters who have received grants from the Trust.

www.gov.uk/browse/working/finding-job

Similar to the above are training schemes supported by the government, as detailed on this site.

Chapter 6 — Frameworks for management and leadership

(Continued)

At the point of registration, the registered nurse will be able to:

5.5 safely and effectively lead and manage the nursing care of a group of people, demonstrating appropriate prioritisation, delegation and assignment of care responsibilities to others involved in providing care.

Chapter aims

After reading this chapter, you will be able to:

* identify the features of leadership and management;
* discuss what features of management and leadership are appropriate in nursing;
* relate some management and leadership theories to your own experiences of practice;
* consider which aspects of leadership and management you would like to develop in yourself.

Introduction

The purpose of this chapter is to provide some definition and enable you to understand what it means to be a leader or manager in health and social care. To appreciate leadership and management for nursing fully it is important that any definition of the roles leaders and managers hold includes not just a theoretical explanation of what they do, but also some explanation of how they might be applied in nursing as well as why they are important to practice.

This chapter will advance some of the ideas seen in Chapter 1, where the key characteristics of leaders and managers as might be experienced by student nurses were explored.

Are leadership and management different?

Some commentators on leadership and management regard them to be totally different from each other – a manager is a manager and a leader is a leader. More commonly, and perhaps more correctly, one could say that leadership is one of the roles of a manager in health and social care, whereas leadership can be everyone's responsibility depending on their position, the roles they are given and the situations in which they find themselves.

This may seem a difficult idea to grasp, but consider all the people who display leadership qualities, or who undertake leadership roles, in the clinical setting. These people may include individuals who have responsibility for leading a small team, some of whom may be at the same grade. Other leaders may have specific roles in the team, such as a wound care or moving and handling co-ordinator. On occasions people may have to show leadership because of a situation that arises. Such individuals are not perhaps always managers, but they are leaders, even if that leadership is transient and only applies to certain tasks or situations.

Managers on the other hand are most often defined by their position and job title, e.g. a ward manager, community team manager or outpatients manager. While such individuals are managers, part of their role will include displaying some of the activities of leadership, as described later in the chapter.

Pascale (1990, p65) memorably suggests that: *Managers do things right, while leaders do the right thing.* The proposition here is that managers are bound by and follow policy and procedures, while leaders follow their intuition and understanding of people to get things done. In 1989, Bennis famously explored the comparisons between what he saw as the key features of leadership and listed 12 key differences between managers and leaders:

1. Managers administer; leaders innovate.
2. The manager is a copy; the leader is an original.
3. Managers maintain; leaders develop.
4. Managers focus on systems and structure; leaders focus on people.
5. Managers rely on control; leaders inspire trust.
6. Managers have a short-range view; leaders have a long-range perspective.
7. Managers ask how and when; leaders ask what and why.
8. Managers have their eye always on the bottom line; the leader's eye is on the horizon.
9. Managers imitate; leaders originate.
10. Managers accept the status quo; leaders challenge it.
11. Managers are the classic good soldier; leaders are their own person.
12. Managers do things right; leaders do the right thing.

We can see in these comparisons that managers are regarded as having the interests of the organisation at heart and that they achieve this by following the rules and maintaining the status quo.

Daft (2001) further expands on Bennis' ideas:

13. Managers plan and budget; leaders create vision and set direction.
14. Managers generally direct and control; leaders allow room for others to grow, and change them in the process.

15. Managers create boundaries; leaders reduce them.

16. The manager's relationship with people is based on position power; the leader's relationship and influence are based on personal power.

17. Managers act as boss; leaders act as coaches, facilitators and servants.

18. Managers exhibit and focus on: emotional distance, expert mind, talking, conformity and insight into the organisation; leaders exhibit and focus on: emotional connectedness, open-mindedness, listening, non-conformity and insight into self.

19. Managers maintain stability; leaders create change.

20. Managers create a culture of efficiency; leaders create a culture of integrity.

What we can see in these definitions is the focus on emotional connections with the team on the part of the leader, and remoteness and a controlling attitude from the manager. What seems clear from these distinctions is that some of these qualities will suit some situations at different times, but it is unlikely that one or the other approach will always be the right way to deal with all situations that arise in nursing.

It is worth noting again that leadership is also one of the roles of the manager and so the distinctions drawn here may be somewhat artificial. Nurses in the care setting need to demonstrate the qualities of both leaders and managers.

Activity 6.1 Reflection

Think back to some of your experiences in clinical practice and consider the types of leaders and managers you encountered while there. What were the characteristics of the people in charge you admired? Why did you admire these characteristics?

There are some possible answers and thoughts at the end of the chapter.

Considering the differences in the above comparisons and the answers you gave to the activity, you may start to form the opinion that leaders are better than managers in the ways in which they connect with people. You may feel that managers perhaps miss the bigger picture and are more remote and removed from the realities of practice. You may also note that some situations require management and therefore some of the key skills of management are appropriate to certain situations.

In exploring different management and leadership theories in the rest of the chapter, we hope that you will start to see, as we have already suggested, that leadership and management styles and activities can co-exist in, and be practised by, the same person. We further hope that you will also come to the conclusion that perhaps the art of good leadership and management is knowing what style of supervision to apply in what situation. So being a good manager may also mean being a good leader.

You may find it useful to look back at the answers you gave to some of the activities in Chapter 1 (especially Activities 1.2, 1.5 and 1.6) and consider what role values play in helping to shape leadership and management behaviours. Consideration of the 2018 Nursing and Midwifery Council (NMC) *Future Nurse: Standards of Proficiency for Registered Nurses*, notably Platform 5: Leading and managing nursing care and working in teams (see the start of this chapter), should be at the forefront of your mind as you read the rest of the chapter and engage with the activities and case studies. (At the time of writing, these were still being completed.)

While we argue that leadership and management cannot be divorced from each other, it is worth considering theories of management and theories of leadership to see what we, as nurses, can gain from them and when it might be appropriate to adopt one approach or the other in supervising care.

Theories of management

Unlike biochemistry, microbiology and physiology, the study of leadership and management is neither precise nor based on scientific principles. This means there are many theories about what it means to be a leader or a manager, but none of these are proven; they are **theories** (i.e. logical attempts to explain an observation) but not, in the scientific sense, facts.

The purpose of the theories in the discipline of studying management and leadership is to act as a guide to the important tasks and roles of the manager. Interestingly for nursing, a profession that is increasingly driven by an emphasis on evidence-based practice, little of the work of the manager, especially the health and social care manager, is informed by any meaningful research and so, as explained above, it remains theoretical. What this means is that we have theory and observation for guidance, but there is a large amount of scope within these theories for personal interpretation and adjustment to the individual management tasks and contexts within which these are applied. There is a large amount of research into leadership and management styles and behaviours from disciplines other than nursing which can be used to inform your thinking.

In part, the lack of meaningful research into the management function is itself a product of the diversity of people, staff, managers and settings in which nurse management takes place. The uniqueness of each individual, manager, team, group and organisation, as well as the ever-changing political, social and technological climate in which they work, mean it is difficult to produce research-informed strategies for management that have any real, long-lasting meaning. This means that being a manager requires a constant engagement with the people being managed, the organisation and the wider political and social context.

What this implies for theories of management is that they are just that, theories. Theories are ideas about a topic which are supported by some evidence; they are not substantively proven. Even if management theories were proven, they would not all apply in the same way in every management situation.

Mintzberg's management role theory

Mintzberg (1975) produced one of the most enduring descriptions of the roles of the manager. Mintzberg suggests strongly that if managers are to be effective at what they do, they need to recognise the nature and scope of the work they are undertaking and they must apply their own natural abilities to it. Mintzberg further suggests that the management function is complex and involves an intricate balance of three key roles. The power which the manager possesses arises from a recognition of his or her formal authority and status within the organisation. There are three categories within which the roles of the manager sit, as Mintzberg describes them, are the *interpersonal*, the *informational* and the *decisional*. Within each of these categories there are a number of roles which together constitute the larger role; that of management.

Interpersonal roles

- Figurehead – the manager performs some more basic functions which may be part of the routine of day-to-day work.
- Leader – including recruitment, staff development and motivating staff.
- Liaison – including communication with people and organisations not directly related to the immediate team.

Informational roles

- Monitor – in this role the manager collects information about the team and the wider environment in which the team works. Some of this information comes from official sources and some from sources such as staff room gossip.
- Disseminator – managers share some of the information they have gathered from formal and informal sources from inside and outside the team with the team. There is a need for discretion here as to what information is shared, with whom and when.
- Spokesperson – essentially information sharing outside of the direct team and organisation.

Decisional roles

- Entrepreneur – the manager seeks opportunities to improve what s/he does.
- Disturbance handler – the manager has to respond to external pressures and make changes that have not come from within the team.

- Resource allocator – as well as managing his or her own time, the manager allocates tasks, equipment and jobs to the team.
- Negotiator – this may mean within the team, with service users, other professions or other agencies. Sometimes this is planned; sometimes it is a response to immediate pressures.

Source: Adapted from Mintzberg (1975).

What is apparent from the description of the manager Mintzberg presents is that management requires a fair degree of adaptability on the part of the manager. Mintzberg regards the interpersonal elements of the role as being integral to the task of managing and places leadership within the description of the functions of management.

Activity 6.2 Reflection

Consider how the manager on your last placement/current place of work exercises the various roles of the manager as described by Mintzberg. How does the manager adopting a particular role at a particular time affect you and the rest of the team? Can you identify them moving between roles throughout the day? Perhaps you are, have been, on your management placement, are you conscious of the need to do different things at different points in the day? Is the switch between roles something which you consciously do?

As this activity is based on your own reflection, there is no specimen answer at the end of the chapter.

Theories such as Mintzberg's can help to add some clarity to what it is managers actually do. In Chapter 1, the case study 'The newly qualified nurse' demonstrated that the student (Julius) had little idea about what it was that the ward sister (Deirdre) did all day. Sometimes an understanding of the roles and pressures others have to work under, in this case the very many roles the manager has to practise within a day, allows us to understand better what it is they do and therefore our place in the team.

Contingency theory

Contingency theory refers to the idea that managers have to take into account a number of factors when making management decisions; that is, decisions are situation-dependent. Management decisions are therefore seen as being dependent on what is happening, where it is happening and who is involved. This is perhaps best thought of as applying as much to the way in which a decision is made as to the decision that is made. Such an idea fits well within Mintzberg's scheme, where the manager is busy juggling a number of roles in order to fulfil the task of managing dependent on the situation they find them self-managing.

Activity 6.3   Reflection

Reflect on the management decisions made on a day-to-day basis in the area in which you are/have most recently been on placement. What are the factors that influence the way in which these decisions are made/communicated and therefore the impact they have on the team? Are these decisions always communicated in an appropriate way? How does the team respond to the manner of the communication?

Since this is based on your own experiences, there is no specimen answer at the end of the chapter.

Contingency theory is similar to the different ways in which you will interact with clients and their relatives according to the nature of the care they are receiving, their age, mental capacity and how well you know them as individuals. As a manager, successful action relies on your understanding of a situation which in turn relies on good communication. Griffin (1999) makes the useful point that what works as a manager in one situation cannot be generalised to all such situations. As such, managers have to be adaptable to the demands of their various roles as well as the environment they work in and the people they work with.

Systems theory

Systems theory identifies that managing people, resources and care delivery requires the manager to recognise the contribution all of these elements make to the effective running of an organisation or team. Systems theorists see the world of work as a set of interdependent subsystems which interconnect to form what is a whole (or holistic) system. Von Bertalanffy (1968), the initial and most famous system theorist, recognised that systems (teams, groups, organisations) are characterised by the interactions of their components (people and their environments) and the unpredictability of those interactions.

What this means for the management of people is that the role each plays within the functioning of a team has to be recognised, supported and directed with one eye on the bigger picture. When one part of the system fails, then the whole system is affected. It is important therefore for the leader or manager to consider the role of each member of the team in achieving the team's goals.

The Hawthorne experiments (see the useful websites at the end of this chapter) provide an interesting insight into how people are motivated at work by the feelings of belonging and of being paid attention to: the so-called **Hawthorne effect**. Essentially the experiments undertaken at the Hawthorne factory involved making both positive and negative changes to people's working conditions and recording the impact this had on productivity. What the experiments demonstrated is that what is done is not as important as the fact that workers are being paid attention to, which alters their behaviour. A similar effect is seen in research, where people react in ways which they believe a researcher wants them to because they are under scrutiny (Ellis, 2016a).

Activity 6.4   Research and finding out

Consider the practice area you are most recently familiar with. Make a list of all of the people you have come into contact with who play a role in the day-to-day activity of the area. List what these people do and who is affected by this. Ask a colleague or your mentor to do a similar list so that you can compare. Consider together what difficulties the rest of the team face when individual members of the wider team are away from work. What does this say about the way in which that system works?

Since this is based on your own experiences, there is no specimen answer at the end of the chapter.

The important message for the manager here is the need to demonstrate to all members of the team that the role they play, however minor it may seem, can have a much wider impact.

Case study: The wrong mop

George is a new ward orderly who is responsible for cleaning Juniper Ward. The ward has three side rooms. In side room two is a patient with methicillin-resistant *Staphylococcus aureus* (MRSA), who is being nursed in isolation. George mops side room two and then continues to use the same mop to clean the open ward areas. Within a few days there is an outbreak of MRSA on the ward.

This case study reminds us that even the most mundane task can have a significant impact not only on the nursing team, but also the patients that we care for. The nurses on the ward may have been meticulous in their hygiene and infection control procedures when caring for the MRSA-positive patient, but one component of the system, in this case George, was not and so the system, which includes the ward and the hospital at large, is affected by this single action. Of course, there are a number of potential explanations for George's lack of understanding about the impact of his actions, which include poor training, poor leadership or perhaps his feeling of not belonging in the ward team.

What should be clear to you in thinking about systems theory is that the team is only as good as the weakest of its members and that the team, those people a manager manages, all have to play a part in achieving a task no matter how mundane that task is. One of the lessons from this for the nurse on their journey to leadership and management is to consider, and pay attention to, all of the members of the team not just the 'most important' or the most senior.

Workload management

Within the role of the manager there are a number of tasks which need to be undertaken. Some of these tasks reflect on the roles identified in the model by Mintzberg discussed earlier; others are more singular and are worthy of some discussion here.

The role of the manager in co-ordinating the work of a team was alluded to in Chapter 1, especially in the case study 'The newly qualified nurse'. The management of workload is perhaps one of the key skills for the new or aspiring nurse manager who needs to satisfy his or her own developmental and work–life balance needs; the needs of the team members; the needs of the organisation; and the needs of the people who use the service.

To achieve this balance the nurse manager must learn and consolidate a number of skills and, while this is not an exhaustive list, some of these skills are discussed here:

- Learn to say 'no'! The need to prioritise workloads as a manager is very real. Taking on more than you or the team can manage will mean that no one is satisfied.
- Learn to delegate. People are the greatest resource for the nurse leader and manager. Knowing your team, what they are capable of and what individuals enjoy doing means that you can delegate tasks and everyone benefits (Ellis and Abbott, 2010).
- Learn to kick the door shut (Templar, 2011). When you have a pressing task to attend to, an open-door policy (which allows anyone in at any time for any reason) means you cannot concentrate on what is in front of you and so are unable to finish anything. Clearly this is not always appropriate; emergency situations may require immediate attention and shutting yourself away during a crisis is not helpful.
- Learn to go home. If your job cannot be done in the time allotted to it, you have too much work. A tired nurse manager is likely to make mistakes and be unhappy. This is no good to anyone. Failure to achieve everything in the allotted time may also indicate the need to become more organised, delegate more effectively and manage time more wisely.

By managing their time through prioritising, saying no and sensible delegation, managers can achieve their goals and develop team members at the same time. In Chapter 5 we discussed burnout. Some burnout can be attributed to not taking care of oneself as a manager, working too many hours and not having a good work-life balance.

Of the roles of the nurse manager, drawing up the roster is one which can often lead to disagreement and create disharmony in the team (as we saw in the case study 'The rota' in Chapter 4). For the manager who is concerned with doing things right, there are a few simple rules to follow in undertaking this task and which contribute to successful workload. The lessons from these translate well into other management tasks.

There is a need to be open and honest about the process: people have no need to speculate, and gossip, about what they can see. An open process will involve observing two important principles: being fair and being consistent. The morally active manager is described by Dawson and Butler (2004, p237) as acting *on the basis of internal values, or standards, rather than (or as well as) … on the basis of externally imposed codes of conduct.* Clearly, as well as being transparent in the process of work allocation, it is important for the manager to allocate staff so that there are appropriate levels (the skill mix) and numbers of staff on duty at any one time.

The sorts of principles associated with moral management are also the sorts of principles associated with moral and ethical nursing practice. Fairness dictates that all staff are given equal opportunity to request days off and consistency that these are all considered according to the same criteria. Whatever tasks the manager faces, be this acting as a spokesperson or as a role model (see the NMC's Platform 5, at the start of the chapter), there is a need to demonstrate moral and ethical awareness. Managers who are unable to demonstrate moral activity in their day-to-day management practice cannot reasonably require the same from their team. Moral and professional conduct is perhaps the main cornerstone of good nursing and good management practice.

Resilience and management

One of the features of modern nursing management is the need to be resilient. Resilience is the ability to cope with, and even thrive as a result of, the stresses and challenges that being a twenty-first-century nurse manager throw up. In Chapter 9, we will discuss strategies for developing confidence as a leader or manager and how this will enable you to make the transitions from student to qualified nurse and nurse leader and thereby develop the ability to cope with the challenges that nurse management and leadership create.

There are some key strategies that enable nurse managers to become more resilient and in so doing role model to their team how to cope with the challenges that nursing creates. Where a manager is able to deal with situations clearly, fairly and ethically, there will be trust within the team.

The most important strategy in being resilient is your own ability to make sense of what is happening in the world around you. In part, this ability comes from a strong understanding and belief in your core values (as discussed in Chapter 1). A positive attitude to reflecting on and learning from situations (see 'The learning organisation' in Chapter 5), changes and challenges is a core element of being a good nurse and later a good nurse manager. This understanding is exercised and communicated through the use of emotional intelligence (as described in Chapter 4, as well as later in this chapter) in which the leader recognises and responds to his or her own, and other people's, emotional responses to a situation rather than dealing with it on purely a cognitive (thinking) level.

Being positive and using new situations as opportunities to learn mean in turn that you will develop problem-solving abilities. The ability to solve problems means that you are in control, not only of the situation, but also of yourself. Understanding the effects of stress on yourself and on others is a key element of emotional intelligence, discussed further later, which is a necessary skill for successful managers and leaders.

Ellis and Abbott (2017, p289) caution: *Resilience requires the manager to understand themself and the things which affect them because in this way the manager can manage their response to situations. It is important here to understand that the manager who develops a thick skin does not learn, does not see what is going on around them and will lack the emotional intelligence and empathy to deal with the people elements of the role.* So resilience is not about hiding away and disengaging from one's emotional responses to situations; it is about learning what your responses are and then learning how to manage them.

Activity 6.5 Reflection

Consider how reflection on critical incidents throughout your training as a nurse has enabled you to make sense of some aspects of nursing practice. What strategies did you find helpful during this process – perhaps discussion with peers, tutors, mentors or managers, reading articles, textbooks or attending lectures? How did this process help you to develop? What was it about reflection that enabled you to cope in untoward circumstances? Compare how you cope with untoward incidents now with how you coped before you started to train as a nurse; what are the differences? How might these strategies translate to the need for resilience as a leader or manager?

There are some possible answers and thoughts at the end of the chapter.

Your reflections on this activity will have led you to the conclusion that being prepared emotionally and intellectually is one of the key strategies for surviving as a student, as a nurse and in the long term as a manager. As with all aspects of leadership and management, understanding your own responses to a situation will mean you are better prepared for, and more understanding of, the emotional responses of others. That is one of the fundamental requirements of effective people management.

Theories of leadership

Leadership can be regarded as one facet of the management role or as an entity in itself. It is a people-focused activity that requires engagement with a team – the followers.

House (2004) describes leadership as the ability to motivate and enable other people to achieve the goals of the organisation for which they work.

Being a leader can arise out of an individual's position within an organisation or team, or it may result from a natural ability a person has to inspire other people to follow him or her (charisma, perhaps). There are a number of approaches to leadership, some of which take account of the nature of the interaction between the leader and followers and others which take a more comprehensive view of the nature of leadership and the tasks of the leader as well as the interpersonal aspect of the role.

Transactional leadership

Transactional leadership is leadership at its most basic. As the name implies, there is a transaction taking place. The followers do what the leader asks of them in return for a reward, at its most basic a salary or perhaps praise or recognition. The role of the leader in this model is to state what needs to be done and who will do it and then allow them to get the job done.

This approach to leadership is very much focused on getting a task done, rather than on the people undertaking the task. It is easy to imagine how this approach to leadership may be appealing in an emergency situation or when there are serious time constraints. In nursing, it does hark back to the days of task allocation, when patient care was perhaps less holistic than is common today.

Relating the theory to good leadership practice, the leader who understands and communicates effectively with the team will gain the respect and trust of that team and for the team the reward for getting the job done will come from the sense of shared purpose and belonging that co-operative working brings.

Transformational leadership

Transformational leadership is about having a vision (a view of how things should or could be) and being able to communicate this vision effectively to others. The vision of how things should be may come from leaders themselves, from their managers or following discussion within a group or team. What is important about transformational leaders is that they believe, and are seen to believe, the vision.

For transformational leadership to work, there are some assumptions which need to be made and need to be true. First, people will follow a leader who can inspire them; second, a passionate leader with vision can get things done; and third, getting things done is a matter of instilling energy and enthusiasm into a group.

Transformational leadership requires there to be a relationship of trust between the leader and the followers. This trust means that the followers will do whatever it is that the leader envisions for them. As in all relationships, the best way to generate trust is to show people you care about them and be consistent in your approach to achieving the management task (Scholtes, 1998 – see below).

Transformational leaders succeed in what they do by having faith, not only in what they want to achieve and what they do, but also by generating and displaying trust in those they work with. Clearly one of the central focuses of the transformational leader is change. Transformational leaders who are successful in sharing their vision with their team will doubtless be able to lead their team through change more successfully than a leader who does not have the full support of the team.

It is worth considering whether transformational leadership is suited to health and social care, and more specifically within nursing. The simple answer is that the most successful nurse leaders will retain a vision of how things should be in terms of high-quality and successful patient care provision. The shared values of care and compassion are the key to generating the trust which transformational leaders need in order to improve (transform) care provision.

Of course, having the faith and trust of the team is not of itself enough to make a person a transformational leader. There is also a real need for a vision that is correct and workable as well as inspiring. If we can agree that all improvement is a change, but not all change is an improvement, we can see that enthusiasm and vision without some foundation in reality are perhaps not all that helpful. Trust is generated when followers believe both that a leader cares about them as individuals and that the same leader is capable of delivering whatever it is s/he says s/he will deliver. Liking someone as an individual and trusting that person as a leader are not the same thing.

Activity 6.6   Reflection

Think about some occasion when you have met a mentor or lecturer who you have liked because s/he was inspirational. Now think about whether s/he delivered what you expected. Did you learn what you thought you would learn? What was the difference between successful learning and less successful learning? Is a good relationship as important for learning as the content of the learning?

There are some possible answers and thoughts at the end of the chapter.

What this reflection shows is that there is more than one dimension to being an effective leader of people. Being nice is not really enough; there is a need for some substance to underpin activity.

Bass (1985), one of the leading writers on transformational leadership, suggests four essential components of effective transformational leadership. First, leaders must provide intellectual stimulation, challenging the way things are and encouraging creativity among the team. Second, they must demonstrate individualised consideration and by using good communication skills make followers feel able to share ideas and gain direct recognition for their unique contributions. Third, they need to demonstrate inspirational motivation which enables followers to experience the same passion and motivation as the leader to meet the team goals. Fourth, they need to have idealised influence; that is, they must act as a role model who followers wish to emulate while taking on the values of the leader.

Reflecting on the nature of the leaders we respect and trust, the sorts of people we choose as role models, we can see they have many of the characteristics which suggest them to be exercising values which are central to nursing. The requirement of a transformational leader closely reflect what Jane Cummings, the Chief Nurse for NHS England, in 2012 coined as the 6 Cs (see the useful websites at the end of the chapter).

1. care
2. compassion
3. competence
4. communication
5. courage
6. commitment.

Transformational leaders who have the ability to exercise, and be seen to exercise, these essential values in their dealings with colleagues and service users can expect others to see these as a template for how they ought to act. One of the core learning points for anyone moving into a leadership or management position in the caring professions is not to put aside all of the qualities and values they worked to while in clinical practice (as embodied in the 6 Cs), since their continued exercise reflects strongly on who we are and putting aside our values, as we discussed in Chapter 1, especially in the scenario about Julius and Deirdre, can lead to dire consequences for all concerned.

Activity 6.7   Researching and finding out

With some colleagues, go online and find some more information about transformational leadership. What are the key qualities of a transformational leader? What examples can you find of transformational leaders in history, now or in healthcare? What attributes do you share with these great transformational leaders? Which might you be able to cultivate for yourself in the coming years?

Since this is based on your own experiences, there is no specimen answer at the end of the chapter.

Adair's action-centred leadership

Adair (2010) describes leadership as being made up of three interlocking and inter-dependent activities (often portrayed as interconnected circles (see Figure 6.1) which leaders must pay attention to in their role: the task, the team and the individual. The role of the leader is to achieve the task (in nursing, this may be the provision of good-quality care) through building and developing the team while developing the individuals that make up the team.

The functions of the leader, as described by Adair (2010), which enable them to achieve the task are defining the task, planning how the task will be achieved, briefing the team and controlling the process. In order to achieve the task the leader also needs to pay attention to the human elements of what they are doing through evaluating, motivating, organising and providing an example to both the team as a whole and the individuals in it. The elements of the various activities include:

Task

- organising duties
- focusing on goals
- controlling quality
- checking performance
- reviewing progress.

Team

- building and maintaining morale
- maintaining communication
- setting standards
- supporting the team.

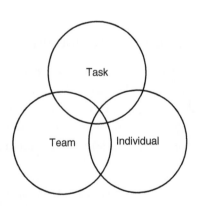

Figure 6.1 Action-centred leadership

Source: Adapted from Adair (2010).

Individual

- praise and recognition
- developing and training
- meeting human needs.

Ignoring or underemphasising any one of these areas of activity will mean the leader is not doing what the team, individual or task require. Overemphasis on any one element of these three leadership activities will lead to imbalances in the ways in which work is done and can be to the detriment of all concerned. Leaders need to learn to balance all three activity areas as a general rule, increasing their attention in any one area for short periods as required. So, for instance, if there are problems with the team the effort put into this needs to increase but – and this is important – this should not mean the leader neglects the task or the individuals within the team as a result.

The servant leader

Many classic models of leadership identify the leader as the individual out in front with the followers coming along behind. Some modern theories of leadership take a different view of the role of leaders, who have a more interdependent relationship with their team (Howatson-Jones, 2004). The role of the leader in this view is that of a leader who also has the ability to follow. This idea of the 'servant leader' is described as an individual who wants to serve first and to whom the decision to lead comes later. Servant leaders seek leadership as a means of expanding their ability to serve. In some respects there is a relationship between this and systems theory, in that the servant leader appreciates their role as leader is to coordinate the activity of the system (the team/ organisation) in order to achieve the shared (system) goals of the team or organisation.

Throughout history there have been a number of individuals who can be said to have been servant leaders. Well-known examples include the Dalai Lama, Mahatma Gandhi and Mother Teresa. These individuals, whose motivation lies in serving others, have managed to expand their ability to do so by taking on leadership roles. While it can be argued that each was motivated by religion or political change, they share the value of care for other people, which is a value common to many healthcare managers and leaders.

Activity 6.8 Critical thinking

Think about the nurses, and other health professionals, who you have worked with and who hold positions of power. Consider those individuals you most admire. Think about what it was that you admired about them most.

(Continued)

(Continued)

Consider whether they were the sort of individuals who got their hands dirty, who led by example, who seemed to lead so that they could improve the care of the people that they care for.

Conversely consider the leaders you least admired, what was it about them that you did not like? Were their motivations in question? How did this show in the ways they spoke and worked?

Now think what this means for you as a nurse and how you might continue to hold the focus on patient care you have now as you progress into more senior roles.

As this is based on your own thoughts and reflections, there is no specimen answer at the end of the chapter.

We can see from this example that servant leadership could be a natural progression for nurses who start their career in positions where they deliver patient care. This model of leadership allows there to be some consistency in who they are and what they do as their career progresses.

This should not be seen as justification for leaders and managers who continue to deliver nursing care much of the time while neglecting the role which they are paid to perform. While we have highlighted the person-centred nature of health and social care, this does not always mean for leaders or managers that they have to deliver face-to-face patient care. What it does mean is that they need to support their staff to do so by leading by example, providing environments conducive to learning and improving care (see Chapter 8) and by creating and supporting policies which underpin person-centred care.

The NHS Leadership Model

Partly in response to the Francis report (2013) and partly to update an old leadership framework, the NHS Leadership Academy launched the new Healthcare Leadership Model in 2013. The emphasis of the model is on personal qualities and behaviours. The authors argue:

> *The way that we manage ourselves is a central part of being an effective leader. It is vital to recognise that personal qualities like self-awareness, self-confidence, self-control, self-knowledge, personal reflection, resilience and determination are the foundation of how we behave. Being aware of your strengths and limitations in these areas will have a direct effect on how you behave and interact with others, and they with you.*

(NHS Leadership Academy, 2013)

The argument continues to highlight how the behaviours of the leader set the culture of the workplace and subsequently, the tone of patient care. In their view, workplace culture is partly a product of the behaviours and dispositions of the leader. Ideas regarding personal qualities are not explicit in the model but are a core theme throughout. Being able to lead with reference to personal qualities and exhibited behaviours requires self-awareness and emotional intelligence. The model is divided into nine interdependent and interlocked dimensions.

The nine dimensions of the Healthcare Leadership Model

1. Inspiring shared purpose
2. Leading with care
3. Evaluating information
4. Connecting our service
5. Sharing the vision
6. Engaging the team
7. Holding to account
8. Developing capability
9. Influencing for results.

Activity 6.9 Research and finding out

Go online and find the NHS Healthcare Leadership Model; use the web address given at the end of this chapter. Read each of the descriptors for each dimension and reflect on how they describe what each dimension is, is not and why it is important. Look at the four part scale which describes a person's engagement with each dimension of the model (essential, proficient, strong and exemplary) and consider which description best fits you.

Since this is based on your own experiences, there is no specimen answer at the end of the chapter.

The role of emotional intelligence

The concept of emotional intelligence has gained an increasing following over recent years. Emotional intelligence in relation to leadership and management refers to the ability of leaders or managers to understand the role that their emotions play in their decision-making and the ability to recognise the emotions of the individuals within the team and how this affects the work they do (Goleman, 1996).

Recognising the influence of emotions on decision-making means that leaders and managers may be in a better position to understand what motivates and what constrains staff in their work. Leaders and managers who have well-developed emotional intelligence are said to be better at communicating with their team and therefore at achieving better outcomes.

Goleman (1998, p317) defines emotional intelligence as the capacity *for recognizing our own feelings and those of others, for motivating ourselves, and for managing emotions well in ourselves and in our relationships.* He further states that emotional intelligence is a learned capability. Goleman's emotional intelligence framework comprises five elements: self-awareness, motivation, self-regulation, empathy and social skills. It is probably fair to comment that emotional intelligence is one dimension of what it is to be a good nurse and that this learned skill translates well into leadership and management roles.

It follows from this, however, that people who rely heavily on their emotions to guide their actions will tend to base their decisions on their emotional responses to a situation rather than on more objective empirical evidence and that in some situations this may be detrimental to the decisions they make (Croskerry and Norman, 2008). That said, the failure of leaders and managers to understand the role of their own emotions and those of their staff in shaping decision-making and behaviours at work will mean that important issues are overlooked which may affect patient care.

Case study: The grieving staff nurse

Blossom had always been a self-confident and able staff nurse. She was friendly with staff and patients, but on the whole tended to keep very much to herself. Blossom had seemed a little withdrawn in recent weeks, but had said nothing to anyone until one day she went into an unexplained rage. Blossom shouted at the students and her fellow staff nurses and was rude and abrasive towards patients and visitors. Kathy, a fellow staff nurse, decided she should take control of the situation and took Blossom to one side. Once in the ward office Blossom started to cry. She confided to Kathy that her father had died some weeks previously and she was finding it hard to cope.

There are two interesting elements to this case study: first, Blossom had not shared her grief with anyone and did not know how to deal with it herself; second, no one on the ward team had picked up on her distress. On two levels, then, emotional intelligence was seen to be lacking: in Blossom recognising the effects of grief on her behaviour and in her colleagues recognising that Blossom was grieving. Clearly, for emotional intelligence to work for leaders or managers of people, they need to develop an awareness of the effects of their own emotions before they can recognise and respond to the emotions of others.

Chapter 4 looks at emotional intelligence in the context of conflict management.

Gaining support

What we have seen in this chapter is that one of the key roles of leaders or managers in nursing is working with and through their team. In order to achieve this, nurse managers and leaders need the support of their team. How this support is gained and maintained is through a mixture of good communication, good interpersonal skills and developing a sense of achievement. The team will support a leader that they trust.

Scholtes (1998) identifies trust as arising out of the feeling that leaders or managers both care for their staff and are capable of doing the job (Figure 6.2).

The model presented in Figure 6.2 demonstrates to novice leaders or managers the importance not only of getting the technical, procedural and policy elements of their role right, but also the need to take their team with them. This returns us to one of the key themes of the chapter – that to be a successful nurse manager there is a clear need not only to know what you are doing, but also to nurture and develop your staff and team while you are doing it – good management and good leadership.

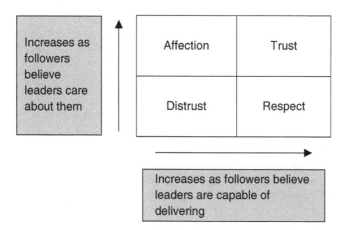

Figure 6.2   Trust, respect and affection

Source: Adapted from Scholtes (1998).

> ## Chapter summary
>
> This chapter has introduced some of the different theories of management and leadership as well as some of the ways of acting that contribute to their success. We have seen that leadership and management, while often viewed as separate entities, can co-exist in the same individual and that when they do they can add to the success of the manager.
>
> The chapter has identified that some of the key values of nursing translate well into good nurse leadership, that managers or leaders need both resilience and the ability to influence people if they are to be successful. The need for resilience clearly comes from the requirement for managers and leaders to manage what can be difficult situations, and part of the toolkit of successful leadership and management in terms of resilience is the ability to connect with people on the human level and thereby influence what they do and how they do it.
>
> For nurses, who enter the profession to care for others, we have suggested that maintaining the focus on care as a fundamental part of developing as a leader and manager both sets a good role model to the team and helps to develop trust. Developing trust means that nurse leaders or managers can effectively lead their team in the delivery of high-quality nursing care.

Activities: Brief outline answers

Activity 6.1 Reflection (p106)

You may remember meeting senior nurses who were able to let you know what they were doing and why you should do things in the way they wanted. Other nurses may have told you to do things because that is how things are done here. The first example is of leadership, as the senior nurse lets you see why and how you should behave in a certain way. The second example is more managerial in telling you what to do because this is policy. The best senior staff will be able to swap between being a leader and manager according to the situation and this change will appear appropriate; for example, during an emergency situation it may be best to be told what to do rather than why.

Activity 6.5 Reflection (p114)

Using reflection as a tool and utilising the experience and understanding of others allow us to see situations in a context. Understanding the context of a situation and why things happen as they do enables us to make sense of them, and cope emotionally with things which might otherwise prove too difficult. Part of the reflection process is planning how we will meet challenges in the future, namely, action planning, which is how we become prepared. When we are prepared, we know not only how we will feel, but also how we will act and, more importantly, why. This means that when we meet similar situations in the future they will be less daunting. That is resilience.

Activity 6.6 Reflection (p116)

How you feel about an individual that you have to work with or follow is often affected by whether you like him or her as a person and whether you feel s/he cares about you as an individual. This is certainly an important first step in any relationship. When these same people deliver what they promise, when you learn from them what they said you would learn, it generates a feeling of great trust and gratitude. When an individual that you like is unable to deliver what s/he promised, you may not stop liking that person, but you question whether your trust in him or her is well placed and you will think twice before following whatever s/he says in the future.

Further reading

Adair, J (2010) *Develop Your Leadership Skills.* London: Kogan Page.

A really short and useful introduction to leadership as Adair sees it.

Grint, K (2002) Management or leadership? *Journal of Health Services Research and Policy*, 7 (4): 248–51.

A useful discussion of leadership and management.

Henderson, J and Atkinson, D (eds) (2004) *Managing Care in Context.* London: Routledge.

A good overview of management in health and social care.

Jones, L and Bennett, CL (2012) *Leadership in Health and Social Care: An Introduction for Emerging Leaders.* Banbury: Lantern.

A good primer for people interested in the idea of leadership.

Useful websites

www.kingsfund.org.uk/Leadership

The King's Fund – a good leadership and management resource website.

www.bbc.co.uk/programmes/b00lv0wx

A podcast and explanation of the Hawthorne effect which is worth listening to.

http://www.leadershipacademy.nhs.uk/resources/healthcare-leadership-model

Look here to do the Healthcare Leadership Model activities alluded to in the text.

https://www.healthcareers.nhs.uk/about/working-health/6cs

Explanation of the 6 Cs.

Chapter 7 Improving care and change management

Platform 4: Providing and evaluating care

Registered nurses take the lead in providing evidence-based, compassionate and safe nursing interventions. They ensure that care they provide and delegate is person-centred and of a consistently high standard. They support people of all ages in a range of care settings. They work in partnership with people, families and carers to evaluate whether care is effective and the goals of care have been met in line with their wishes, preferences and desired outcomes.

At the point of registration, the registered nurse will be able to:

4.3 demonstrate the knowledge, communication and relationship management skills required to provide people, families and carers with accurate information that meets their needs before, during and after a range of interventions.

Platform 6: Improving safety and quality of care

Registered nurses make a key contribution to the continuous monitoring and quality improvement of care and treatment in order to enhance health outcomes and people's experience of nursing and related care. They assess risks to safety or experience and take appropriate action to manage those, putting the best interests, needs and preferences of people first.

At the point of registration, the registered nurse will be able to:

6.4 demonstrate an understanding of the principles of improvement methodologies, participate in all stages of audit activity and identify appropriate quality improvement strategies.

6.7 understand how the quality and effectiveness of nursing care can be evaluated in practice, and demonstrate how to use service delivery evaluation and audit findings to bring about continuous improvement.

6.9 work with people, their families, carers and colleagues to develop effective improvement strategies for quality and safety, sharing feedback and learning from positive outcomes and experiences, mistakes and adverse outcomes and experiences.

6.11 acknowledge the need to accept and manage uncertainty, and demonstrate an understanding of strategies that develop resilience in self and others.

Chapter aims

After reading this chapter you will be able to:

- describe different organisational structures;
- appreciate organisational requirements to maintain standards;
- compare change theories and their use in the change management process;
- evaluate the appraisal tools available to improve work performance;
- appreciate a new approach to changing practice through entrepreneurial skills.

Introduction

This chapter will help you understand how the organisation for which you work is structured and operates to maintain and improve standards. It looks at the structure and practice of organisational clinical governance and explores how you can contribute to the planning and implementation of change. Included in this chapter are methods to improve standards of working through performance appraisal, supervision and 360-degree reviews. The final section looks at how entrepreneurial nurses can use a business-minded approach to improving patient care.

Understanding your organisation

Once you have qualified, you will be busy adapting to your new responsibilities and getting to grips with a new working environment. You will have little time to think about the 'powers that be' or the 'upper echelons' of the organisational structure in which you work. But as this structure has an impact on your daily working life it is worth spending a few minutes figuring out who controls what.

Organisational structures influence the manner in which they operate and perform. The structure, which will vary according to the mission and culture of the organisation, provides a framework for distributing responsibilities for the different activities the organisation undertakes between the different services and departments. Factors influencing the shape of this structure include organisational size, main purpose and skills of the workforce. The historical origins of a hospital (e.g. as a Victorian workhouse) or location (e.g. in an industrial area, close to a medieval leper colony or monastery),

Activity 7.1   Evidence-based practice and research

1. Ask your mentor if they know the origins of the organisation where you are currently on placement. Consider whether this has had any impact on the functions of the organisation today.

2. Go to the web page of the organisation and look for the welcome page. See if there is a strapline which outlines the main priorities of the organisation. There may be a statement which says 'Our main objective is to …' or 'Our mission is to …'; often the best place to look for this is within the 'About Us' tab. Finding these key messages helps you understand what the priorities are for the organisation. If there is no web page, each organisation will produce an annual report. Seek this out to see what the main priorities for the organisation are.

As this answer is based on your own research and reflections, there is no specimen answer at the end of the chapter.

although distant from the modern demands of current NHS, or private-sector health-care, may nevertheless influence the organisation's culture.

An important factor in any organisational structure, whether historically derived, a private healthcare company or small-scale organisation (such as a charitable foundation supporting a hospice), is the **span of control**. Used to describe the number of employees each organisation manager or head of department is responsible for, this can also be expressed in financial terms such as the budget or annual financial turnover of a department. The span of control will determine issues such as the structure, number of departments and managers in an organisation. There will usually be a chief executive, managing director or hospital director or similar post and a governing board with a number of board members, some of whom will be external to the organisation to provide expert advice or represent other organisations. In the NHS, for example, these would be patient organisation and local authority representatives from the council or regional government offices.

Activity 7.2   Evidence-based practice and research

Find out the structure in the organisation you have a placement in or hope to work in when you qualify. Try to get hold of a copy of the structure or ask your mentor to sketch one out.

Identify who sits on the board of the organisation as this is the main decision-making body with the power to agree or prevent service developments; also usually found within the 'about us' section of the website.

Find out if there is a nurse member of the board who represents your professional interests.

As this answer is based on your own research and reflections, there is no specimen answer at the end of the chapter.

Organisation structure

The Learn Management website (**www.learnmanagement2.com**) describes five main organisational structures: tall, flat, hierarchical, matrix and centralised/decentralised. On this website you will find descriptions of each type of structure, along with some of its advantages and disadvantages. In brief, a *tall* structure is one that has many levels of management, with each line manager having a small number of people reporting directly to him or her, so that the people on the lower levels may have no contact at all with those higher up. This can have implications for accountability and communication, but it does provide employees with a clear management structure with ample opportunities for promotion.

By contrast, a *flat* structure has fewer management layers, but each manager has quite a large number of people (all at more or less the same level) reporting to them. This can encourage team spirit and a sense of collective belonging, but it can be difficult to manage if the organisation is large. A *hierarchical* organisation has much in common with a tall organisation, but there are likely to be more people reporting directly to managers on each different level, particularly at the lower levels (thus giving them a pyramid shape). The most important decisions tend to be taken by the most senior people.

The *matrix* structure could not be more different. In an organisation with this type of structure, the important unit is the team. Each team will be led by a project manager or team leader, and will be responsible for a specific project or aspect of the organisation's work. In some organisations, the team will only exist for the duration of the work required by the project (e.g. a team of engineers working to develop a new type of vacuum cleaner). In others, the team becomes an established department within a whole organisation structure (e.g. with responsibility for distribution of the items being made). In many cases, the matrix organisation would consist of a mixture of permanent teams and project-specific teams.

Tall structures can be contrasted with flat structures, and hierarchical organisations with matrix-based organisations. Another important contrast is between centralised and decentralised structures. In a *centralised* organisation, a small group of senior managers (or a 'head office', which will be in a specific location) retains the major responsibilities and powers. In a *decentralised* organisation, these powers are devolved down to various lower-level managers, perhaps spread over a wide geographical area. Many supermarkets and chain stores are excellent examples of the decentralised structure. Each outlet is a management unit in itself, but, although the manager is relatively autonomous on a day-to-day basis, he or she will be ultimately answerable to the head office – either directly or through an interim (or regional) manager.

Some organisations may find a combination of centralisation and decentralisation to be most effective. For example, functions such as accounting or warehousing may be centralised to save costs. The Department of Health uses a mixture of centralisation and decentralisation, with central policy decisions being made to influence local health services. At the same time, local NHS Trusts have functions and responsibilities to respond to local population health needs and to manage their organisations according to the workforce they require to deliver those services.

Nurses at board level

An influential government report in the early 1980s observed that *If Florence Nightingale were carrying her lamp through the corridors of the NHS today she would almost certainly be searching for the people in charge* (Griffiths, 1983). In the wake of this, the Royal College of Nursing launched a campaign with the slogan 'Nursing should be managed by nurses' and, indeed, the first nurse general managers were appointed shortly afterwards (*Nursing Standard*, 1985). Nurse managers should be well placed to improve the business of caring by helping boards not only to understand the quality of care patients receive on the wards, but also to make positive decisions which improve care.

During the 1990s and early this millennium, the management of NHS organisations had started to focus on financial measures (e.g. cost management and budgets) and performance targets (e.g. waiting times and operations done) rather than on the quality of clinical care. However, the Darzi report (Darzi, 2008) has reversed this trend, describing the improvement in quality of care as *the basis of everything we do in the NHS*. The business of caring was brought to the forefront in the review and considered just as important as financial management.

This produces a raft of different issues for managers and leaders, especially in senior roles, where the emphasis has shifted from cost efficiency (i.e. money management) to effectiveness (i.e. good quality care) to what is now more common in that they need to think of both. That is the emphasis in modern healthcare management is on achieving both effectiveness and efficiency; the best care for the best price.

Nurses are now represented at board level in almost all healthcare facilities. The post of nurse executive (or nursing director) was established alongside the first wave of NHS Trusts in 1991. In 2007 the Burdett Trust commissioned the King's Fund to develop an intensive programme of work to support executive nurses and NHS boards in raising the quality of clinical care and giving a central place to patients and how they experience healthcare.

This work has resulted in two reports:

1. *From Ward to Board* (Machell et al., 2009) sets out the key questions and findings from the first phase of the programme and identifies good practice that can be easily replicated. Key areas to be built on are identified, along with the key skills and qualities nurse executives need to fulfil their role effectively.

2. *Putting Quality First in the Boardroom: Improving the Business of Caring* (Machell et al., 2010) is based on observations of how nurse executives and their boards work together. This report builds on themes that emerged from the previous one, and addresses long-standing concerns about the way in which financial and administrative performance indicators have taken precedence over issues relating to the quality of clinical care.

Commitment to the patient experience and the role of the NHS in the wider community is further recognised in the 2014 *Five Year Forward View* plan published by NHS England which reiterated this position, stating that patients and communities need to be at the heart of care. Other indicators of the NHS's commitment to improving the patient experience include the widespread use of satisfaction survey tools such as the 'friends and family test' (NHS England, 2013).

Activity 7.3   Research and finding out

Go online and find a copy of the 'Friends and family' test. Consider how you might respond to the questions contained within it with regard to your last experience as a healthcare user as well as how people might respond to it in the area you are currently working, or last worked.

As this answer is based on your own research and reflections, there is no specimen answer at the end of the chapter.

Governance

This section examines the regulatory bodies responsible for ensuring quality and good **governance** in health and social care organisations. The White Paper *Equity and Excellence: Liberating the NHS* (Department of Health, 2010) proposed changes to the governance, regulation and accountability arrangements of the NHS in England. The Care Quality Commission (CQC) is a regulatory body with responsibility for monitoring the quality of health and social care provision in England. It was created in 2009 through a merger of the Healthcare Commission, the Mental Health Commission and the Care Service Inspection Service. Scotland, Northern Ireland and Wales have separate governance arrangements.

Activity 7.4   Research and finding out

If you are in placement in an NHS organisation in England there will have been a CQC inspection within recent years. This activity will help you find the most recent report. Go to the website: **http://www.cqc.org.uk**.

In the 'Search whole website' box put a place name or postcode and select a service you wish to find out about. You can also find out about independent nursing homes and social care providers who are registered, and therefore licensed to provide services, with the CQC. Read the most recent report, paying special attention to the elements of quality as identified by the inspectorate, as well as the type of evidence to support the conclusions they have come to about the service.

As this answer is based on your own research, there is no specimen answer at the end of the chapter.

Case study: Investigating quality of care (CQC, 2011)

In February 2010 the CQC investigated Cambridgeshire and Peterborough NHS Foundation Trust and warned it to improve the standards of its mental health services or face enforcement action. In 2011 the CQC published a report which drew attention to its findings and made recommendations for improvements. The inspectors found the Trust was contravening five regulations regarding care and welfare, staffing, safeguarding people, assessing and monitoring service provision and safety and suitability of premises. The Mental Health Act Annual Statement report (2010) presented recommendations as to how the Trust should continue to conform to the Mental Health Act and Codes of Practice when detaining patients (CQC, 2011).

Some concerns identified in the 2011 review had not been fully addressed by the Trust. These were as follows:

- Care and welfare of people who use services:
  - o Not all care plans were person-centred or included information regarding individuals' wider care and inclusion needs.
  - o The seclusion suite on one ward is not meeting environmental requirements or the requirements of the Mental Health Act 1983 Code of Practice.

- Safeguarding vulnerable people who use services from abuse:
  - o Policies in relation to adult safeguarding and incident reporting do not clearly set out arrangements that ensure consistent reporting, investigation and dissemination of learning in relation to matters regarding cases of abuse allegations and incidents.
  - o Incident reporting and auditing systems are not robust.

- Safety and suitability of premises:
  - o Poorly designed fixed furniture and the presence of potential ligature points in some parts of the premises pose a risk to people who use services.
  - o The standard of décor and maintenance of one ward does not promote the dignity and well-being of people using services.

- Staffing:
  - o There are not always sufficient numbers of staff with the right competencies, knowledge, qualifications, skills and experience available to meet the needs of patients.
- Assessing and monitoring the quality of service provision:
  - o There is a lack of consistency in grading of incidents and no safety mechanism to ensure that inconsistencies are identified and resolved.

(Continued)

(Continued)

    o   There are delays in the time it takes between staff reporting incidents and their managers signing off the processes (CQC, 2011).

At the time the Trust submitted positive action plans addressing how they planned to meet the essential standards. As a result of the inspection and the subsequent improvement plans, a re-inspection of the trust in 2015 by the CQC led to an overall good rating for the Trust which reflected improvements in the quality of the care provided to patients and service users.

This real-life case illustrates the power of the CQC and its ability to act swiftly and responsively if concerns are raised about a regulated service.

Concept Summary: Governance

The term governance is widely used throughout all aspects of life. In healthcare the term **clinical governance** is heard almost every day. At its simplest, clinical governance promotes good practice. There are however as many definitions of what clinical governance is as there are people writing about it.

The term 'clinical governance' initially emerged in the white paper 'The New NHS: Modern and Dependable' (DH, 1997) and came into effect in 1998 being, as it was, central to ongoing NHS reform. Later its principles were more widely adopted for use in the healthcare sector (see the Health and Social Care Act, 2008).

Brennan and Flynn (2013) suggest CG is a way of promoting integrated quality improvement across administrative and clinical functions within a framework providing the basis for clinical accountability and clinical professional performance. Therefore all activity which challenges, promotes and records professional practice including performance, continuing professional development and regulatory activity fall within the remit of clinical governance.

Improving standards

Improving the quality of clinical care occurs at many levels, organisationally, within services, within teams and individually. NHS Improvement (formed in 2016) exists specifically to 'support foundation trusts and NHS trusts to give patients consistently safe, high quality, compassionate care within local health systems that are financially sustainable'. This is achieved through providing 'strategic leadership and practical help to the sector, supporting and holding providers to account to achieve a single definition of success'.

Activity 7.5 Evidence-based practice and research

Go online and find the NHS Improvement website. Browse the site paying specific attention to the pages in 'Resource' and the 'improvement hub'. Think about how you may have seen some of the tools within here in practice and what they mean for the quality of the care the patients receive.

If you also read the sections within 'about us' you will better understand the roles and functions of NHS Improvement.

As this answer is based on your own research, there is no specimen answer at the end of the chapter.

In Chapter 5, we discussed how staff development could enable individuals to develop their skills further. Performance appraisal is one method that managers use to regulate how well individuals carry out their responsibilities. The Chartered Institute of Personnel and Development (CIPD, 2011) claims it is important to distinguish between performance management and performance appraisal. Performance management is undertaken through supervision and achievements are observed against a specific set of objectives or goals, whereas performance appraisal is a dialogue between manager and subordinate to discuss an individual's performance, past and future development and the support required from the organisation and manager to achieve optimum performance. Marquis and Huston (2009) suggest the process of performance appraisal can also be a motivator towards improving performance. In this sense, performance appraisal is a tool to be used in performance management.

The CIPD (2011) recommends five key elements in the process:

1. measurement – assessing the performance against agreed targets and objectives;
2. feedback – providing information to individuals on their performance and progress;
3. positive reinforcement – emphasising what has been done well and making only constructive criticism about what might be improved;
4. exchange of views – a frank exchange of views about what has happened, how appraisees can improve performance, the support they need from their managers to achieve this and their aspiration for their future career;
5. agreement – jointly coming to an understanding by all parties about what needs to be done to improve performance generally and overcome any issues raised in the course of the discussion.

Appraisal tools

There are several tools that can be used for performance appraisal. The simplest is a trait-rating scale where individuals are rated using a numerical score against a set of standards, including their job description, knowledge, behaviours and personal traits – such as attitude to work. This method invites a subjective decision, which is open to potential bias, and, if a point scale is used, a tendency to score to the midline, making the process meaningless.

Self-assessment methods involve individuals submitting a portfolio of achievements and productivity. While introspection and self-awareness can result in growth and achievement, feedback on achievements is essential for a positive result.

Management by objectives is a technique seldom used in healthcare. It incorporates a process that negotiates both the organisation's objectives and the individual's assessments. It is a very specific form of appraisal, with individuals measured against the objectives on a regular basis. In public healthcare organisations the appraisal is usually an annual event, whereas management by objectives is often quarterly and therefore far more intensive and oriented towards action by observable results.

Peer review is, as the name suggests, a process whereby professional colleagues monitor and assess each other's performance. It is used widely in medicine and education, and less widely in wider healthcare. The NMC uses this approach to review nursing and midwifery education. Peer review events take place on an annual basis with a group of colleagues from other, similar organisations or professional groups conducting a review of systems and processes set against publicly available criteria. The process requires data to be collected from a variety of sources, such as charts, patient care plans, information systems, other professionals and patients.

An adaptation of the peer review process is 360-degree feedback. This is an assessment of performance that provides information from a variety of sources and often includes a group of colleagues who work with an individual. Usually, eight to ten people complete questionnaires that can also include a self-assessment, and which are submitted anonymously to an independent observer to collate the responses into a report for the individual. The report should demonstrate a synthesis of information about performance in a role. In healthcare, this could include patients as well as co-workers to provide all-round information, which is where the name originates. This allows the individuals being assessed to understand how other people view them (as in the Johari window, discussed in Chapter 1) and can enable the developing leader to work on areas of their behaviour which they might otherwise not be aware of.

We have previously discussed clinical supervision and coaching (Chapter 5) as a means of supporting individuals to develop new skills. These are also tools that a manager can utilise to improve work performance and standards.

Activity 7.6   Reflection and critical thinking

1. How do you feel about being appraised? What are your fears and anxieties about appraisal? Think about the expectations you have. Now put yourself into the shoes of the manager and try to understand his or her expectations of the process.

2. Consider each of the appraisal tools discussed above and draw up a table that compares the advantages and disadvantages of each method. You may need to look again at Chapter 5 on clinical supervision and coaching.

Further guidance is given on this activity at the end of the chapter.

Rewards

Performance appraisal can also be used as a means of assessing an individual's ability to be promoted or moved to another pay band. The now simplified Knowledge and Skills Framework, defined in the Agenda for Change (AfC) pay agreement (**http://www. nhsemployers.org/SimplifiedKSF**), paved the way for a Gateway Policy to be formulated by NHS Trusts to ensure that staff covered by the AfC would obtain a transparent opportunity to move to a higher pay band. Under the AfC, progression from one pay point to another is assessed each year against the skills identified in the Knowledge and Skills Framework bands. At defined points, known as Gateways, management decisions will be made about progression to higher levels of pay and responsibility. There are two Gateways in each of the nine pay bands: Foundation, which takes place no later than 12 months after an individual is appointed to a pay band, and Second Gateway, which is set at a fixed point towards the top of a pay band.

Planning change

Change, or service improvement, is a constant feature of health and social care. Changes are sometimes driven by policies to restructure organisations, by improvements in medical science such as the development of stem cell research, or advances in society's attitudes to rights, such as with the Human Rights Act (1998) and changes in legislation such as the Mental Capacity Act (2005). In the day-to-day running of a ward or unit the types of change that take place can be personal (such as when staff change) or organisational (such as changes in shift patterns) or the way in which internal services are delivered (e.g. bed management, portering services, catering services or discharge-planning methods).

There are many forces driving change in healthcare that are not just related to the UK. Rising costs of medical treatments, shortages of skilled workforces, increasing technology, availability of information and a growing elderly population have led, in some cases, to extreme destabilisation and a constant need to upgrade structures, promote better quality and manage workforce constraints. Whatever the changes to the work environment, there are those who embrace the changes and those who find it very difficult to adapt. Nurses in the future will need to be even more adaptable than they have been in the past to keep up with change.

Activity 7.7   Reflection

What is your personal perspective on change? Below is a short rating scale for you to self-assess your attitude to change. Place a mark in the score that most fits your perspective: 1 = low agreement; 5 = high agreement.

	1	2	3	4	5
1. I always embrace change					
2. I look for opportunities to change things					
3. I accept change reluctantly					
4. I avoid change at all costs					
5. My response to change is the same as that of my friends and family					
6. Have you always responded to change in this way or have you changed in your lifetime?					
7. What events have altered your views and responses to change?					

As this answer is based on your own experience and reflections, there is no specimen answer at the end of the chapter.

Initiating and co-ordinating change requires well-developed leadership and management skills. It requires vision and expert planning skills because neither skill alone is sufficient.

Many of the best ideas for changing practice fail because of inadequate preparation and planning. Poor preparation results in problems during implementation, frustrated staff and lack of successful outcome. Others fail at the first hurdle or later in the process because the team, the people having to implement and live with the change, do not understand the vision.

Change theory

Most of the contemporary research into change management originates from the work of social psychologist Kurt Lewin in the mid-twentieth century. There are other theories; however, we will concentrate on Lewin's theory in this book and will compare it briefly with newer developments in complexity theory and chaos theory. If you are interested in other theories, please go to the useful websites at the end of this chapter for further information.

Lewin (1951) identified three stages through which change must proceed before any planned change will become embedded in an organisation or system of working. The stages are unfreezing, movement and refreezing.

Unfreezing is when the change agent proposes a convincing plan for change to the team or management. It is also when team members who are not keen on the change can be helped to draw out their anxieties or concerns about the change. At this stage people become either discontented about the proposal or increasingly aware of the need to change. The skilful leader will be able to work with these conflicting views to build up trust in the change proposal's worth and the value of putting effort into the proposed change. Cummings and McLennan (2005) claim an essential leadership role is to understand the different perspectives of individuals and **stakeholders** and *to align the changes to be meaningful for them* (p65).

During unfreezing leaders need to take account of the balance between change and stability, as too much change leads to instability, which results in feelings of lack of control, insecurity and anxiety. A good leader will assess the relative merits of the forces for and against change, such as extent of the proposed change, nature and depth of motivation of stakeholders and the environment in which the change will occur; this last could be physical (e.g. buildings) or political (e.g. local or national policy). The driving forces for change will need to exceed the opposing forces for change to be successful (Beckhard and Harris, 1987). This idiom is something which managers need to focus on throughout all phases of the change process.

In the second stage there is *movement* towards accepting the change, and a plan of action and implementation is instigated. Change takes time as people adjust to the idea, come to understand the benefits of the change and eventually become adopters of the change. Part of the planning process for change management involves including time for recognising, addressing and overcoming resistance to the proposal arising from stakeholders' attitudes, perceptions and personal values.

The final stage, according to Lewin (1951), is *refreezing*. Change needs time before it is accepted as part of the system. This means that, after the change is implemented, support will still be needed to embed the change. The leader's role is to help the continued integration of the change into practice to ensure refreezing – that is, the change becoming part of normal practice; if this does not occur, the previous behaviours will emerge.

A good way of understanding Lewin's theory is to think of how you might create a spherical ice block from a cube shaped one. There are two main approaches to achieving this. The first is to chip away and try to achieve the change in shape. This is time-consuming, takes effort and the outcome is not guaranteed. The second approach is to melt the ice cube, pour the resulting water into a new mould and refreeze it. This approach is simple and guarantees that the desired result is achieved.

One method to ensure the effects of change are perceived as beneficial is to measure the outcomes of change or make improvements to the change as a result of feedback from outcome measures. Thus a plan to evaluate the change should be incorporated in the overall change management plan.

Steps of change

Stage 1: Unfreezing

1. Gather data and information about the planned change.
2. Accurately and objectively describe the issues that are causing the problem or reason for change. Use evidence and hard facts, not supposition or 'finger in the air' tactics.
3. Decide if change is really needed and identify the reasons for change. This could be a pilot for your ideas by testing on your team or one or two close colleagues.
4. Make others aware of the need for change. This also involves highlighting discontent with the current system, i.e. what is wrong or not productive. Progress to the next stage should not happen until sufficient discontent is expressed about the current system.

Stage 2: Movement

1. Develop a change management plan – this could take the form of a project plan (use a **Gantt chart** if it will help you visualise what you want to achieve – see Further reading at the end of the chapter).
2. Set goals and objectives.
3. Identify areas of support and resistance.
4. Include everyone who will be affected by the change in its planning; however, you may want to have a small project group or reference group to help manage the project with you.
5. Set target dates and timelines.
6. Develop appropriate strategies.
7. Implement the change.
8. Be available to support others and offer encouragement through the change process.
9. Use strategies for overcoming resistance to change.
10. Evaluate the change.
11. Modify the change if necessary.

Stage 3: Refreezing

Support others so that the change is sustainable and remains in place to achieve improved outcomes.

Source: Adapted from Marquis and Huston (2009), p171.

Case study: Change management

Cummings and McLennan (2005) outlined four steps in a change management project to introduce advanced practice nurse roles into a traditionally, medically oriented tertiary care oncology centre. Their main aim was to engage stakeholders in the change process and use an evidence-based approach. Step one was to identify a change model to guide the project. They did this by using Lewin's theoretical change model and adapting it to connect action research and policy drivers for change. The policy drivers challenged stakeholders' values and beliefs (i.e. the value of advanced nursing) and competence, standards of practice, financial savings, medical and nursing workloads.

The second step was to assign a 'champion' or change agent to the project to work closely with staff through the unfreezing stages of the project and enable the final stage, which is beyond the change itself. In the third step a forum was created, involving members from all the professional groups involved in the change, to facilitate open communication between everyone who would be affected by the change and change process. The final stage was to support staff through and beyond the change process to ensure the change became embedded into the working practices of the team.

Cummings and McLennan (2005) found that multidisciplinary team work, already established in the unit, was an important lever to help implement and embed the change. You will have noticed that, all the way through the change process, communication of intentions and plans, which ensures individuals and teams are engaged and informed in the change plan, has been paramount to creating an effective change strategy.

Activity 7.8 Decision-making

Identify a change you would like to make in your personal life. List the driving forces that you think are your reasons for wanting to change. Then list the restraining forces that you think will inhibit you making the change.

(Continued)

(Continued)

Work out a plan, utilising all of the steps of change in the box above, to achieve the change.

Hint

Remember the driving forces will need to exceed the restraining forces and you will need to feel sufficient discontent with how things currently are for the change process to tip from unsuccessful to successful. You will also need to plan time for the change to be embedded into your everyday life. This means it will take longer than you originally planned; especially if you were hoping for quick results.

As this answer is based on your own decision-making, there is no specimen answer at the end of the chapter.

Complexity theory and chaos theory

Lewin's change theory is a linear approach to change, with an optimistic view that change, once implemented, will be refrozen and equilibrium re-established. In this current world, where science is moving the frontiers of knowledge forward at an increasing pace and organisations respond to change more rapidly, the linear approach may not always work. This is particularly evident in UK healthcare, where long-term planning is problematic due to fluctuating economic and political influences. Consequently, non-linear change theories such as complexity theory and chaos theory now influence contemporary thinking about change.

Complexity theory maintains that we inhabit a complex world where individuals are multifaceted and situations are forever dynamic and changing. The theory originates from physics, where the natural order of science is challenged by systems that are constantly adapting because of the interaction between parts and feedback loops that change things and do not maintain the status quo. An example of this is that an individual may have behaved in a certain way in the past but that person's future behaviour may not be predictably the same.

Olson and Eoyang (2001) developed a theory of complex adaptive systems which maintains that we should not focus on the large changes taking place but on the effects of change at a micro level between individuals. It is at the individual level where relationships, and simple expressions of rules, are responsible for change. When applying this theory to changes in healthcare it suggests we should concentrate on the individuals who work in the organisations and understand these relationships before attempting to unfreeze, as in Lewin's theory. They also suggest that continual monitoring and adaptation are needed for refreezing to be achieved.

Research summary: Complexity theory and organisations

Anderson et al. (2004) undertook a study, underpinned by complexity theory, to analyse the effects of organisational climate and communication patterns on high staff turnover in nursing homes. They surveyed 3,449 employees in 164 randomly selected nursing homes in North Carolina, USA, to identify the perceptions of staff about organisational climate and communication. They also asked questions about the characteristics of the homes' facilities, allocation of resources and turnover. The results were analysed statistically using a hierarchical regression technique (to examine the relationship between variables).

They found that there was a lower turnover in the lower-paid staffing groups (which had the highest overall turnover rates) when the climate was viewed positively and communication was open. Where there was a reward-based climate and high levels of open communication, staff performed better than in those homes with unclear and confusing communication methods. They also found that, where there were good levels of staffing, and senior staff who had been in position for a long time, there was more likely to be lower staff turnover. Thus, a stable leadership situation enhanced staff satisfaction with workplace conditions through the influence of the leadership style. A reward-themed climate and open communication were aspects of this style.

Chaos theory was first described in 1963 by Edward Lorenz, a meteorologist working on the problem of weather predictability. It is related to complexity theory in that it refers to the unpredictable and adaptive factors that affect events. Lorenz discovered that a minor change in a part of an experiment could change the whole outcome. A practical example is where a slight rise in the temperature of the ocean in one place in the world may have an effect on the airflow that will eventually lead to a change in temperature in another part of the world.

Chaos theory is a relatively new science that helps us understand why a small change in a situation can alter how a system functions. Chaos theory also suggests that it is impossible to know what this change may be because there are so many different variables that can affect a situation. For example, even if you know everything about football – the players, strategies, ground conditions and everything involved – you still cannot accurately predict the outcome. Yet, if you watch repeated games you would be able to predict some elements of the game.

The application of complexity theory to change management in organisations provides a means of understanding why change does not always go to plan because of unpredictable multifactorial influences and, secondly, that understanding small effects, as chaos theory suggests, can have a big effect in a change management plan. For example, individuals who do not trust the change plan or do not think it can work could jeopardise the change plan. However, if they are brought into the change process and their ideas given a hearing, they may not feel the need to jeopardise the plan. A major lesson for managers is that they cannot completely control a change plan because there will always be some elements that cannot be predicted in advance that will affect it. Managers need to learn how to manage the anxiety that accompanies change as well as flexibility and the ability to think on their feet so that they can manage the unexpected. In Chapter 9 we talk some more about the impact of change on individuals and their self-esteem.

There is of course a further complication within healthcare and nursing: people. As well as staff, of which there are many professions and grades operating within any one team, patients are all unique. The uniqueness of individuals and increasing awareness of healthcare rights and responsibilities can mean that different people will ask, and deliver, different things even in the same circumstances. People are complex and their unpredictable responses to challenges and change can provoke chaos even within the best managed system.

Living in a constantly changing world where there is rapid technological, social, cultural and political change, we have to be prepared to adapt, be willing to learn and test our assumptions. Things that worked in the past may not work in the future and nurses have always been able to find new ways of managing problems and being creative. That is why in the next section we will explore how nurses can use this creativity to improve patient care.

Tools for change: entrepreneurship

In 2004 the International Council of Nurses (ICN) produced a monograph that gives guidance on the scope for nurses to become self-employed using expert skills and knowledge. In the UK there has been limited uptake of independent practitioners of nursing and midwifery; however, the skills of entrepreneurship are now being debated as a potential, valuable contribution to innovative healthcare initiatives. The ICN sets out how this can be understood by describing three different types of nursing entrepreneur:

1. Entrepreneur: an individual who assumes the total responsibility and risk for discovering or creating unique opportunities to use personal talents, skills and energy and who employs a strategic planning process to transfer that opportunity into a marketable service or product.

2. Nurse entrepreneur: a proprietor of a business that offers nursing services of a direct care, educational, research, administrative or consultative nature. The self-employed nurse is directly accountable to the client, to whom, or on behalf of whom, nursing services are provided.

3. Nurse intrapreneur: a salaried nurse who develops, promotes and delivers an innovative health/nursing programme or project within a given healthcare setting based upon the skills of entrepreneurism (ICN, 2004).

It is this last role that we will be exploring in this chapter. Within these definitions it is clear that the only difference between an intrapreneur and entrepreneur is the setting in which the skills of entrepreneurship are used.

The NMC (2018) *Future Nurse: Standards of Proficiency for Registered Nurses* Platform 6: 'Improving safety and quality of care' proficiency 6.9 requires the graduate nurse to: 'work with people, their families, carers and colleagues to develop effective improvement strategies for quality and safety, sharing feedback and learning from positive outcomes and experiences, mistakes and adverse outcomes and experiences'. As such 'effective improvement strategies' are changes made in real time, they are entrepreneurial, or more correctly intrapreneurial, solutions to day-to-day problems seen in the clinical setting. Nurse are therefore required to be equipped with many of the skills needed to be entrepreneurs, but often we fail to recognise them.

To understand the influence of entrepreneurism on the concept of intrapreneurism, we need to consider its antecedents. There is no commonly accepted definition of the terms 'entrepreneur' and 'entrepreneurship' and furthermore the meaning is shifting as it is applied to healthcare endeavours as intrapreneurism. In business or commercial terms an entrepreneur is someone who has a new idea and wishes to undertake a new venture with a responsibility for the risks that may result and the outcome. There is an implicit sense that the entrepreneur will personally gain from the venture. Entrepreneurs will see opportunities for developments and take advantage of those opportunities; they can act as a catalyst for change and research and innovation, introducing new technologies, increasing efficiency and productivity, and generating new products or services. An intrapreneur will essentially do the same but within the confines of an organisation and will benefit less from the outcomes, but will be exposed to less attendant risk.

Traynor et al. (2006) reported on a research project that investigated the extent and potential for entrepreneurial activity in nursing, midwifery and health visiting (NMHV). In 2007, Drennan et al. published the findings and claimed that, while they found a range of NMHV entrepreneurial activity in the UK, there is very little in relation to the total numbers of nurses, midwives and health visitors registered in the UK. This reflects the international picture. The examples of nurse entrepreneur activity that were found involved nurses being creative and flexible in their working environments to solve problems or substituting for medical roles. The researchers found that nurses in certain fields (such as public health or specialist nursing) were more likely to have carried out entrepreneurial activity. Specific examples of activity were found through knowledge transfer (through training and consultancy), invention of healthcare products and small-business provision of infrastructure services to healthcare and self-employed and small-business provision of direct healthcare services.

The study attempted to find a relationship between entrepreneurial activity and patient choice but found this to be weak, except in the case of independent midwifery. Yet in 20 per cent of the documents they analysed, this was an aspiration, along with seeking autonomous practice and achieving personal and professional accomplishment. Financial incentives were not a prominent feature; however, this was not borne out by seminar participants, who felt that financial gain was a hidden agenda due to the lack of a commercial culture within the NHS.

Activity 7.9   Skills development

Think of an area of practice, service delivery or patient care that you would like to see improved. Imagine you are going to present this idea to a *Dragons' Den*-type panel of peers. (If you are not familiar with the television programme *Dragons' Den*, please generate an idea for presentation to a panel of peers.)

1.   Who would you have on the panel? What skills and knowledge would you expect them to have to make a decision about your idea?
2.   Design a simple presentation that 'sells' your idea to the panel.

Hint

Go to the BBC web page **http://news.bbc.co.uk/1/hi/business/2943252. stm**, for tips on writing a business plan.

As this answer is based on your own research and reflections, there is no specimen answer at the end of the chapter.

The debate is still open on whether or not entrepreneurialism can drive forward a culture of innovation and creativity, benefiting patient care. There remain several obstacles, such as the prevailing ideology of the NHS as a public-sector organisation and therefore by default a 'not-for-profit industry', and the socialisation of NMHVs that does not include a business frame of reference. As Drennan et al. (2007) point out, there has been no systematic measurement of the outcomes of NMHV enterprise activities to support the effectiveness of entrepreneurial activity. Yet there are examples of where it has made a difference (Drennan et al., 2007).

Chapter summary

In this chapter we have examined different organisational structures that you can map out in your own organisation. You can then identify where the decisions are made in your organisation which will, in turn, help you understand where to find information about the decisions. Nurses are playing an increasingly pivotal role in organisational decisions as government policy recognises that nurses can represent not only their profession but also the patient's point of view. We have studied the governance requirements for NHS, and other healthcare, institutions to ensure they are meeting the standards required and also looked at the regulatory arrangements starting in 2012. While looking at standards we considered how to improve care on a personal level through performance appraisal and compared some of the methods that can be used.

The chapter has also looked at the theory underpinning change management and contemporary theory developments. Change management is a huge subject and we have only briefly touched on the change-planning process to raise your awareness of the methods available. Finally, we looked at the potential for a newer approach to introducing change and improving standards with an emphasis on social enterprise and entrepreneurial skills.

Activities: Brief outline answers

Activity 7.6 Reflection and critical thinking (p137)

1. Preparation for appraisal is the best method of ensuring levels of anxiety are minimised on the part of both the appraisee and the appraiser. This means ensuring the method and purpose of the appraisal are clearly articulated and agreed beforehand, standards are transparent and evident in the organisation's policies, strengths as well as weaknesses are explored and the paperwork is available and prepared in advance by both parties. Further support for conducting appraisals can be found on the CIPD website listed in the useful websites section below.

2. Comparison of appraisal methods:

	Advantages	Disadvantages
Clinical supervision	Personal and focused	Could become too intense
	Deeper trusting relationship can be established	Personalities may not match
	Can specifically match specialty area to improve performance	More resources required for time
Coaching	Personalised	Takes time
	Identifies specific goals	Needs in-depth coaching training to be effective
	Enhances personal motivation	
Trait-rating scales	Uses a set standard that is transparent	Can lead to subjective assessments
	Incorporates personal behaviours such as attitudes	Central tendency in scores
		'Halo' or 'horns' effects from rater

(Continued)

(Continued)

	Advantages	Disadvantages
Self-appraisal	Collects examples of impact on standards and is achievement-oriented Enables personal growth and awareness	Gives little scope for feedback – positive or negative May have focused on goals that do not correspond to organisational targets for improvement
Management by objectives	Determines individual progress, incorporating both employee and organisation's goals Promotes individual growth and excellence	Authoritarian and directive managers find this approach difficult due to the negotiated nature of the goal setting Some employees may set easily achievable goals
Peer review	Has the potential to increase accuracy of performance appraisal as collects data from wider range of sources Can enhance team working and improve understanding between different teams, especially interdisciplinary teams Provides increased opportunities for professional learning and sharing of good practice	Requires high levels of trust to share data More time consuming than one-to-one appraisals Takes time to orient staff to the process, requires training and has high administration costs Shifts authority away from manager, which can be threatening to the manager, who may feel exposed
360-degree appraisal	Feedback from a variety of sources Provides a broader perspective on an individual's performance	Requires questionnaires to be designed and administered, data collected anonymously and collated into a report, which is costly and time consuming Could be threatening to have such a wide selection of subjective opinions about an individual's performance

Further reading

Dwyer, J, Stanton, P and Thiessen, V (2004) *Project Management in Health and Community.* London: Routledge.

Gantt, HL (1910) *Work, Wages and Profit,* published by *The Engineering Magazine,* New York; republished as *Work, Wages and Profits.* Easton, PA: Hive Publishing Company, 1974.

Johnson, S (1999) *Who Moved my Cheese? An Amazing Way to Deal with Change in Your Work and in Your Life.* London: Vermilion.

Kritonis, A (2004) Comparison of change theory. *International Journal of Scholarly Academic Intellectual Diversity*, 8 (1).

Marquis, BL and Huston, CJ (2014) *Leadership Roles and Management Functions in Nursing: Theory and Applications* (7th edition). Philadelphia, PA: Lippincott, Williams and Wilkins, Chapter 24: Performance Appraisal.

Standing, M (ed.) (2010) Chapter 2 on complex systems theory. In: *Clinical Judgement and Decision-Making in Nursing: Theory and Practice*. Milton Keynes: Open University Press.

Traynor, M, Davis, K, Drennan, V, Goodman, C, Humphrey, C, Locke, R, Mark, A, Murray, SF, Banning, M and Peacock, R (2006) *A Report to the National Co-ordinating Centre for NHS Service Delivery and Organisation Research and Development of a Scoping Exercise on 'The Contribution of Nurse, Midwife and Health Visitor Entrepreneurs to Patient Choice'*. London: National Co-ordinating Centre for Service Delivery and Organisation.

Yoder-Wise, PS (2014) *Leading and Managing in Nursing* (6th edition). St Louis, MO: Mosby Elsevier. See especially Chapter 17: Leading Change.

Useful websites

www.businessballs.com/change-management/

A good overview of change, change tools and the impact of change.

www.cipd.co.uk/hr-resources/factsheets/performance-appraisal.aspx

Performance appraisal: Chartered Institute of Personnel and Development performance appraisal: guidance and processes.

www.learnmanagement2.com

Organisation structures: The Learn Management website gives lots of theory and useful explanatory diagrams.

www.scottlondon.com/interviews/wheatley.html

The New Science of Leadership: an interview with Margaret Wheatley by Scott London.

www.bbc.co.uk/programmes/p00548f6

Chaos theory: BBC broadcast of radio programme chaired by Melvyn Bragg in 2002 with Susan Greenfield, Senior Research Fellow, Lincoln College, Oxford University, David Papineau, Professor of the Philosophy of Science, King's College, London and Neil Johnson, University Lecturer in Physics at Oxford University, discussing chaos theory. The broadcast explains chaos theory and its roots and application to modern-day usage. You will need Realplayer software to listen to the broadcast, which lasts for 45 minutes.

www.nurse-entrepreneur-network.com

US Nurse Entrepreneur Network web page: advice and tips on setting up a nursing business.

www.youtube.com/watch?v=ZxuwVqyyrmM

Wendy Miles, entrepreneurial nurse 'Nurse Joey': Example of a nurse entrepreneur success that has improved nurses' working lives, benefited the organisation and released time for patient care. Wendy developed a handy pocket-like pouch to assist nurses; it saves time for nurses to carry small essential equipment about with them while they work.

www.entreprenurses.net

A website for UK nurses wishing to learn more about developing entrepreneurial skills and links to short learning modules, podcasts and relevant literature.

Chapter 8

Creating a learning environment

5.9 demonstrate the ability to challenge and provide constructive feedback about care delivered by others in the team, and support them to identify and agree individual learning needs.

5.10 contribute to supervision and team reflection activities to promote improvements in practice and services.

Chapter aims

After reading this chapter you will be able to:

- identify what a learning environment is;
- explain why a learning environment is important;
- discuss how a learning environment might be created;
- consider your role in developing a learning environment.

Introduction

Nursing, in common with all health and social care, is evolving. In great part this evolution is driven by the society and culture we live in and by the changing technology we work with, developing understandings of the nature and experience of care. Within this changing environment there is a need for nursing, and individual nurses, to keep pace with developments. The increased professionalisation of nursing, clearly demonstrated by the move to an all-graduate profession, further requires nurses to be engaged with their own development and learning in order to meet the demands of twenty-first-century care provision. As can be seen in the descriptor for Platform 5, each nurse has the responsibility to act as 'a role model for best practice in the delivery of nursing care'. This can only be achieved if we stay up to date with the latest learning and understanding.

Learning and developing are therefore constant and enduring requirements for all nurses and the need to facilitate this is a key function of nurse leaders and managers. This chapter describes how the creation and maintenance of a learning environment in the clinical setting can contribute to the development of nurses and nursing. You will be challenged within this chapter to consider what this means for you as an individual, as well as how you might take the messages contained in it forward in your career as a leader or manager of nurses; that is in the development of others. It is important to remember that your orientation to learning and the generation of learning environments have a direct, positive impact on patient care. In this respect, environments of care which are 'learning environments' allow us to express some of the values of care we discussed in detail in Chapter 1.

What are 'environments of care'?

Before we go on to consider what is meant by a 'learning environment', let's take a moment to consider what is meant by the term environments in the sense used here. Environments refer to many things, including the physical nature of a building and its surroundings, as well as the meanings different people attach to the same physical space.

Activity 8.1 Reflection

To understand the ways in which different people attach different meanings to spaces, let's begin by reflecting on the nature of the work environment. When you are working in the hospital setting, consider the different ways in which people may experience the area in which you work. Consider how you experience the area, how the permanent staff experience it, how visiting staff experience it, how patients experience it and how patient visitors experience it. What are their different interpretations based on? Why is this important?

If you do not work in the hospital setting, consider the same questions in the context of the area in which you do work.

There are some possible answers and thoughts at the end of the chapter.

The interpretation of what an environment is, using the answers to the reflection, very much hinges on the function of the area concerned and your role in relation to that function. Different people experience the same area in a different light and have different views about the nature and workings of the same place. This gives us some clues as to what an environment of care is about, but this is not the whole story.

Environments, especially care environments, are very much the product not only of what goes on there, but of how people behave and interact. In this sense environments can be considered to reflect the psychosocial nature of a place. Many commentators refer to environments as *cultures* (Handy, 1994) and in many ways this term is as useful as environments, if not more so; this is because the word culture conjures up an image of something more ingrained, natural and all-encompassing than the term environment. In this sense a culture is not about nationality, race or ethnicity; it is about a shared sense of the psychosocial nature, *the feel*, of a place. This nature of the place is very much tied to the ways in which people interact and behave within the place and is therefore a product of the human interaction and activity which take place there.

The psychosocial feel of a ward, clinical area or team is closely related to the ways in which the people there talk about, and to, each other, and the way in which they interact with people who are visitors to the area – the general ambience, if you like. In many respects, the environment or culture (we will use the terms interchangeably) created in a care area reflects the *values* of the people who work there.

As nurses, and especially as leaders or managers, we have the ability to affect the environment in which we work. Understanding the impact we have as individuals and as leaders and managers is essential to understanding how to manage environments; you may find it useful to revisit the Johari window discussed in Chapter 1 at this stage to remind yourself about how others see us and how we see ourselves and what impact this has on relationships. The important aspect of the Johari window for the manager is how we manage the elements of the window which are shared with others; in particular the open area, in which we allow others to see who we are. It is people's interpretation of who we are and how we behave which sets the tone for the team and the wider organisation.

As a leader of people, the tone and nature of your interactions with others will set the benchmark by which others act. If you are seen not to care about where you work, or the people who work there, neither will the team. If you are brash, loud or condescending, then members of the team will be too. It is almost impossible to overestimate the impact that leaders have on their immediate environment. The message about the impact of leaders on the environment of the team they lead is therefore clear – in most instances leaders create the culture.

Activity 8.2   Reflection

Think about the values you identified yourself and a leader as having in Activity 1.2. Now you understand a little more about leadership and management how do you see those values as being important to you, not only as a nurse but as an emerging leader? Rather than just thinking about what values you and the nurse leader have in common, think about how the exercise of those values has an impact on the people around you. Consider this both for the leader you identified in Activity 1.2 and for yourself.

As this is based on your own observations, there is no specimen answer at the end of the chapter.

The Nursing and Midwifery Council (NMC, 2002) states that lifelong learning *requires an enquiring approach to the practice of nursing and midwifery, as well as to issues which impact on that practice.* With the advent of revalidation for nurses, all nurses need both to engage with and to record their continuing professional development activities (NMC, 2017). These activities contribute to the proof nurses requires to demonstrate that their practice is contemporaneous, informed by the current state of knowledge.

The role of the manager and leader in developing environments of care that support such learning development is critical. Creating a learning culture is something leaders must therefore do by setting an example, not only in undertaking formal education themselves, but by learning from their team, their clients, from complaints and from their own practice. The action of learning from others is an example of the exercise of the value of being 'other-regarding'. Being alert to sources of information as well as having the disposition to continually engage in learning with others is described in Chapter 1 of *Evidence Based Practice in Nursing* (Ellis, 2016b). In the model of evidence based nursing described there, patient centredness relies on the nurse being open to continual learning and development. The same is true of the leader who in acting in this way also acts as a role model to their team.

Learning from and with others is also a requirement of revalidation in that nurses have to demonstrate that they have gained practice related feedback, written reflective accounts based on practice and undertaken a reflective discussion with a peer (NMC, 2017). In following the template set out for revalidation by the NMC the aspiring leader or manager can show how they demonstrate lifelong learning to the team.

Lee et al. (2010, p475) state: *By practising the knowledge builder role, leaders create opportunities and processes that stimulate and encourage knowledge sharing amongst team members.* This knowledge-building role is achieved by offering new ideas and solutions to problems and by encouraging dialogue in the team. The key message here is that, for a team to develop a learning culture, the leader or manager must take the lead in that learning by role modelling learning behaviour.

What a learning environment is

A learning environment is essentially a set of attitudes, values and their corresponding actions that creates a culture in which learning and development can take place. Quinn (1995) suggests that the learning that takes place in the clinical setting is more meaningful to nursing students than that which occurs in the classroom setting. The proposal here is that the opportunities for learning and development which occur in the clinical setting are invaluable to the development of students. We would argue this point can be stretched further to include all of the staff who work in a particular setting.

A ward, clinic or community team whose members are empowered to learn and develop will be able to provide meaningful care which not only reflects current clinical trends but which puts the patient at the heart of care. A team which operates in a learning environment will seize every opportunity to grow and develop and as a result, their ability to care will be enhanced. In this sense, a learning environment is one which fosters positive development and change.

Bersin (2010, p16) argues that a learning environment is *the collective practices that encourage sharing of information and all forms of people development.* This idea further supports the idea that learning is more than an optional extra within the team; it is fundamental to the development of all members of the team and therefore the improvement of what they do. As such the creation, adoption and maintenance of a learning environment is a fundamental approach to addressing the standards and proficiencies for registered nurse education highlighted at the start of the chapter.

What this means for you as an individual student or nurse will be discussed later in the chapter.

Why learning environments are important

Increasing emphasis is being placed on the benefits associated with work-based learning in today's health and social care provision. In some part, this is evidenced by the increase in the number and range of foundation degrees available and in the increasing provision of workplace learning modules in post-registration and postgraduate continuing professional development programmes for health and social care professionals.

The emphasis on work-based learning has been described by Spouse (2001) as arising from the need to generate workers who have moved on from being skilled and technically competent to becoming active problem solvers who are able to adapt and develop in tandem with their environment. Think of it this way; someone who is trained to change a dressing will do just that, while someone who understands how to change a dressing and what to look for in the way of healing will both change the dressing and be aware of alternative ways of doing the dressing, what infection might look like and what the nutritional needs of the patient might be. This latter way of working is an example of the activity which takes place in a learning environment where care is constantly evolving. Care which is the best it can be allows the nurse to exercise the values of providing high-quality, holistic care and in this sense, at least, the generation of a learning environment is a fulfilment of nursing values.

Developing a learning environment in the workplace also has the potential to bring many benefits to the team and to the individuals within the team. A team established in a learning culture can rapidly adapt to change and develop new ways of working that are consistent with best practice. Staff who work in and adopt the values of a learning organisation both feel, and are, more empowered to do their job and as a consequence have the ability to be more effective at what they do.

This is not about learning and changing for learning and changing's sake, it is about the advancement of care. One of the key complaints from nurses in any setting is that there

Activity 8.3 Reflection

Reflect on the times in the classroom setting when you have engaged with the conversation around whatever it is you were learning. How did your engagement in the debate around the topic affect your learning? Did your contribution have an impact on what you learnt and how you felt about what you learnt?

There are some possible answers and thoughts at the end of the chapter.

are constant changes taking place. In a learning culture, change is seen as the norm when that change advances practice and brings about improvements in patient care.

Your answers to the above reflection probably demonstrate that on the occasions you engaged in what was happening in the classroom you learnt more, felt happier and were clearer about the subject matter. What is more important is that engaging in what is going on probably helped you to feel more involved, part of something if you like, as well as feeling you contributed to the learning and development of the group as a whole.

Case study: The same practice supervisor

Paul is a student nurse in his first year of training. Paul has a clinical placement on a care of the elderly ward and is not at all happy with it as there is not enough high-tech care going on. Paul comes into work each shift, as he knows he must, and goes through the motions of caring for the elderly patients. He washes and helps to feed patients, but does little in the way of communication and does not attempt to understand the care needs of those he nurses. Paul's practice supervisor offers little in the way of teaching, support or advice to Paul. Overall, it is a pretty poor experience and Paul does little more than endure it.

Mary, also a first-year student, is placed on the same ward as Paul. Mary is keen to understand the care she is giving and what it means for the patients. She too would prefer to work somewhere more exciting, but has decided to get what she can in the way of learning from her experience. Mary talks to her patients and asks them about their lives. She observes them closely when washing and dressing them and takes note of issues such as the development of pressure areas. Mary listens when patients explain their symptoms and makes mental notes to look things up when she is off duty. Mary asks questions of her practice supervisor and explores ideas and tries to understand the new experiences she is having. Mary's practice supervisor is the same person supervising Paul, but offers Mary different learning opportunities and looks for ways to enhance her learning experience. Mary quickly starts to enjoy her placement and learns a lot about good-quality nursing care provision.

Certainly the same ideas translate into the practice setting, where engaging in learning, rather than being the passive recipient of knowledge, will greatly affect the learning which you are able to take from a situation. Consider this scenario:

This case study may reflect some of the experiences you have had either as a student or a mentor. What is important to understand is that the learning opportunities for both Mary and Paul are the same. What makes the difference is their approach to learning. Mary adopts a positive and open approach to learning. You might say she embodies a learning culture in herself, and as a result she gets a lot from her experience. Paul, on the other hand, closes himself off to learning and therefore gets little from his placement.

The reward for Mary in adopting this positive approach to her own development is enjoyment of the placement and enhanced learning. It is clear her mentor also gained something from mentoring Mary and therefore sought opportunities to support her development. Again, this is all about attitude. Mary shows her mentor that she is engaged and values the experience. The extra effort the mentor makes for her is in recognition of this.

As well as the opportunities that arise for self-development, learning cultures bring other rewards to the team and the organisation at large. Consider again the case study above. In being more diligent about her care provision and in seeking not only to provide care but to understand the care she is giving, Mary has the opportunity to identify and prevent some potential complications arising in the patients she cares for. Such proactive nursing will benefit Mary, her patients, the team and the wider organisation in reducing complication rates and the time patients stay in hospital.

From the perspective of the ward manager, the constructive approach to learning Mary has adopted demonstrates benefits for the team in the creation of a positive environment. For the team leader or ward manager the fostering of a positive learning culture will benefit the team in helping with staff recruitment and retention as well as the potential reduction in absences from work.

What is fascinating about this is the impact that allowing people to ask and answer questions can have on both morale and clinical outcomes. It seems so insignificant a thing to do, but clearly the effect is great.

Case study: Being alert to learning opportunities

Felicity was working with her mentor Maxine caring for Mr King. While helping Mr King to transfer from his bed to a chair Felicity noticed him wincing but thought very little of it. Maxine had also noticed Mr King wincing and, unlike her mentee, thought something was not right. Maxine went and checked Mr King's notes to be sure she understood his condition, she then asked Felicity to accompany her while they asked Mr King what is was that made him wince. Mr King said that it was when Felicity had supported him near his armpit, she was not rough though. Maxine considered this for a moment and then, after gaining Mr King's consent, examined his axilla where she found some swelling of his lymph nodes.

The swelling did not fit with Mr King's diagnosis so Maxine reported her finding to the ward doctor. The doctors examined Mr King and after ordering a chest x-ray were able to see that he had asbestosis which had not been previously diagnosed.

What this real life case study shows is that working in a learning environment and being alert to what is going on in it can be of benefit to everyone but most especially the

157

patient. Felicity learned as a result of this episode to not ignore things she saw about her, but to adopt a questioning approach to care.

Elements of the learning environment

So far we have identified a definition of a learning culture and have explored some of the benefits for the individual, team and organisation. In order to understand better the notion of learning environments it is now worth exploring the elements which go towards creating and sustaining them.

Peter Senge (1990), one of the leading writers on learning organisations, identifies five key elements – he calls them disciplines – which need to be in place for a learning organisation to be generated and maintained.

The five disciplines needed to create a learning environment

1. Systems thinking – this is essentially the ability to see the bigger picture. Seeing the big picture is an important element of nursing and leadership because of the complex nature of caring for people. Jackson and Ellis (2010) argue that whole-systems thinking in complex environments requires us to: identify all of the components of the system (people) and their roles as well as the nature of the interrelationships between them; recognise that working in a whole system is beneficial; and understand the risks of whole-systems working. The idea is that we see the interconnectedness of what each component (individual) of the system does and work to maximise its input (in much the same way as we explored team working in Chapter 2 and when we explored systems theory in Chapter 7).

2. Personal mastery – this is about the commitment of the people in the system to self-development. Self-development in this sense is about realising our potential and striving to be the best that we can be through constant and consistent self-development – clearly this relates to the exercise of our personal values, as we explored in Chapter 1.

3. Mental models – this requires us to identify and acknowledge the values, issues and beliefs that prevent us from being all we can be. This process involves reflection on ourselves and our motivations and becoming open and receptive to new ideas and ways of working; this often requires a change in both personal and team cultures.

4. Building shared visions – for the leader or manager, this is about gaining consensus on the view of how things should be from all of the members of the team. When the team can agree to a vision of how things should be, they can work consistently and supportively to achieve it. As well as understanding your values, as a leader you will need to understand and acknowledge the values of the team.

5. Team learning – this is the final and fundamental aspect of creating a learning culture. One person does not make a culture alone. Nursing involves the co-operative working of nurses and other care professionals. Learning together facilitates the creation of relationships which enable the wider team to work together more effectively.

Source: Adapted from Senge (1990).

What Senge's model demonstrates is that the creation of learning cultures requires the ability to see how things fit together, personal commitment, a change in thinking, shared drive and a willingness to learn together. So some of the messages here are about us as individuals and others about us and the way we interact in, or lead, teams.

Senge (1996) further identifies that the first step on the road to becoming a learning team or organisation is a willingness to allow people of all levels to lead in different ways. This requirement points to the need for each individual within the learning environment to commit to the values and practice of learning together.

What this means for you

The teams that work within a learning environment are made up of many individuals. As we have discussed, to a great extent the culture of the team derives from the actions and values of the leader or manager. The message is therefore clear for the leader or manager who wants to create a learning culture: lead by example. But what if you are not the manager or leader? What do the messages of this chapter hold for you?

As with all aspects of leading and managing, the first port of call is self. We saw in Chapter 4 that to deal with conflict effectively you must first of all ensure you are not the problem; we saw in Chapter 1 that to be an effective leader you must first know yourself and what drives and motivates you. Similarly, if you want to develop into the sort of leader who can promote learning and development, you must first of all develop yourself. Such development is not all about learning new things and ideas: it is more about your attitude to learning and development – the exercise of your values. For the student nurse this may mean adopting a more proactive approach to learning. You have made an important first step in choosing to read books such as this. If you are a trained nurse your attitude to your own continuing professional development is equally important.

For the manager, this might include learning and understanding the strengths and weaknesses of your team so that you can use the strengths and develop the weaknesses to the benefit of the individuals, team and the patients you care for. Again this is also about being a role model, being ready and willing to learn, to adapt and to ask questions pertinent to what is going on around you.

Not only is your attitude to self-development important, but so too is your attitude to the learning and development of others. Are you happy to share what you know?

Do you support colleagues and friends who need to understand something you know already? Are you willing to listen to and learn from others, perhaps even those you consider to be your juniors? Are you comfortable asking questions?

Activity 8.4   Critical thinking

In order to develop as a nurse learner, and contribute to the development of learning environments of care, it is important you understand your journey as a nurse. In order to understand better what you need to do to develop, you must first reflect on your learning journey to date. Write a short biography of your learning as a person and a nurse to date: what have you learnt, where have you learned it and how what you have learnt has changed you. You should write this as if you are explaining who you are to someone meeting you for the first time.

As this is based on your own observations, there is no specimen answer at the end of the chapter.

There are some key challenges here about the way in which you present yourself to others as well as understanding what truly motivates you and your practice. There are multiple influences on what and how we learn; reflecting on these may start to tell us something about the type of environment we might want to create in order to promote learning. Certainly the culture of the place in which you work now will impact on how you answer Activity 8.4 as well as how you feel about learning. Once again the onus rests with you as to how you will react to new learning opportunities. For the leader, the message about leading by example is clear: if you are comfortable about asking questions and developing your learning, your staff will be too; if you make people feel valued when they ask questions, they will ask them, and with questioning will come learning and development.

A word of caution here: leaders who are not serious about learning and developing with their staff create cultures which are the very antithesis on learning cultures. Such cultures are impoverished, they do not support development, they engage in outdated and outmoded practices, and good staff leave.

Developing a learning environment: The challenge

Now we have some understanding of the nature of learning environments, their benefits to the individual, team and wider organisation, the challenge is to understand for ourselves how we might create and develop such an environment. For the remainder of this chapter, this challenge takes the form of a series of activities to help you identify your orientation to learning environments, your experience of learning environments to date and your understanding of how a learning environment might be created.

It is important that you explore these issues in order to address the requirement of the 2018 NMC *Future Nurse: Standards of Proficiency for Registered Nurses*: Platform 5: Leading and managing nursing care and working in teams:

5.7   demonstrate the ability to monitor and evaluate the quality of care delivered by others in the team and lay carers.

5.8   support and supervise students in the delivery of nursing care, promoting reflection and providing constructive feedback, and evaluating and documenting their performance.

5.10 contribute to supervision and team reflection activities to promote improvements in practice and services.

Activity 8.5   Reflection

Reflecting on how you feel about learning in general and learning within the practice setting in particular will say something about your orientation to learning environments. Consider these questions and answer truthfully. You may find that some of the comments from mentors in your practice assessment document will help you to identify how others perceive your learning behaviours: you might like to reflect on the learning biography you wrote in Activity 8.3.

- How do you feel about new situations in the practice setting?
- Do you like new experiences or are you only comfortable with things that you know?
- How do you feel about asking questions?
- Does it matter who you are asking the questions of?
- Are you comfortable asking questions in front of others?
- When a patient asks you a question that you do not know the answer to, do you make up an answer, say you don't know and find someone else or tell the patient that you will find out?
- When you come across something that you do not understand, do you ignore it, ask questions of people who do, go away and look it up for yourself, ask questions and look it up?

As this is based on your own observations, there is no specimen answer at the end of the chapter.

What these questions will help you to appreciate is what you value in the way of learning and understanding in the clinical setting. While there are no wrong answers as such, primarily because these questions do not ask you what is the right thing to do but ask you what it is *you* do, there are some states of behaviour and responses which are perhaps more in line with the values needed to engage in a learning environment.

What is needed from you in terms of engaging in self-development which makes you fit for lifelong learning and engagement in, and potentially future creation of, learning environments is: keenness to engage in and understand new situations and ways of working; a willingness to admit when you do not know something; a willingness to ask questions and a desire to increase your understanding and the understanding of others when you are in a position to do so.

When we fail to embrace these key values as individual nurses, or nursing students, it is not only ourselves that we fail, but also the wider team, organisation and ultimately our patients.

Activity 8.6   Critical thinking

Your orientation to learning environments will influence your understanding and feelings about learning environments. Think about how the environments in the various clinical areas that you have worked in have affected your learning. Consider how you have responded to the various learning opportunities presented to you:

- What have you done when the learning opportunities appear poor?
- Do you ask questions?
- Do you try to supplement this with your own reading and finding out?
- When faced with a poor learning environment, do you try to help more junior staff or students with their learning?
- What factors in the ward environment affect the learning opportunities available?
- Can you identify personal or group behaviours which appear to make a difference?

As this is based on your own observations, there is no specimen answer at the end of the chapter.

The questions in this activity point to the role you might play in creating your own learning opportunities regardless of the culture of the place in which you are working. They ask questions about whether you role model positive learning behaviours and take a proactive stance in your own learning and that of others.

You are also asked to reflect on individual and group behaviours which impact on your learning and that of others in the area. Reflecting on and being aware of the behaviours and attitudes that promote, or hinder, learning equip you with ideas about how you might behave in order to promote a positive learning environment. What is important is that you realise that issues you have reflected on as a student or junior member of staff become action points for your future career. When you see good practice you might choose to mirror it when you are a leader or manager; when you see poor practice, or practices which do not work very well, you learn from these and do not repeat the same mistakes when you are in a position of influence.

Activity 8.7   Critical thinking

Given your orientation to learning environments and your experience of them to date, consider how you might go about creating a learning environment in the clinical setting:

- What strategies might you use to promote the change?
- How will you sell the idea to others?
- What strategies for learning might you promote to others?

The project management template below might help you plan your answer to this activity in a constructive manner.

Project management template

What is the purpose of the project? What do we do now and what is it we are trying to achieve?

Who is responsible for what aspect of the project? What skills and resources do we have available to us?

Who are our stakeholders? Who will this project affect and how will we get people on board with the idea?

How will we make a start? What do we need to do to start the change process?

What are the possible outcomes, both positive and negative? Consider here personal, team, organisational and patients.

What things might hinder the project and what might help it progress? What are the personnel and financial costs attached?

What should we have achieved by when and how will we know we have achieved these goals?

(Continued)

(Continued)

Project management template

What will this look like when it is implemented? How will we know we have achieved our ultimate goals?

How and how often will we audit what we have done and maintain impetus, assuming we achieve our goals? What measure, both direct and indirect, might there be of our success?

As this is based on your own observations, there is no specimen answer at the end of the chapter.

The purpose of this activity is to demonstrate the thinking, planning, communicating and team working that need to go into the initiation of a change project. Committing to becoming more learning-oriented for yourself and developing a learning culture in a team require commitment, time, effort and good communication. By working through the template you should now be more familiar with the sorts of processes required to make such an important change.

Learning environments and values

One of the fundamental messages of this book has been about how we can develop as managers and leaders who exercise the values which brought us into nursing in the first place. As we have seen throughout the book, there are many values which we need to exercise as leaders of care. As we saw in Chapter 6, the most famous current example of these values are Cummings' (2012) 6 Cs: care, compassion, competence, communication, courage and commitment.

The development of a learning environment which is underpinned by the values of good care, compassion and communication requires us as leaders to exercise courage and commitment in developing ourselves to become more competent at what we do and in supporting the developing competency of others. In this sense we can see that learning environments contribute strongly to enabling nurses to express their values.

Chapter summary

In this chapter we have seen that environments or cultures of care are important in the functioning of health and social care teams. We have identified that learning cultures are important for the sustained development of nursing teams, and the wider healthcare system. We have identified that for learning cultures to succeed there is a need for engagement of all of the members of the team. The role of the individual leader, nurse or nursing student within the team has been identified as being fundamental to the success of any culture.

We have also seen how developing learning environments serves to develop environments in which nursing values, as embodied in the 6 Cs, can thrive, to the benefits of staff, individual nurses and, most importantly, patients.

The challenge that has been presented in this chapter has been one of engaging in self-development as a learner for yourself before considering taking on the extended task of creating a learning environment in your place of work.

Activities: Brief outline answers

Activity 8.1 Reflection (p152)

As a student transiting through an area as part of your training, you may see the area as a place of learning while having a feeling of being an outsider. Permanent staff may be comfortable with the area and regard it very much as a place of work. Visiting staff, such as physiotherapists and social workers, may experience the area as an extension of a bigger area of work. Patients may experience the environment as one in which they do not belong and which is somewhere they can at least leave.

When working in the community, your place of work is often someone else's home, a place where you are both at work and a visitor, and where your patient is both patient and home owner.

Activity 8.3 Reflection (p155)

When we engage in open conversation about a topic, we become involved. Being involved in something brings a sense of belonging and worth. This sense of worth helps us to understand our place in contributing to something bigger than ourselves, in this case the collective understanding of the topic. This reflects nicely the concept of the learning environment, where people feel that they belong because they are not only learning together, they are also contributing to that learning.

Further reading

Clarke, A (2001) *Learning Organisations: What They Are and How to Become One.* Leicester: National Institute of Adult Continuing Education.

A comprehensive guide to learning organisations.

Handy, C (1994) *Understanding Organizations.* London: Penguin.

A great and classic text on organisational cultures.

Mullins, LJ (2011) *Essentials of Organisational Behaviour* (3rd edition). London: Prentice Hall.

A comprehensive guide to understanding organisations.

Useful websites

https://www.cipd.co.uk/knowledge/culture/working-environment

An interesting selection of resources about workplace cultures from the Chartered Institute of Personnel and Development.

www.pmis.co.uk/free-project-management-templates.htm

A wide collection of interesting and adaptable project templates.

https://www.investorsinpeople.com/resources/share-inspire

A useful website with many resources including ones about culture. Register for access to some of the guides including some on employee engagement.

Chapter 9 — Developing confidence as a manager and leader

NMC Standards of Proficiency for Registered Nurses

This chapter will address the following platforms and proficiencies:

Platform 1: Being an accountable professional

Registered nurses act in the best interests of people, putting them first and providing nursing care that is person-centred, safe and compassionate. They act professionally at all times and use their knowledge and experience to make evidence-based decisions about care. They communicate effectively, are role models for others, and are accountable for their actions. Registered nurses continually reflect on their practice and keep abreast of new and emerging developments in nursing, health and care.

At the point of registration, the registered nurse will be able to:

1.1 understand and act in accordance with the Code (2015): Professional standards of practice and behaviour for nurses and midwives, and fulfil all registration requirements.

Platform 5: Leading and managing nursing care and working in teams

Registered nurses provide leadership by acting as a role model for best practice in the delivery of nursing care. They are responsible for managing nursing care and are accountable for the appropriate delegation and supervision of care provided by others in the team including lay carers. They play an active and equal role in the interdisciplinary team, collaborating and communicating effectively with a range of colleagues.

At the point of registration, the registered nurse will be able to:

5.4 demonstrate an understanding of the roles, responsibilities and scope of practice of all members of the nursing and interdisciplinary team and how to make best use of the contributions of others involved in providing care.

5.6 exhibit leadership potential by demonstrating an ability to guide, support and motivate individuals and interact confidently with other members of the care team.

(Continued)

(Continued)

5.7 demonstrate the ability to monitor and evaluate the quality of care delivered by others in the team and lay carers.

Platform 6: Improving safety and quality of care

Registered nurses make a key contribution to the continuous monitoring and quality improvement of care and treatment in order to enhance health outcomes and people's experience of nursing and related care. They assess risks to safety or experience and take appropriate action to manage those, putting the best interests, needs and preferences of people first.

At the point of registration, the registered nurse will be able to:

6.1 understand and apply the principles of health and safety legislation and regulations and maintain safe work and care environments.
6.2 understand the relationship between safe staffing levels, appropriate skills mix, safety and quality of care, recognising risks to public protection and quality of care, escalating concerns appropriately.
6.4 demonstrate an understanding of the principles of improvement methodologies, participate in all stages of audit activity and identify appropriate quality improvement strategies.

Chapter aims

After reading this chapter you will be able to:

- discuss the practice–leadership continuum;
- demonstrate an awareness of some of the issues with transition to leadership and management roles;
- discuss some of the key challenges which face new leaders and managers;
- explain how confidence might be developed in the new manager.

Introduction

Throughout this book we have introduced you to ideas and theories about leadership and management and some of the tasks leaders and managers undertake; you may have formed the impression there is a lot to learn, and indeed there is. You will also have noted many of the tasks of management start with understanding yourself and your orientation to a situation, role or task as well as having a clear appreciation of your values and those of the organisation in which you work. Clearly understanding yourself and being aware of your strengths and weaknesses are as important for succeeding as a leader or manager as for nursing in general.

This chapter will look at some of the issues facing the new leader or manager and identify and focus on some strategies that might be used to help develop ability and confidence. Other issues which commonly confront the new manager will also be addressed, with some ideas about how these might be handled both proactively and reactively. As with all of the chapters in this book it is important that you engage with the activities as they represent tools for self-development which may help to enhance both your learning and your development as a manager as well as your confidence to lead.

The transition to leadership

When you first thought about being a nurse and when you were interviewed for your nurse training, it is likely you thought and talked about all of the ways you could help people as a practising nurse. As you progress through your training and into your nursing career you may start to aspire to leadership and management and start to see this as a way of extending the scope of what you can do for and with patients.

It is worth reflecting here on the different stages of professional life we adopt as we move from practising nurse through to leadership and management roles. Causer and Exworthy (2003) identify six stages on the path from practice to management which they regard as being stages on a continuum of roles which health and social care professionals may find themselves on.

Roles within the professional–management continuum

1. The practising professional: The main task of the practising professional is the provision of care. Within this definition there are two groups of people:

    (a) the pure practitioner – who undertakes professional roles but has no supervisory role;

    (b) the quasi-managerial practitioner – who undertakes a professional caring role, and has some responsibility for supervising others or allocating resources.

2. The managing professional: The main function of these professionally trained managers is the supervision of other professionals and the allocation and management of resources. Again, this group is split into two groups:

    (a) the practising managing professional – who still works in the delivery of care as well as managing others and resources;

    (b) the non-practising managing professional – who does not deliver care, but supervises other professionals and manages resources.

3. General managers: These are managers who manage others who are involved in the delivery of professional care, but not at the day-to-day (**operational**) level. Again, these are subdivided into two categories:

   (a) non-professionally grounded general managers – who are not part of the profession they are managing;

   (b) professionally grounded general managers – who are part of the profession they are managing.

Source: Adapted from Causer and Exworthy (2003).

What Causer and Exworthy (2003) identify is that the transition from being a practitioner to being a manager can be one that is subtle and takes place over a series of stages. The move from practice to management is therefore not a stark one, whereby one day you are a nurse practising on the ward and the next day you are a general manager, far removed from the realities of day-to-day care. The process identified here will most certainly allow for some adaptation and personal and professional development to take place. This notion links well with the ideas around being a learning organisation and individual, identified in Chapter 8.

Activity 9.1   Critical thinking

Taking the categories of professionals and managers that Causer and Exworthy identify, consider all of the people who work in the team in the clinical area in which you are, or were last, placed. Which of the roles identified in the model do they fit into, if any? What characteristics of Causer and Exworthy's descriptions do they display? What was their previous role? You may want to take this activity a step further and discuss the changing nature of the individual roles with them.

As this is based on your own observations, there is no specimen answer at the end of the chapter.

Undertaking this activity will help you to discover that there are layers of responsibility, leadership and management in the clinical setting. The degree of certainty people have in the roles they undertake can grow and develop as they move from one position to another within the team, or between teams, and as they learn from their own practice and from those around them. What is important in the transition from practice to management remains the focus on the values which you came into nursing with (see Chapter 1) and a willingness to develop both yourself and others around you (see Chapter 8).

Self-esteem and transition

As with all development, the changes which need to occur for you to move from school, or from another job, to becoming a nursing student, to qualifying and beyond, require some psychological adjustment. Even when we are excited about something, there are adjustments to make to the ways in which we think and behave as we move on to something new. Sometimes the adjustments we have to make are in response to whatever it was we aspired to not quite living up to what we expected from it. Either way, it is worth considering the nature of change and transition from being a practising nurse to being a leader.

Activity 9.2   Reflection

Think about how you felt during your first few weeks in a care environment. One day you were a member of the public and the next a carer or a student nurse. Taking responsibility for the welfare of other human beings requires some adjusting to and is the cause for some soul searching; reflect on your feelings at this time and think about how you managed to cope with this transition.

There are some possible answers and thoughts at the end of the chapter.

Some of your answers to the above reflection will show that the emotions experienced during a change can be quite overwhelming, even if it is a change which we want and are on the whole excited about. What this tells us for planning to make the change from practitioner to leader or manager is that there are a host of normal emotions and responses to change that we need to prepare for.

Perhaps the first lesson is that an emotional response to change is normal and not something we should be shy or embarrassed about. You should therefore not be surprised if you are a little stressed by a promotion or when you are given a leadership role; it is normal!

It is worth stopping again here and considering the nature of the emotional responses that people have as they adapt and evolve.

Bridges (2003), a leading thinker and writer about the change process, reminds us that things change, but people go through transitions. A fundamental tenet of Bridges' position is that transition involves loss and letting go, as well as developing a new understanding of how things are. In the case of the nurse making the transition from practising nurse to leader or manager, this involves a redefining of his or her professional and personal identity. Bridges' model of transition captures these ideas in a three-stage process.

Three-phase process of transition

1. Ending, losing, letting go: at this stage people have to make the adjustment to not being who they were before. For example, a student nurse on the point of

qualifying must adjust to being a qualified and accountable nurse; or a staff nurse being promoted to being a junior sister may have to adapt to being more visible to others and the hub of questions and responsibility.

2. The neutral zone: at this stage people try to make sense of who they are now and how things are going to be. Student nurses start to accept they are now qualified and begin to adopt the persona of someone who is accountable for what s/he is doing; junior charge nurses start to understand they have to be the one to find solutions to problems and act as a role model to the team.

3. The new beginning: a new identity is forming and there is increased clarity about what is expected in the new role. There is a sense of urgency and of wanting to get on with the job. New staff nurses start to feel confident in their own ability and what they are doing; the new sister or charge nurse feels comfortable about being a role model and overseeing the work of the team.

Source: Adapted from Bridges (2003).

While progressing through the process of changing identity – what we have called transition – it is normal for people to experience a whole range of different emotions. These emotions, as we discussed earlier, can arise even if the change is something that is wanted. Understanding these emotions and recognising them in yourself, as well as others, is a good way of helping maintain and develop your confidence as you progress through your nursing and leadership career. When these emotional responses feel like they might become overwhelming, it is worth harking back to our discussion of values in Chapter 1; what is important about the values of caring and of leading care is that they are the same values. All that changes, and therefore what healthcare leaders and managers have left of their caring identity, is how the values are expressed. You may find it useful here to revisit the case study from Chapter 1, 'The newly qualified nurse', in which Deirdre, the ward sister, explains to Julius, the newly qualified nurse, how what she has to do as the ward manager supports the ward staff in the delivery of care, which she is often unable to participate in because of the various other roles she must perform.

Hopson and Adams (1976) propose a useful, and enduring, model which helps identify some of the stages people go through when they are subject to transition. This model, presented below, is not a linear one (people move through it in different directions at different rates and may skip stages), nor does it necessarily apply to all transitions people go through; nevertheless, it is a useful model for helping us to understand the emotional response to transition.

Changes in self-esteem during transitions

- Immobilisation: the feeling of being unable to act and being overwhelmed because of a transition. Transitions for which people are unprepared and ones associated with negative expectations may intensify this stage.

- Minimisation: a coping mechanism. People often deny the change is happening. This reaction is common in a crisis which is too difficult to face head-on.
- Depression: some people become depressed when they have to face the reality of change.
- Accepting reality: occurs when a person going through a transition begins to let go of how things were and starts to accept the reality of the change.
- Testing: begins when the reality of the change has been accepted. At this stage people start to try out new behaviours to cope with the new situation.
- Seeking meaning: a reflective stage, during which people try to work out how and why things are different.
- Internalisation: the final stage of the process, during which the new situation becomes accepted. The new understanding then becomes part of the person's behaviour.

Source: Adapted from Hopson and Adams (1976).

When making the transition from student nurse to trained nurse and then on to leader and manager it is useful for us to be aware of the ways in which we react to change as individuals. Being aware of our own responses enables us to make sense of and progress through the various stages of emotional response to change as well as managing how we behave around and towards other people.

Being aware of the range of emotions experienced during times of transition also allows us to provide appropriate support to staff during periods of change and transition in their lives. Change and transition are not only confined to the workplace: changes in home circumstances, bereavement and ill health will all impact on how managers and their staff feel and behave. Being aware of this and maintaining good channels of communication will allow the leader or manager to develop skills and confidence in people management which are closely associated with emotional intelligence.

Often emotional intelligence is exercised by the leader or manager before the person identifies to them that they are stressed or upset by a particular occurrence or event. This is because the emotionally literate manager is sensitive to the verbal and non-verbal cues given off by their staff rather than waiting to be told that someone is upset or stressed. The best managers anticipate an emotional response to change and are therefore ready to address it with their staff when it arises.

Activity 9.3 Evidence-based practice and research

Hopson and Adams' model of the changes in self-esteem during change is similar in content to a very famous model of the stages of grief by Elizabeth Kubler-Ross. Go online and find the Kubler-Ross model and read what it says about how the stages of grief work (see the useful websites at the end

(Continued)

(Continued)

of the chapter). Compare and contrast what you learn about the stages of grief in this model with the Hopson and Adams model, what important similarities and differences do you notice? What does this tell you about the psychological impact of change in the work place?

There are some possible answers and thoughts at the end of the chapter.

Clearly, being prepared for the emotional response which you may have to a change in your role or work circumstances means you will be able to reflect on what is happening and better prepare yourself mentally for the challenges ahead. As a leader or manager, providing support to your team through supervision, information giving and being generally supportive will mean you can help reduce some of the impact of negative emotional responses to transition.

Activity 9.4   Evidence-based practice and research

To understand better the nature of the emotional responses to change people have, look up the **Holmes–Rahe Life Event Rating Scale** (see the useful websites at the end of the chapter) and read the categories of change that people find most stressful in their lives; some of the listed changes may surprise you.

As this is based on your own observations, there is no specimen answer at the end of the chapter.

Having a growing understanding of your own responses to change will enable you to face the transitions required to progress throughout your career in nursing with a renewed degree of confidence. Preparing yourself mentally and emotionally for the impact of transition will mean you are better prepared for some of the challenges of leadership and management.

Developing yourself as a leader

The purpose of this book has been to prepare you for some of the challenges being a leader or manager can present. This section will present and examine some of the strategies you can use to prepare yourself better for a leadership or management role whilst being aware of, and managing, your own emotional response to change. All of the ideas presented here are tools and tactics that can be used while a student, staff nurse, charge nurse or beyond in order to improve and enhance your own confidence, understand yourself better and develop some self-discipline in your approach to managing yourself.

Williams (2007, p51) tells us: *exceptional leaders have the ability to honestly assess their leadership skills – and the discipline to improve their weaknesses and build upon their strengths.* Only you can truly know whether you are willing to put effort into your self-development.

Set incremental goals

Target setting is a key factor in self-motivation. If you cannot be bothered to write an essay or to complete an application form, then whatever it is you are aiming to do will not happen. Motivation is an interesting tool, both in personal and professional development as well as from the point of view of the leader or manager. Herzberg (1959), the most enduring and famous theorist in this area, proposed the motivation–hygiene theory of job satisfaction. In essence, Herzberg's theory suggests that people will work hard in order to achieve the hygiene needs, as without them they are unhappy. Once the hygiene factors are achieved, people are happy, but only for a short time. It is only the true motivators which keep people happy and motivate them and offer a true sense of meaning for individuals.

Motivation–hygiene theory of job satisfaction
Hygiene factors

- Quality of relationships with supervisors
- Working conditions
- Salary
- Status
- Job security
- Quality of relationship with subordinates
- Personal life.

True motivators

- Achievement
- Recognition
- Opportunity for advancement
- Work itself
- Responsibility
- Sense of personal growth.

Source: Adapted from Herzberg (1959).

What we can see both for ourselves and for others is that motivation lies in taking responsibility and improving on what we do and therefore who we are. For the student this may mean getting better at writing essays, by learning from feedback to achieve better marks and hence recognition. For the leader it may be important to ensure the hygiene factors are all in place before worrying too much about the motivators; although some things remain outside the sphere of influence of most nurse leaders.

Case study: Recognising the value of motivation

Jacinta had recently been promoted to Modern Matron in the surgical care team. Jacinta had worked her way up through the team over a period of years and was very much aware of the issues which preoccupied the staff. She knew that staff morale was very low as the team felt overworked, understaffed, poorly cared for and generally neglected. Jacinta understood the team felt the need for further professional development as well as some clarity about promotion opportunities. Jacinta was also aware that the whole team were fed up with the state of their coffee room, which had been allowed to deteriorate over time. She knew she needed to do something fast to raise the morale of the whole team and to consolidate her position as the team leader, but she also knew she had limited funds with which to do anything.

Jacinta considered her options and decided there were some things she could do collectively for the team as well as some things she needed to do for individuals within the team in order to raise morale, gain trust and improve motivation. Jacinta decided to spend some of the capital budget available to her to buy new furniture for the coffee room. By doing so she improved working conditions for the whole team and addressed a hygiene need.

Jacinta quickly realised she could not provide the motivation the staff needed purely by spending money (which was not available to her anyway), so she identified new roles for various members of the team as link nurses for infection control, diabetes and wound management, providing some of the junior staff with a sense of increased responsibility, recognition and personal growth. Furthermore, Jacinta took it upon herself to try to make sure staff went home when their shifts ended. She praised effort and cultivated her relationships within the team, addressing key hygiene and motivational needs.

This case study, which is based on a real-life experience, demonstrates how easy it can be to grow as a leader or manager in the eyes of the team by making small but important changes. What is important about these changes is that they demonstrate to the team that the manager cares about them as individuals. As we saw in Chapter 6, demonstrating that you, as a leader, care about people is a key strategy for gaining the trust of the team.

Facilitating and bringing about the changes meant that not only did the team feel happier, but Jacinta's confidence as a manager grew as she started to notice a change in the morale of the team and that the team had started to trust her as someone who both cared about them and was able to get things done.

Trust is an important element of the role of the manager, ensuring the work which the team needs to get done is actually done. We saw in Chapter 4 how the meta-analysis by Dirks and Ferrin (2002) demonstrated that trust is important in the prevention and management of conflict; their work also showed two other important findings pertinent to goal setting and motivation in the personal and team setting. The first is about attitude to work, where attitude is seen as contributing both to achieving your goals and to the exercise of values. Having a positive attitude as a leader will reflect in your orientation to work, the *manner* by which you achieve goals, and this in turn leads to the other important observation, which is about citizenship.

Because the team learn to trust you in the way you work and in the types of goals you set yourself, they start to feel responsibility towards the things you find important. This citizenship is in essence about the ways in which we behave towards each other and how we share some common values and aspirations. In turn this means that the leader can be confident the members of the team will also work toward achieving the goals the leader has set not because they have to, but because they want to.

Learn to listen

For the nurse as much as the leader or manager, listening is a fundamental skill. When we learn to listen to others, be it in a formal context or by listening to informal sources of information, we can understand the true context of situations. Listening also enables us to find solutions to problems which we may not have identified for ourselves.

Listening is a key skill for the leader or manager in understanding what the team are thinking and what is important to them. Managing information was identified in Chapter 6 as one of Mintzberg's (1975) roles of the manager. Information allows us to make decisions which are well grounded and learning to listen and to be enquiring will enhance your ability both to understand what is going on around you and to make sound decisions.

In this context listening is more about taking the time to hear what people are saying, and trying to understand it, while placing what we are hearing in the context of what we know. As an active skill, listening is important for personal growth and for professional development within healthcare, which is a complex and evolving environment within which to work (Jackson and Ellis, 2010). For the developing leader, listening means you can be confident you understand what is going on around you.

Activity 9.5   Evidence-based practice and research

Go online and find some websites which talk about the skills you need in order to become an active listener. Make a list of the skills and tips the websites identify and think about how they compare to how you are when you are listening to other people. Take the time to then practice some of the skills you identify when talking to friends, colleagues and patients.

As this is based on your own observations, there is no specimen answer at the end of the chapter.

Understand, then communicate

The ultimate aim of listening properly and effectively is to understand. Understanding situations and new ideas is a good way of developing your confidence. Part of understanding is the ability to ask the right questions at the right time as well as being able to communicate your ideas in an effective way. Communicating effectively hinges on your ability to understand what other people know as well as what it is they want.

As a leader or manager your confidence will develop as people become aware that you are able to communicate clearly. Clear communication will mean members of the team understand what it is you want from them; it allows you to delegate effectively and explain ideas. Learning to think and understand before speaking is a key skill for the aspiring leader or manager; we have all been in situations when individuals have made themselves look silly because they have said something or asked a question which clearly demonstrates they have not been listening; being thought of as silly is not a good place to be for the new leader or manager!

Believe in yourself

Self-belief is not the same as arrogance or being egocentric. Self-belief is having the confidence you can do something well and doing it. Self-belief comes only from practice, from exercising your leadership muscles by developing and maintaining good relationships with staff and understanding yourself. When you believe in what you are doing as well as believe you have the ability to do it, other people will see this self-belief and feel able to follow your lead.

Leaders and managers who are confident in their own abilities are better able to develop their team and are comfortable with members of the team having better skills and knowledge in certain areas than they do. The manager who has self-belief will recognise that the team is more important than self and this team-focused attitude will help develop trust within the team.

Don't be afraid to make mistakes

Making mistakes is part of life. This is as true for the leader or manager as it is for individual team workers. Learning to reflect enables us to make sense of what has happened as well as learning how to do something better in the future (see Howatson-Jones, 2016, *Reflective Practice in Nursing*). Learning from our mistakes can make us stronger as individuals and as leaders as we develop new ways of working which take account of what we have learnt as well as where we want to be. Failure often precedes success, as it is through trying new ways of working that we are able to be innovative (Farson and Keyes, 2002).

Part of the process of growing as a person and a leader is the ability to accept responsibility for the things we get wrong. When, as leaders, we develop the ability to accept responsibility for our own actions we can role model responsibility and accountability to our team.

Within the team context, supporting others who make mistakes empowers them to make decisions and take actions with the confidence that they will be supported; again, this is a key element of trust. SanFacon (2008) reminds leaders that in order to achieve success they need to trust in their staff and allow them to make mistakes. So being brave enough to try new things and new ways of working is useful in developing your confidence in yourself and in your ability to lead others.

Learn to manage your time effectively

As a leader or manager how you use time is important. The pressures on time for leaders of people come in all shapes and forms and can quite easily disrupt the working day. Time management is the art of getting the most from your time by developing an awareness of what time is and how it is used. Understanding how to use time wisely will help you understand what you can achieve and in what time frame. This will translate into the confidence to take on new roles and tasks or allow you to explain why you cannot.

John Adair (1990), whose model of action-centred leadership we looked at in Chapter 6, suggests leaders and managers need to learn to manage time before they can manage anything else. He sees good time management as a requirement for allowing us to focus on what we do and achieve our goals. Time management is therefore about being focused on attaining our goals and achieving results and, in Adair's view, there are ten principles by which good time management can be achieved by a leader or manager.

Theory summary: Adair's ten principles of good time management

1. Develop a personal sense of time: this is about understanding where your time goes and therefore understanding where it is wasted and where it could be better used. For the leader it may also uncover areas of work which might be better delegated to someone else.

2. Identify long-term goals: this is about knowing what it is you want to achieve in life and work. Adair recognises values as being a key driving force behind setting such goals.

3. Make medium-term plans: understand what things you need to do in order to prepare you to achieve your long-term goals and plan what you need to do now to achieve them. Medium-term plans involve setting realistic goals which are measurable.

4. Plan the day: without planning what you will achieve today, you cannot know whether you have used your time wisely at the end of the day. Learning to say no to things which are a poor use of your time or which interfere with you achieving your goals is important here.

5. Make the best use of your best time: understand what times of day you work best and work during them. Take time to think about issues and ideas which need planning while doing other more mundane activities.

6. Organise office work: make sure that you organise your life and your working space so things you need are at hand when you need them.

7. Manage meetings: understand what you want from a meeting or other period of communication with other people and stick to the time available for this.

8. Delegate effectively: consider what things you need to do and what might be better done by someone else.

9. Make use of committed time: plan to use time that is usually wasted waiting or travelling and be prepared to use this to good effect, perhaps reading something, making phone calls or thinking constructively about an issue.

10. Manage your health: things are easier to achieve when we are well, so look after yourself and make time to do things that are necessary for your physical and mental well-being.

Source: Adapted from Adair (1990).

For Adair, understanding and being aware of time and how we use it is key to personal success. Making good use of time and being aware of what we can achieve in a given time frame are key to developing confidence in ourselves both as individuals and as leaders or managers. Knowing what you achieved and why is a great motivator.

Activity 9.6   Evidence-based practice and research

Keep a diary of all the things you do for one week. Split the time into 15-minute slots and record what you do: be careful to record wasted time as well as activities. After a week review the diary and identify times during which you could have done something useful if you were prepared. Consider how you might adapt some of your ways of working and habits to allow you to achieve more in the time available to you.

You may wish to use this exercise as a springboard for planning your personal development and planning what you want to achieve, how and by when. Understanding how you use time will enable you to plan this more effectively.

As this is based on your own observations, there is no specimen answer at the end of the chapter.

Once you understand how you use time and where you can fit in tasks to make your use of time more efficient, you will start to see that it is possible to fit more into your day. When you free up time you can decide how to use it, perhaps undertaking more work or engaging in a hobby or other interest.

Know your values

You may feel we have discussed values too much in this book; however, since our values shape the ways we behave, their importance cannot be overestimated. Knowing what your values are as a human, as a nurse and ultimately as a leader or manager will mean there is some consistency in the ways in which you act. Sticking to your values will not only mean you are happier in whatever you do; it will mean the team will know what to expect from you and, perhaps more importantly, what you expect from them. Trust, which is the means by which leaders get things done, relies on leaders demonstrating their integrity to their followers (Lawton, 1998).

One of the issues which face nurses as they move from practice to leadership and management roles is their lack of clarity about their identity. It is easy to forget things which mattered to you as a student or staff nurse, the values which guided your desire to be a nurse and your subsequent practice as you become more engaged with leadership and management roles. Understanding what your values are now and being able to discuss them in a meaningful way will help you remain grounded and focused as you prepare for leadership.

Issues such as fairness, treating people as equals, being polite and behaving with care and compassion might feature on your list. These are all basic values which are easily forgotten in the milieu of the busy working day. Practising these values and

Activity 9.7   Reflection

Take some time now to consider the things which you value as a human being and as a nurse. Think about what you might have said at interview about why you wanted to train as a nurse, or the skills and attributes which you bring to your current role. Consider the issues in practice which cause you frustration and the behaviours which you think are unacceptable from your colleagues. Write these things down and keep them safe. Spend some time over the next few weeks thinking about and observing these issues in practice and considering what you might do to change poor practice and role model good leadership values when you are in a position to do so.

As this is based on your own observations, there is no specimen answer at the end of the chapter.

ensuring they become part of who you are and how you act will allow you to establish a reputation not only as someone who knows what they are doing but also as someone who knows who they are and what they are about. The NMC (2018) *Future Nurse: Standards of Proficiency for Registered Nurses* document talks about the duty of the nurse to act as a role model to others in a number of places. This bears witness to the fact that as a registered nurse, you must demonstrate not only the proficiencies, but also the positive behaviours the NMC and the public expect of you at all times.

It is important to think about this issue. It is all too simple when you become a leader to forget how it feels to be led, so instead of addressing and rejecting the negative leadership behaviours and values you have witnessed, you adopt the same negative leadership behaviours.

Develop resilience

One of the hallmarks of the strong leader or manager is the ability to be resilient. Resilience is the ability to take criticism constructively, listen to what people are saying about your organisation and team without taking it personally and to understand the meaning of situations.

Resilience is not all about developing a thick skin, not least of all because a thick skin prevents effective empathy. Resilience is more about having the ability to deal with stressful situations. It is important here again to understand yourself. If you understand what things you find stressful and why, you can learn to manage them.

Case study: Developing resilience

Mee-Onn was a newly appointed junior sister on a general medical ward. She had come from a different hospital to take on the new role and did not know any of the team. Mee-Onn found that the staff and the patients on the ward were very free and easy about making complaints, grumbling and suggesting how things might be done better.

As the junior sister, Mee-Onn was often the target of these suggestions and gripes. Mee-Onn found it hard to cope with all of the information and after a few weeks in post started to take all of the negative comments personally, as if they were a reflection on her. She started to feel very stressed and did not want to go to work anymore. Mee-Onn discussed her feelings with the medical matron. The matron, who had come up through the ranks in the hospital, suggested to Mee-Onn that she stopped taking all of the criticism as personal and that she turned issues back to the staff, with questions like 'how would you see this progressing?' or 'what would you suggest we do to improve this?' The matron also suggested Mee-Onn did not accept some of the unfair things people were saying and that she should tell them what they were saying was unfair.

Asking these simple questions reminded Mee-Onn that the problems were not hers alone. She developed the strength to confront some of the situations and issues which plagued the team and started to be seen as someone with solutions. She also developed a reputation for being fair-minded and not someone who would tolerate unreasonable behaviour.

This study, again based on a real-life story, demonstrates that one of the skills of being a leader or manager is learning what a gripe or moan means and who it is aimed at. It also demonstrates how taking on board issues which are not personal, and are not purely your own problem, may lead to a sense of helplessness and futility. Taking charge of such situations by being brave enough to ask for a solution, rather than saying something like 'I know what you mean', try saying 'how might this be resolved?' can help you as the leader develop delegation skills and demonstrate trust. It can also help you move away from being weak and downtrodden.

So in part resilience is about developing strategies to deflect and reflect problems back to where they really belong; although, of course, this does not mean every problem which comes your way belongs to someone else to solve!

Confront challenging situations

Developing resilience leads us into the next skill, which is about not being afraid to get involved. There are times as a nurse when situations arise and people behave in ways which we feel are less than acceptable. Such situations need confronting and learning to communicate your point in a way which links in with your expressed values is a good place to start. For a manager or leader, there is often nowhere to hide and learning to confront difficult situations early is a good idea. One strategy for the novice is to accompany more experienced staff who are, for example, breaking bad news; ask questions about what they did after the event and reflect on the answers. We discussed some strategies in Chapter 4 where we suggested some of the approaches to managing conflict might include: collaborating, compromising, accommodating, competing and dodging (Thomas and Kilmann, 1974). The art of good leadership lies in using the right approach for any given situation and not becoming known for always using the same approach regardless of the nature of the situation which has arisen.

Another sort of challenging situation is one which you do not understand or about which you are uncertain. The key to developing the ability to confront such a situation is developing the ability to ask questions. Asking questions allows for understanding and should not be mistaken for weakness. As an aspiring leader it is important you develop a reputation for being enquiring and that you support others in their efforts to achieve self-awareness and self-development.

Develop your emotional intelligence

Perhaps many of the messages which are contained in this book can be boiled down to one key message: develop your emotional intelligence. Throughout the book we have suggested there is a need to understand yourself and the part you play in many situations before you look at what other people are doing or saying. You also need to understand where other people are coming from and what motivates their actions.

Emotional intelligence requires you to be able to use this understanding of the emotional motivation which you and other people have in order to communicate effectively. Emotional intelligence and awareness of motivations as well as the ability and desire to help others achieve their goals reflect strongly on many of the standards of proficiency for registered nurse education highlighted at the start of this chapter.

From your practice you will know many of the skills, attributes and roles which nurses undertake require them to be self-aware and aware of the needs of others. This awareness, which you are required to develop as a student nurse, will most certainly be a big part of the suite of skill competencies which we have suggested in this book go towards creating effective managers and leaders. What is important for you as you develop from student nurse to staff nurse, sister and beyond is that you conscientiously continue to develop these capabilities in such a way that they become part of how you behave and therefore who you are. Nurse leaders and managers are entrusted with the management and leadership of people delivering care to some of the most vulnerable in society. By becoming a good role model you can be more certain the care you and your team deliver lives up to the lofty ideals of modern nursing practice.

Chapter summary

In this chapter we have explored the journey from student nurse to nurse manager and what this might mean for us in managing our emotional responses to change and transition. We have identified a number of important strategies, skills, tactics and values which, taken together, can better prepare you for the responsibilities that leadership and management bring. We have demonstrated how developing trust can have a positive impact on the development of self and of the wider team.

We have identified that the core values and skills of nursing translate well into leadership and management roles and hence the need for student nurses and junior staff nurses to develop, practise and hone these skills from an early point in their career. The challenge lies in engaging with these ways of being from the start of your career and nurturing them as you developed onward into your career as a nurse and a leader.

Activities: Brief outline answers

Activity 9.2 Reflection (p171)

The emotions that people feel as they experience different changes and transitions in their lives are not purely tied to the sort of change they are experiencing. All change can bring fear and trepidation, even the changes that are wanted and exciting. The move into a caring role requires some thought about who you put first, how you behave, what impact the emotional investment will have on you as a person and how you will adapt.

Activity 9.3 Evidence-based practice and research (p173)

When you compare the model of the stages of grief with the model of changes in self-esteem during transition you will notice they both evoke strong reactions. These reactions include not really accepting what is happening through various stages of frustration and anger through to some sort of acceptance of what is happening. Both models also talk about the fact that people do not necessarily proceed through the various stages, nor do they necessarily move the through the various stages in order, nor in a set timeframe, and people can go backward as well as forward through the model.

For the leader this is potentially tricky as, at any one stage of a process, the staff involved can be at different places in their reaction to the process, and staff who have appeared to have moved on can also move backwards.

Further reading

Bennis, WG (2004) The seven ages of the leader. *Harvard Business Review*, 82 (1): 46–53.

An inspiring and informational look at leadership development.

Davis, N (2011) *Learning Skills for Nursing Students*. Exeter: Learning Matters.

Gives helpful advice for gaining knowledge and confidence.

Howatson-Jones, L (2016) *Reflective Practice in Nursing* (3rd edition). London: SAGE.

Essential advice on how to understand yourself and grow in professionalism.

Jones, L and Bennett, CL (2012) *Leadership in Health and Social Care: An Introduction for Emerging Leaders.* Banbury: Lantern.

An easy-to-read general introduction to growing yourself as a leader.

Useful websites

www.businessballs.com/self-confidence-assertiveness.htm

A useful and interesting take on developing self-confidence.

http://changingminds.org/disciplines/change_management/psychology_change/ psychology_change.htm

A quirky but informative look at the psychology of change and transition.

http://changingminds.org/disciplines/change_management/kubler_ross/kubler_ross.htm

A useful introduction to the work of Kubler-Ross on the stages of grief during the dying process.

www.learnmanagement2.com/managementconcepts.htm

Some good pages on motivational theories can be found here.

www.mindtools.com/CommSkll/ActiveListening.htm

Some insights into active listening.

www.mindtools.com/pages/article/newTCS_82.htm

The Holmes and Rahe stress scale.

https://www.psychologytoday.com/basics/emotional-intelligence

A suite of very useful articles all about emotional intelligence.

Glossary

active listening   listening to, understanding and responding appropriately to what other people are saying.

binary thinking   in the sense used here it refers to a way of defining your identity with reference to the differences between you and someone else.

charisma/charismatic   a facet of personality which is compelling to other people and inspires others to follow the individual who is charismatic

clinical governance   the multiple methods of information gathering used to assess the quality of clinical care leading to improvements in the delivery and experience of care for the patient.

clinical supervision   a process of guided group reflection facilitated by a third party.

emotional intelligence   being aware of your own emotions, the emotions in others and how these modify behaviours and being able to talk about this in a meaningful way with others.

Gantt chart   the most common format for displaying project outlines and progress. Named after Henry Gantt, who developed it in the early 1900s, the chart is a form of bar chart which displays activities or events plotted against time.

generalisability   the extent to which the findings of research apply to a wider population.

governance   the methods by which organisations follow regulations stipulated by higher governing bodies to ensure standards are met through their authoritative structures.

group think   a phenomenon that occurs when the members of a group make a collective decision based on seeking unanimity rather than encouraging individual reasoning or critical evaluation of ideas.

Hawthorne effect   changes which occur in people's behaviour because they know they are being observed.

Holmes–Rahe Life Event Rating Scale   a scale of 43 life events which are scored by the amount of stress they can cause. A high score means more stress. Some of the changes are positive ones but still cause significant stress.

integrity   staying true to your own moral and ethical principles.

learning cultures/organisations/teams   groups of people who learn from, and with, each other in the workplace and use this learning to enhance what they do.

legitimate power   the power to lead and manage that an individual has by virtue of his or her position within an organisation as well as the ability to use that power in a reasonable, perhaps ethical, manner.

mediation   resolution of conflict through the facilitation of an impartial third party.

negotiation/negotiate   the process of reaching a compromise agreement through talking.

operational   referring to the management of the day-to-day tasks of an organisation or team.

othering   the process whereby anyone who does not share the same characteristics as us is seen to be 'other'. If we are nurses, non-nurses are 'other'.

outcomes   in the sense they are used in this book, outcomes refer not only to the result of a care episode but also the individual's experience of care. Quality is therefore seen as achieving health goals as well as providing healthcare in a manner acceptable to and involving the client.

person-centred   referring to care which is provided with the needs and wants of the patients at its core. This is the opposite of providing care which is dictated by what health and social care professionals want to provide or which is rigidly dictated by policy.

quorate/quorum   the agreed number and designations of people needed to be at a meeting in order for it to make decisions usually cited in the meetings/committees terms of reference.

skill mix   an appropriate number of people of various levels of ability on duty at the same time in order to be able to undertake the tasks required during a shift.

social capital   building up a bank of good will that can be called on later when you need a favour or support.

span of control   the number of employees for which each organisation manager or head of department is responsible.

stakeholders   individuals who will be affected directly or indirectly as a result of the organisation's actions, objectives, outcomes.

terms of reference   the purposes and powers of a committee, usually contained within a written document.

theory (pl. theories)   a logical attempt to explain a group of facts, phenomena or observations.

total quality management   an approach to quality management that takes account of both the outcome of the care episode and the ways in which the care episode was experienced by the patient or client.

values   the personal rules and understandings we have about what is right and what is wrong in human behaviour.

whistle blowing   the process of raising the alarm about some poor practice, usually through an established channel.

References

Adair, J (1990) *How to Manage Your Time*. Guildford: Talbot Adair Press.

Adair, J (2010) *Develop Your Leadership Skills*. London: Kogan Page.

Aiken, LH, Clarke, SP, Sloane, DL, Sochalski, J and Silber, JH (2002) Hospital nurse staffing and patient mortality, nurse burnout and job dissatisfaction. *Journal of American Medical Association*, 23/30, 288 (16): 1987–93.

Anderson, RA, Corazzini, KN and McDaniel, RR (2004) Complexity science and the dynamics of climate and communication: Reducing nursing home turnover. *The Gerontologist*, 44: 378–88.

Antai-Otong, D (1997) Team building in a health care setting. *American Journal of Nursing*, 97 (7): 48–51.

Barrick, MR and Mount, MK (1991) The big five personality dimensions and job performance: A meta analysis. *Personnel Psychology*, 44 (41): 1–26.

Bass, BM (1985) *Leadership and Performance*. New York: Free Press.

Beckhard, RF and Harris, RT (1987) *Organisation Transitions: Managing Complex Change*. Boston: Addison Wesley.

Belbin, MR (2010) *Management Teams: Why They Succeed or Fail* (3rd edition). Oxford: Butterworth Heinemann.

Benner, P (1984) *From Novice to Expert: Excellence and Power in Clinical Nursing Practice*. Menlo Park: Addison-Wesley.

Benner, P, Tanner, C and Chesla, C (2009) *Expertise in Nursing Practice: Caring, Clinical Judgment and Ethics* (2nd edition). New York: Springer.

Bennis, WG (1989) *On Becoming a Leader*. New York: Addison Wesley.

Bersin, J (2010) Create a high-impact learning culture. *Chief Learning Officer*, 9 (10): 16.

Bondas, T (2006) Paths to nursing leadership. *Journal of Nursing Management*, 14: 332–9.

Bray, L and Nettleton, P (2007) Assessor or mentor? Role confusion in professional education. *Nurse Education Today*, 27 (8): 848–55.

Brennan, NM and Flynn, MA (2013) Differentiating clinical governance, clinical management and clinical practice. *Clinical Governance: An International Journal*, 18 (2): 114–31.

Bridges, W (2003) *Managing Transitions: Making the Most of Change*. London: Nicholas Brearley.

Butterworth, T, Bell, L, Jackson, C and Majda, P (2007) Wicked spell or magic bullet? A review of the clinical supervision literature 2001–2007. *Nurse Education Today*, 28 (3): 264–72.

Care Quality Commission (2011) *Care Quality Commission Demands Action After Report Identifies Failings at Cambridgeshire and Peterborough NHS Trust.* Available online at: www.cqc.org.uk/newsandevents/pressreleases.cfm?cit_id=37178&FAArea1=customWidgets.content_view_1&usecache=false

Causer, G and Exworthy, M (2003) Professionals as managers across the public sector. In: Bullman, A, Charlesworth, J, Henderson, J, Reynolds, J and Seden, J (eds) *The Managing Care Reader* (pages 213–19). London: Routledge.

Chartered Institute of Personnel and Development (2007) *Managing Conflict at Work: Survey Report.* London: CIPD.

Chartered Institute of Personnel and Development (2011) *Performance Appraisal Factsheet.* Available online at: www.cipd.co.uk/hr-resources/factsheets/performance-appraisal.aspx

Clews, G (2010) *Lack of Support for Nurses Blamed for Mid Staffs Failings.* Available online at: www.nursingtimes.net/whats-new-in-nursing/acute-care/lack-of-support-for-nurses-blamed-for-mid-staffsfailings/5011861.article

Croskerry, P and Norman, G (2008) Overconfidence in clinical decision making. *American Journal of Medicine*, 121: S24–9.

Cummings, G and McLennan, M (2005) Advanced practice nursing: Leadership to effect policy change. *Journal of Nursing Administration*, 35 (2): 61–6.

Cummings, J (2012) *Leadership: What's in a Word?* Available online at: http://www.england.nhs.uk/tag/6cs

Curtis, E and O'Connell, R (2011) Essential leadership skills for motivating and developing staff. *Nursing Management*, 18 (5): 32–5.

Daft, R (2001) *The Leadership Experience* (2nd edition). Florence, Kentucky: South-Western Educational Publishing.

Darzi, A (2008) *High-Quality Care for All: NHS Next Stage Review Final Report.* London: Department of Health.

Davies, C (2004) Workers, professions and identity. In: Henderson, J and Atkinson, D (eds) *Managing Care in Context* (pages 189–210). London: Routledge.

Dawson, A and Butler, I (2004) The morally active manager. In: Henderson, J and Atkinson, D (eds) *Managing Care in Context* (pages 237–58). London: Routledge.

Department of Health (1997) *The New NHS: Modern and Dependable.* London: DH.

Department of Health (2010) *Equity and Excellence: Liberating the NHS.* Available online at: https://www.gov.uk/government/uploads/system/uploads/attachment_data/file/213823/dh_117794.pdf

Dirks, KT and Ferrin, DL (2002) Trust in leadership: Meta-analytic findings and implications for research and practice. *Journal of Applied Psychology*, 87 (4): 611–28.

Drennan, V, Davis, K, Traynor, M, Goodman, C, Mark, A, Peacock, R, Humphrey, C and Fairley-Murray, S (2007) Entrepreneurial nurses and midwives in the United Kingdom: An integrative review. *Journal of Advanced Nursing*, 60 (5): 459–69.

Edwards, D, Burnard, P, Hannigan, B, Cooper, L, Adams, J, Juggessur, T, Fothergil, A and Coyle, D (2006) Clinical supervision and burnout: The influence of clinical supervision for community mental health nurses. *Journal of Clinical Nursing*, 15: 1007–10.

Ellis, P (2015) Delegating for success. *Wounds UK.* 11 (2): 70–1.

Ellis, P (2016a) *Understanding Research for Nursing Students (Transforming Nursing Practice)* (3rd edition). London: SAGE.

Ellis, P (2016b) *Evidence Based Practice in Nursing (Transforming Nursing Practice)* (3rd edition). London: SAGE.

Ellis, P (2017) *Understanding Ethics for Nursing Students (Transforming Nursing Practice)* (2nd edition). London: SAGE.

Ellis, P and Abbott, J (2010) How to learn to delegate effectively in the renal unit. *Journal of Renal Nursing*, 2 (2): 38–40.

Ellis, P and Abbott, J (2017) Developing yourself as a kidney care leader, Part two. *Journal of Kidney Care*, 2 (5): 286–9.

Farson, R and Keyes, R (2002) The failure tolerant leader. *Harvard Business Review*, 80 (8): 64–71.

Foster, S (2017) The benefits of values-based recruitment. *British Journal of Nursing*, 26 (10): 579.

Fowler, A (1996) How to provide effective feedback. *People Management*, 2 (14): 44–5.

Francis, R (2013) *Report of the Mid Staffordshire NHS Foundation Trust Public Inquiry.* Available online at: http://www.midstaffspublicinquiry.com/report

Frankel, A (2008) What leadership styles should senior nurses develop? *Nursing Times*, 104 (35): 23–4.

French, JPR Jr and Raven, B (1960) The bases of social power. In: Cartwright, D and Zander, A (eds) *Group Dynamics* (pages 607–23). New York: Harper and Row.

Gainsborough, S (2009) Risks and benefits: Changing the nursing skill mix. *Nursing Times*, 22 (September). Available online at: www.nursingtimes.net/whats-new-in-nursing/acute-care/risks-and benefits-changing-the-nursing-skill-mix/5006399.article

Gallway, T (1974) *The Inner Game of Tennis.* New York: Random House.

Gallway, T (2000) *The Inner Game of Work.* New York: Random House.

Goleman, D (1996) *Emotional Intelligence: Why It Can Matter More Than IQ.* London: Bloomsbury.

Goleman, D (1998) *Working with Emotional Intelligence.* New York: Bantam Books.

Grant, AM (2001) *Towards a Psychology of Coaching.* Sydney: Coaching Psychology Unit, University of Sydney.

Grant, A and Goodman, B (2018) *Communication and Interpersonal Skills in Nursing* (4th edition). London: SAGE.

Griffin, RW (1999) *Management* (6th edition). New York: Houghton Mifflin.

Griffiths, R (1983) *NHS Management Inquiry: Report to the Secretary of State of Social Services.* London: HMSO.

Grivas, C and Puccio, G (2012) *The Innovative Team: Unleashing Creative Potential for Breakthrough Results.* San Francisco: Jossey Bass.

Handy, C (1994) *Understanding Organizations.* London: Penguin.

Heeb, JL and Haberey-Knuessi, V (2014) Health professionals facing burnout: What do we know about nursing managers? *Nursing Research and Practice.* Available online at: doi:10.1155/2014/681814.

Her Majesty's Government (2008) *Health and Social Care Act: Essential Standards of Quality and Safety.* London: HMSO.

Her Majesty's Government (2005) *Mental Capacity Act 2005.* Available online at: http://www.legislation.gov.uk/ukpga/2005/9/contents

Her Majesty's Government (2010) *Equality Act 2010.* Available online at: http://www.legislation.gov.uk/ukpga/2010/15/contents

Hersey, P, Blanchard, K and Johnson, D (2007) *Management of Organisational Behaviour* (9th edition). Oxford: Pearson Education.

Herzberg, F (1959) *The Motivation to Work.* New York: John Wiley.

Hewison, A and Sim, J (1998) Managing interprofessional working: Using codes of ethics as a foundation. *Journal of Interprofessional Care,* 12 (3): 309–21.

Hocking, BA (2006) Using reflection to resolve conflict. *Journal of the Association of Operating Room Nurses,* 84 (2): 249–59.

Homans, GC (1961) *Social Behavior: Its Elementary Forms.* New York: Harcourt Brace.

Hopson, B and Adams, J (1976) *Transition: Understanding and Managing Personal Change.* London: Martin Robertson.

House, RJ (2004) *Culture, Leadership, and Organizations: The GLOBE Study of 62 Societies.* Thousand Oaks: SAGE.

Howatson-Jones, L (2004) The servant leader. *Nursing Management,* 11 (3): 20–4.

Howatson-Jones, L (2016) *Reflective Practice in Nursing (Transforming Nursing Practice)* (3rd edition). London: SAGE.

International Council of Nurses (2004) *Guidelines on the Nurse Entre/Intrapreneur Providing Nursing Service.* Geneva: ICN Publications. Available online at: www.crnns.ca/documents/Self%20Emp%20Practice/Guidelines%20for%20Nurse%20Entrepreneurs%20(ICN).pdf

Jackson, C and Ellis, P (2010) Creative thinking for whole systems working. In: Standing, M (ed.) *Clinical Judgement and Decision Making in Nursing and Interprofessional Healthcare* (pages 54–79). Maidenhead: Open University Press.

Johnson, M (1994) Conflict and nursing professionalization. In: McCloskey, J and Grace, H (eds) *Current Issues in Nursing* (4th edition) (pages 643–9). St Louis: Mosby.

Kim, S, Buttrick, E, Bohannon, I, Fehr, R, Frans, E and Shannon, SE (2016) Conflict narratives from the health care frontline: A conceptual model. *Conflict Resolution Quarterly*, 33: 255–77.

Kohn, S and O'Connell, V (2005) *6 Secrets of Highly Effective Bosses*. Richmond: Crimson.

Kotter, J (1990) *A Force for Change: How Leadership Differs from Management*. New York: Free Press.

Lawton, A (1998) *Ethical Management for the Public Services*. Buckingham: Open University Press.

Lee, P, Gillespie, N, Mann, L and Wearing, A (2010) Leadership and trust: Their effect on knowledge sharing and team performance. *Management Learning*, 41 (4): 473–91.

Lewin, K (1951) *Field Theory in Social Sciences*. New York: Harper and Row.

Lorenz, EN (1963) Deterministic nonperiodic flow. *Journal of the Atmospheric Sciences*, 20 (2): 130–41.

Luft, J and Ingham, H (1955) The Johari Window, a graphic model of interpersonal awareness. In: *Proceedings of the Western Training Laboratory in Group Development*. Los Angeles: UCLA.

Machell, S, Gough, P and Steward, K (2009) *From Ward to Board: Identifying Good Practice in the Business of the Caring*. London: King's Fund Publications.

Machell, S, Gough, P, Naylor, D, Nath, V, Steward, K and Williams, S (2010) *Putting Quality First in the Boardroom: Improving the Business of Caring*. London: The King's Fund and the Burdett Trust for Nursing. Available online at: www.kingsfund.org.uk/publications/putting-quality-first-boardroom

Mahoney, J (2001) Leadership skills for the 21st century. *Journal of Nursing Management*, 9 (5): 269–71.

Marquis, BL and Huston, CJ (2009) *Leadership Roles and Management Functions in Nursing: Theory and Applications*. Philadelphia, PA: Lippincott, Williams and Wilkins.

Maslach, C (2003) Job burnout: New directions in research and intervention. *Current Directions in Psychological Science*, 12 (5): 189–92.

Mayer, JD and Salovey, P (1993) The intelligence of emotional intelligence. *Intelligence*, 17 (4): 433–42.

Mintzberg, H (1975) The manager's job: Folklore and fact. *Harvard Business Review*, July/August: 66–75.

Mumford, A (1999) *Effective Learning*. London: Chartered Institute of Personnel Development.

NHS Employers (2016) *Tackling Bullying in the NHS*. Available at: http://www.nhs employers.org/your-workforce/retain-and-improve/staff-experience/tackling-bullying in-the-nhs; http://www.nhsemployers.org/your-workforce/retain-and-improve/staff experience/tackling-bullying-in-the-nhs

NHS England (2013) *Friends and Family Test.* Available online at: https://www.england.nhs.uk/ourwork/pe/fft/

NHS England (2014) *Five Year Forward View.* Available online at: www.england.nhs.uk/wp-content/uploads/2014/10/5yfv-web.pdf

NHS Improvement (ND) *About Us.* Available online at: https://improvement.nhs.uk/

NHS Leadership Academy (2013) *The Healthcare Leadership Model.* Available online at: www.leadershipacademy.nhs.uk/discover/leadershipmodel

Northam, S (2009a) Conflict in the workplace: Part 1. Sex, age, hierarchy, and culture influence the nursing environment. *American Journal of Nursing,* 109 (6): 70–3.

Northam, S (2009b) Conflict in the workplace: Part 2. Strategies to resolve conflict and restore collegial working relationships. *American Journal of Nursing,* 109 (7): 65–7.

Nowell, L, White, D, Benzies, K and Rosenau, P (2017) Factors that impact implementation of mentorship programs in nursing academia: A sequential-explanatory mixed methods study. *Journal of Nursing Education and Practice,* 7 (10). Available at: https://doi.org/10.5430/jnep.v7n10p1

Nursing and Midwifery Council (2002) *Supporting Nurses and Midwives through Lifelong Learning.* London: NMC.

Nursing and Midwifery Council (2015) *The Code: Professional Standards of Practice and Behaviour for Nurses and Midwives.* London: NMC.

Nursing and Midwifery Council (2017) *Revalidation.* Available at: http://revalidation.nmc.org.uk/welcome-to-revalidation

Nursing and Midwifery Council (2018) *Future Nurse: Standards of Proficiency for Registered Nurses.* Available at: https://www.nmc.org.uk/globalassets/sitedocuments/education-standards/future-nurse-proficiencies.pdf

Nursing Standard (1985) Editorial: First nurses appointed DHA General Managers. *Nursing Standard,* 385 (21 February): 1.

Olson, EE and Eoyang, GH (2001) *Facilitating Organization Change: Lessons from Complexity Science.* San Francisco: Jossey Bass/Pfeiffer.

Parsloe, E and Leedham, M (2009) *Coaching and Mentoring: Practical Conversations to Improve Learning.* London: Kogan Page.

Pascale, R (1990) *Managing on the Edge.* London: Penguin.

Patterson, C (2005) *Generational Diversity: Implications for Consultation and Teamwork.* Paper presented at the meeting of the Council of Directors of School Psychology Programs on generational differences. Deerfield Beach, Florida.

Quinn, F (1995) *Principles and Practice of Nurse Education.* London: Chapman Hall.

Redshaw, G (2008) Improving the performance appraisal system for nurses. *Nursing Times,* 104 (18): 30–1. Available online at: www.nursingtimes.net/nursing-practice-clinical-research/improving-theperformance-appraisal-system-for-nurses/1314790.article

SanFacon, G (2008) *A Conscious Person's Guide to the Workplace.* Bloomington: Trafford Publishing.

Scholtes, PR (1998) *The Leader's Handbook: A Guide to Inspiring Your People and Managing the Daily Workflow.* New York: McGraw-Hill.

Schuetze, H and Inman, P (2010) *The Community Engagement and Service Mission of Universities.* Leicester: National Institute of Adult and Continuing Education (NIACE).

Schwartz, SH (1994) Are there universal aspects in the structure and contents of human values? *Journal of Social Issues,* 50 (4): 19–45.

Senge, P (1990) *The Fifth Discipline: The Art and Practice of the Learning Organization.* New York: Doubleday.

Senge, P (1996) Leading learning organizations. *Training and Development,* 50 (12): 36–7.

Smola, KW and Sutton, CD (2002) Generational differences in working age women. *Journal of Organizational Behavior,* 23 (4): 363–82.

Spouse, J (2001) Work-based learning in health care environments. *Nurse Education in Practice,* 1: 12–18.

Sullivan, EJ and Decker, PJ (2009) *Effective Leadership and Management in Nursing* (7th edition). Harlow: Pearson International Edition.

Swansburg, RC and Swansburg, RJ (2002) *Introduction to Management and Leadership for Nurse Managers* (3rd edition). Boston: Jones and Bartlett.

Templar, R (2011) *The Rules of Management: Expanded edition.* London: FT Press.

The Work Foundation (2008) *Work–Life Balance.* Available online at: www.thework foundation.com/research/health/worklifebalance.aspx

Thomas, J (2006) *Survival Guide for Ward Managers, Sisters and Charge Nurses.* London: Churchill Livingstone, Elsevier.

Thomas, KW and Kilmann, RH (1974) *Thomas–Kilmann Conflict Mode Instrument.* Sterling Forest, New York: Xicom.

Traynor, M, Davis, K, Drennan, V, Goodman, C, Humphrey, C, Locke, R, Mark, A, Murray, SF, Banning, M and Peacock, R (2006) *A Report to the National Co-ordinating Centre for NHS Service Delivery and Organisation Research and Development of a Scoping Exercise on 'The Contribution of Nurse, Midwife and Health Visitor Entrepreneurs to Patient Choice'.* London: National Co-ordinating Centre for Service Delivery and Organisation.

Tuckman, BW (1965) Developmental sequence in small groups. *Psychological Bulletin,* 63: 384–99.

von Bertalanffy, L (1968) *General System Theory: Foundations, Developments, Applications.* New York: Braziller.

Ward, A (2003) Managing the team. In: Seden, J and Reynolds, J (eds) *Managing Care in Practice* (pages 33–56). London: Routledge.

References

Williams, J (2007) Follow the leader. *Healthcare Financial Management*, 61 (1): 50–5.

Wright, P (1996) *Managerial Leadership*. London: Routledge.

Wuchty, S, Jones, BF and Uzzi, B (2007) The increasing dominance of teams in production of knowledge. *Science*, 316: 1036–9.

Yoder-Wise, P (2007) *Leading and Managing in Nursing* (4th edition). Amsterdam: Elsevier.

Index